JAN 2 6 2010

SUPERMAN BATMAN

ENEMIES AMONG US

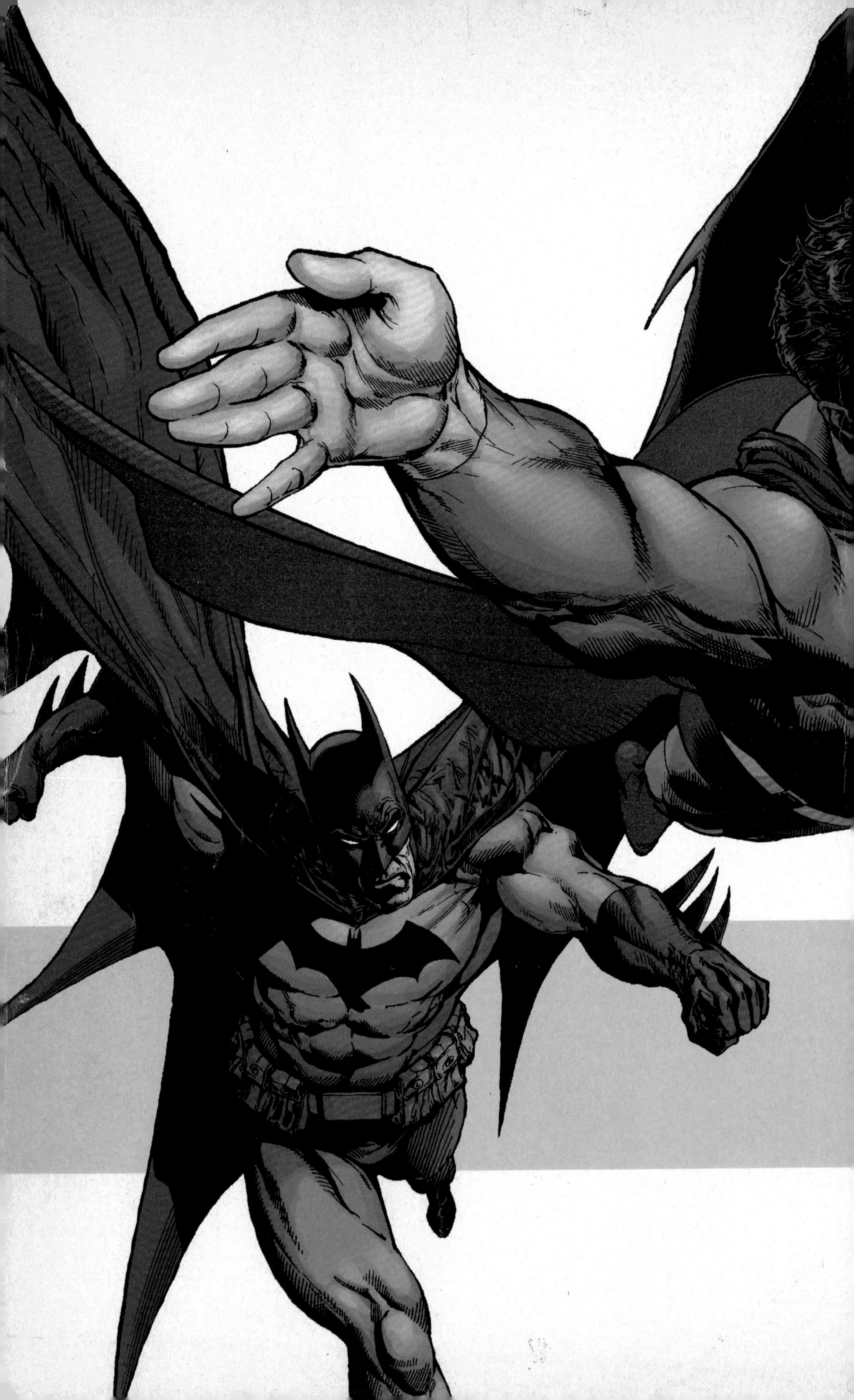

DALY CITY PUBLIC LIBRARY
DALY CITY, CALIFORNIA

DISCARDED

Mark Verheiden
Writer

**Ethan Van Sciver Matthew Clark
Ron Randall Joe Benitez**
Pencils

**Ethan Van Sciver Marlo Alquiza Andy Lanning
Don Hillsman Victor Llamas**
Inks

**Chris Chuckry
Guy Major**
Colors

Rob Leigh
Letters

Batman created by Bob Kane

Superman created by Jerry Siegel and Joe Shuster

SUPERMAN BATMAN

ENEMIES AMONG US

W

DAN DIDIO Senior VP-Executive Editor   EDDIE BERGANZA Editor-original series   JEANINE SCHAEFER Associate Editor-original series   ADAM SCHLAGMAN Assistant Editor-original series
BOB JOY Editor-collected edition   ROBBIN BROSTERMAN Senior Art Director   PAUL LEVITZ President & Publisher   GEORG BREWER VP-Design & DC Direct Creative
RICHARD BRUNING Senior VP-Creative Director   PATRICK CALDON Executive VP-Finance & Operations   CHRIS CARAMALIS VP-Finance   JOHN CUNNINGHAM VP-Marketing
TERRI CUNNINGHAM VP-Managing Editor   ALISON GILL VP-Manufacturing   HANK KANALZ VP-General Manager, WildStorm   JIM LEE Editorial Director-WildStorm
PAULA LOWITT Senior VP-Business & Legal Affairs   MARYELLEN MCLAUGHLIN VP-Advertising & Custom Publishing   JOHN NEE VP-Business Development   GREGORY NOVECK Senior VP-Creative Affairs
SUE POHJA VP-Book Trade Sales   CHERYL RUBIN Senior VP-Brand Management   JEFF TROJAN VP-Business Development, DC Direct   BOB WAYNE VP-Sales

Cover art by Ethan Van Sciver.
Special thanks to Simon Coleby and Don Ho.

SUPERMAN/BATMAN: THE ENEMIES AMONG US
Published by DC Comics. Cover and compilation copyright © 2007 DC Comics. All Rights Reserved. Originally published in single magazine form as: SUPERMAN/BATMAN 28-33 Copyright © 2006-2007
DC Comics. All Rights Reserved. All characters, their distinctive likenesses and related elements featured in this publication are trademarks of DC Comics. The stories, characters and incidents featured in
this publication are entirely fictional. DC Comics does not read or accept unsolicited submissions of ideas, stories or artwork.

DC Comics, 1700 Broadway, New York, NY 10019
A Warner Bros. Entertainment Company. Printed in Canada. First Printing.
Hardcover ISBN: 1-4012-1330-8. Hardcover ISBN 13: 978-1-4012-1330-5. Softcover ISBN: 1-4012-1243-3. Softcover ISBN 13: 978-1-4012-1243-8.

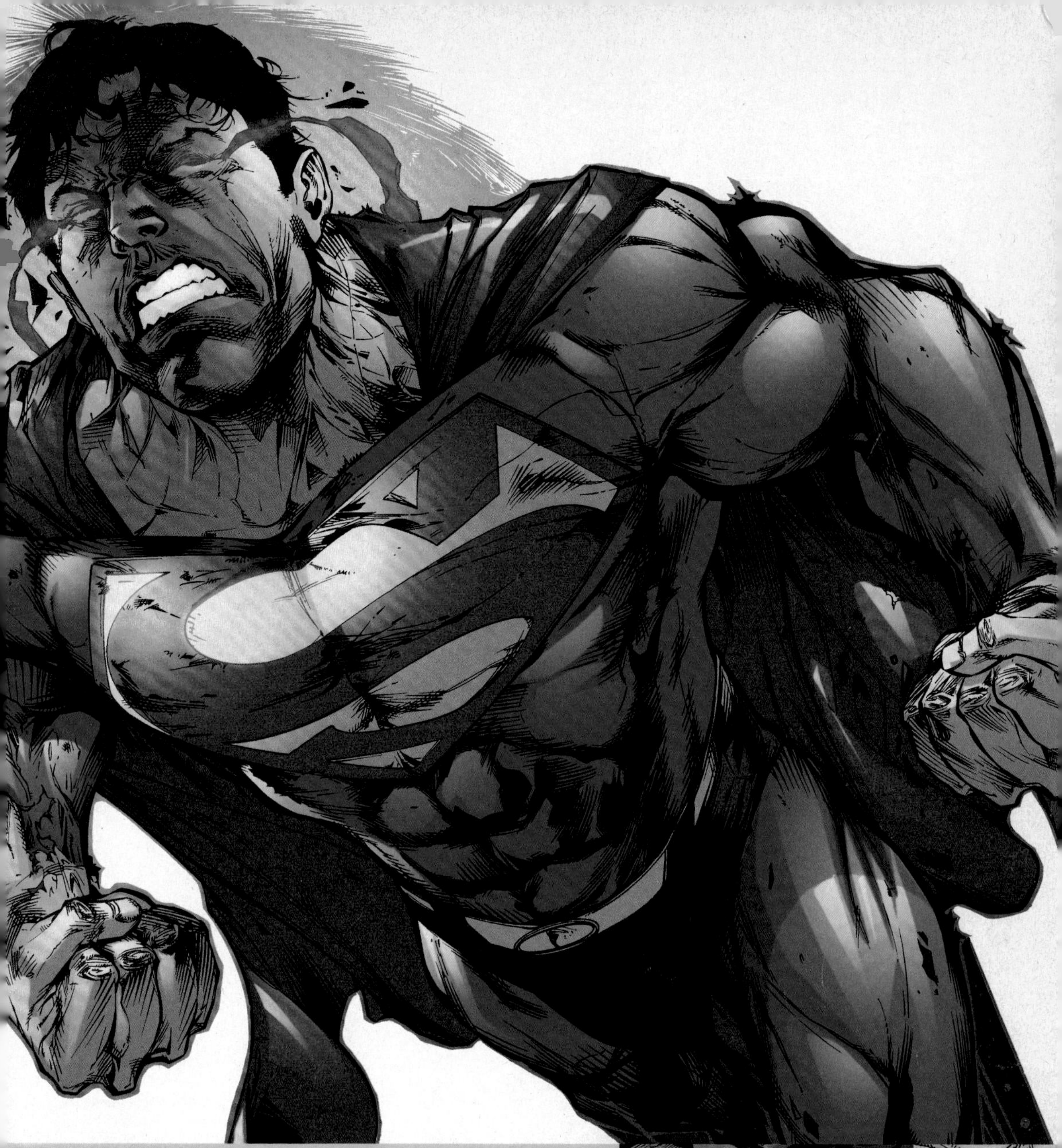
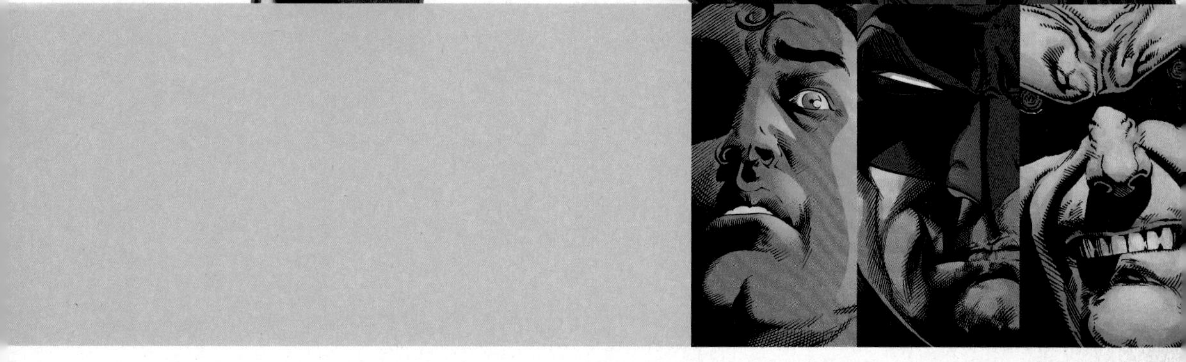

Over the years Earth has become home to many heroes from across the galaxy. Although they have proved their allegiance time and again, Batman has always kept a cautious eye on his extraterrestrial allies, even the ones he considered close friends ...

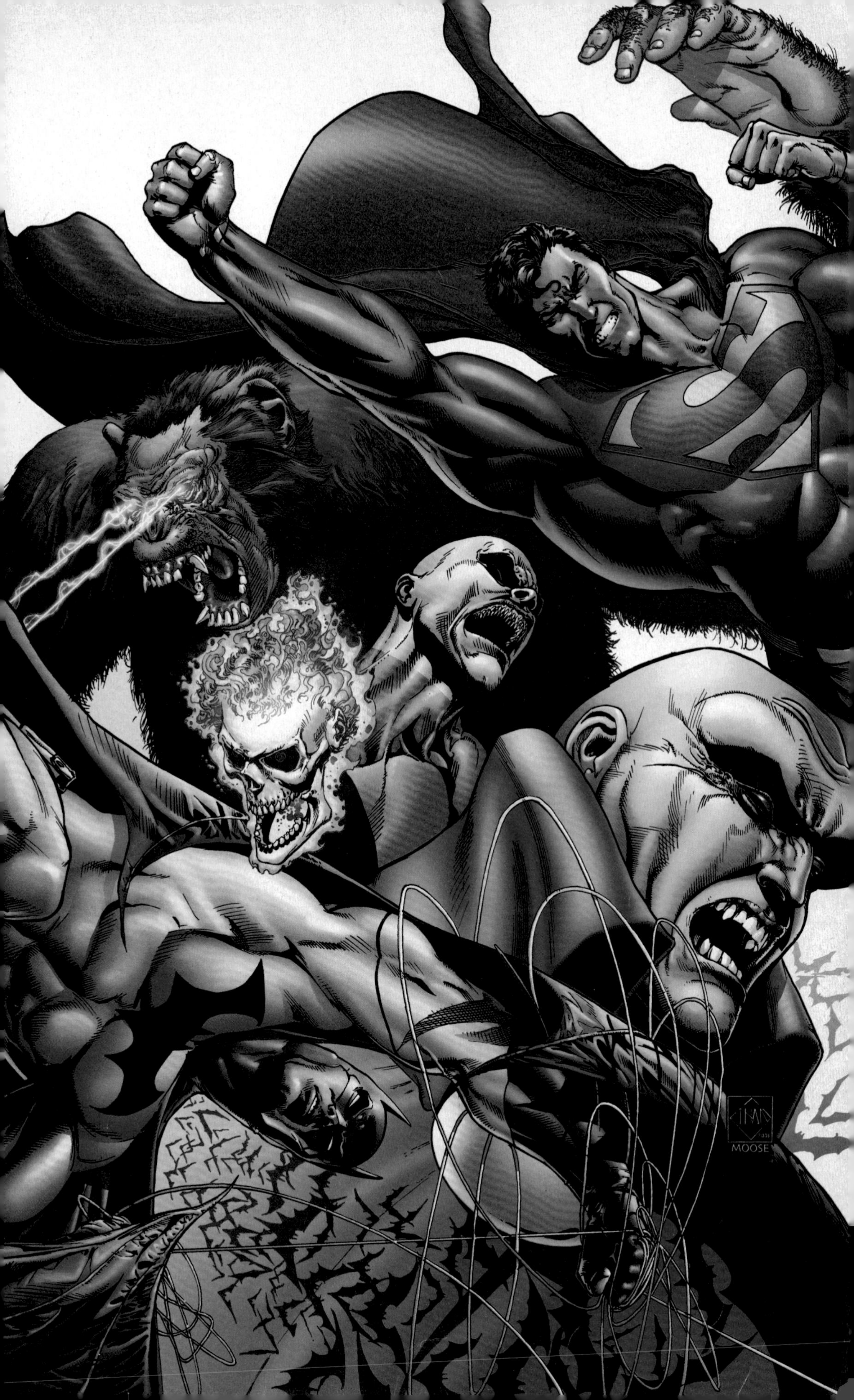
MOOSE

THE ENEMIES AMONG US: PART ONE
From SUPERMAN/BATMAN 28
Cover by Ethan Van Sciver and Moose Baumann

Mark Verheiden
Writer

Ethan Van Sciver
Artist

Chris Chuckry
Colors

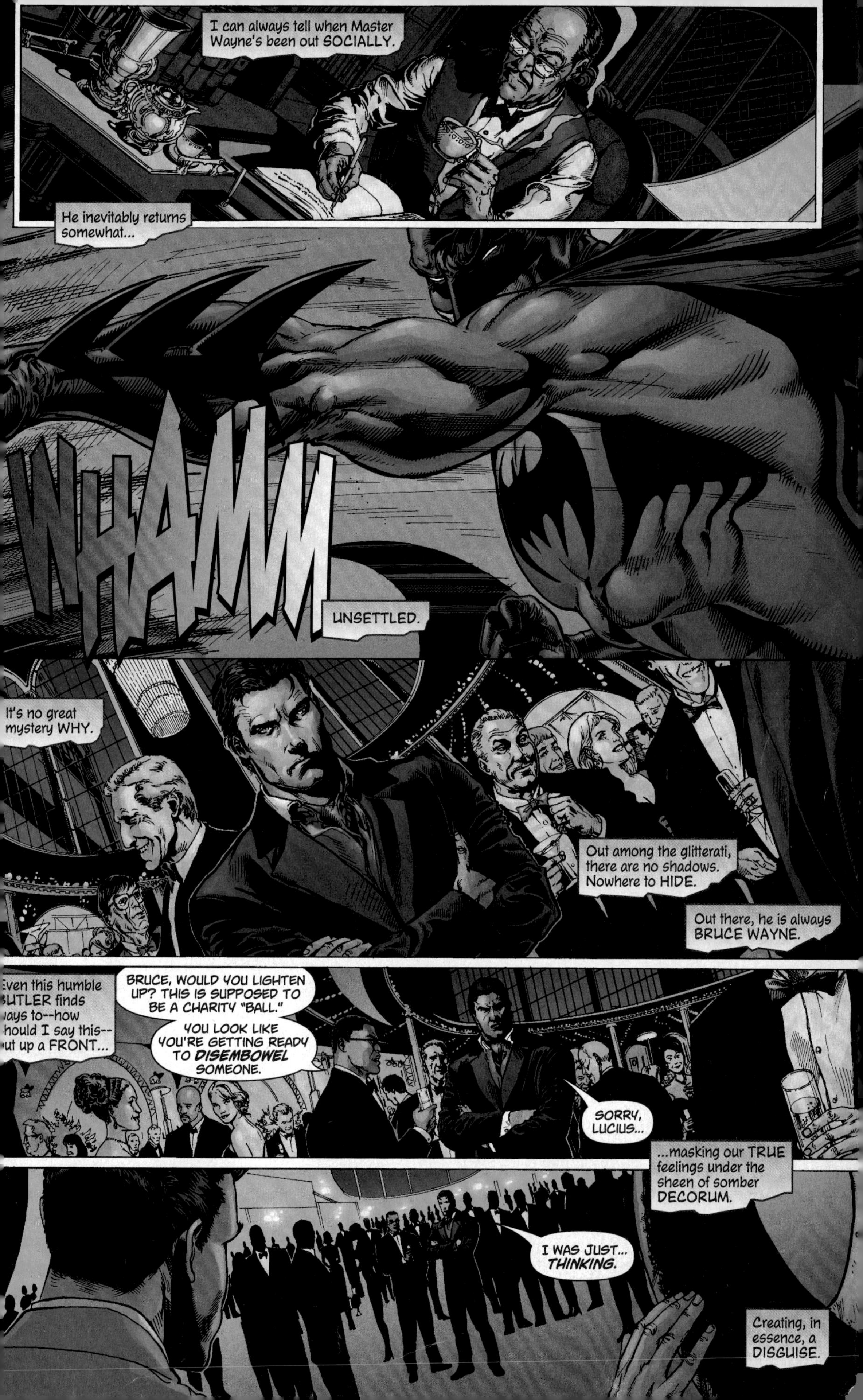
I can always tell when Master Wayne's been out SOCIALLY.
He inevitably returns somewhat...
WHAMM
UNSETTLED.
It's no great mystery WHY.
Out among the glitterati, there are no shadows. Nowhere to HIDE.
Out there, he is always BRUCE WAYNE.
Even this humble BUTLER finds ways to--how should I say this--put up a FRONT...
BRUCE, WOULD YOU LIGHTEN UP? THIS IS SUPPOSED TO BE A CHARITY "BALL."
YOU LOOK LIKE YOU'RE GETTING READY TO DISEMBOWEL SOMEONE.
SORRY, LUCIUS...
...masking our TRUE feelings under the sheen of somber DECORUM.
I WAS JUST... THINKING.
Creating, in essence, a DISGUISE.

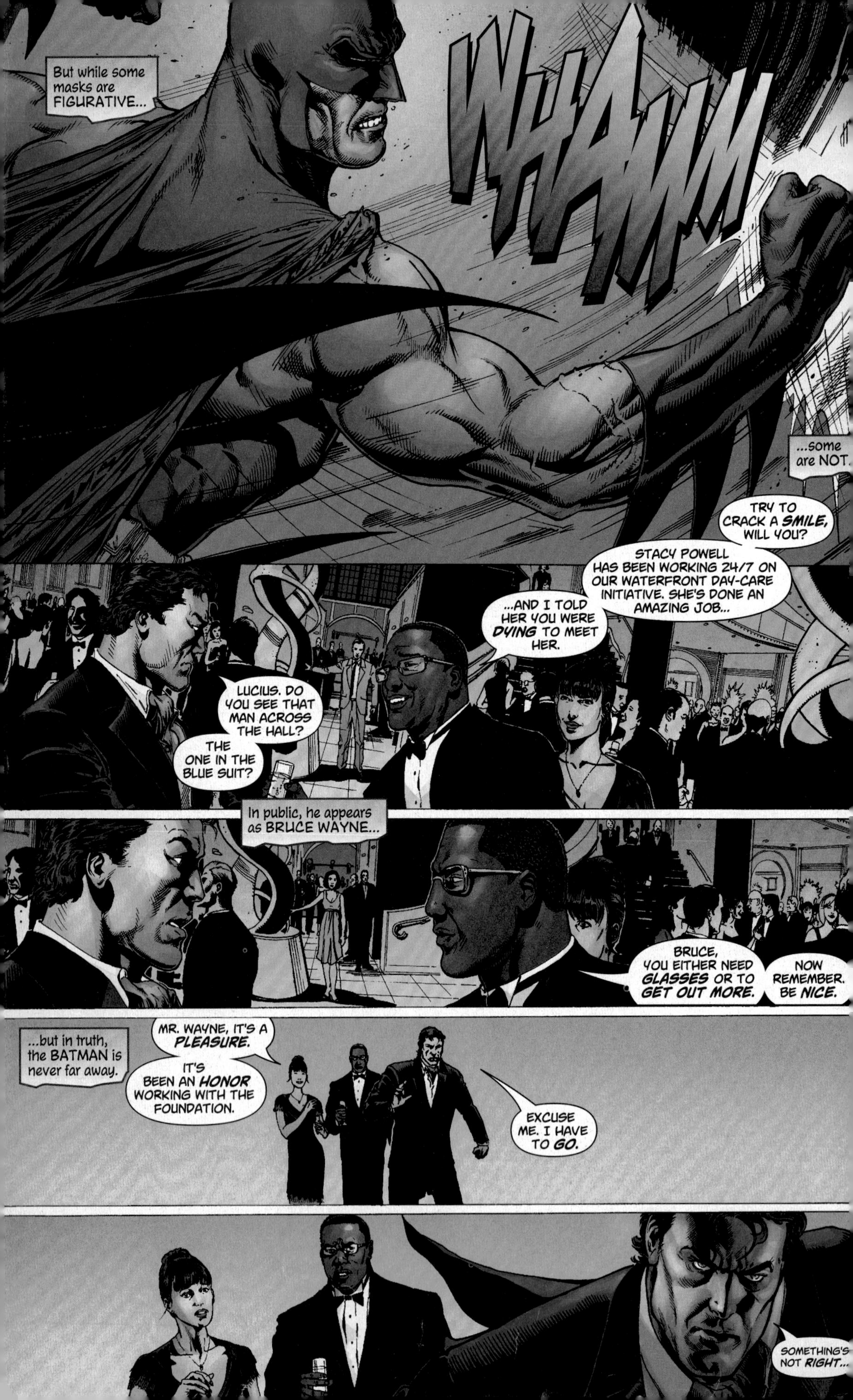

But while some masks are FIGURATIVE...
WHAMM
...some are NOT.
TRY TO CRACK A SMILE, WILL YOU?
STACY POWELL HAS BEEN WORKING 24/7 ON OUR WATERFRONT DAY-CARE INITIATIVE. SHE'S DONE AN AMAZING JOB...
...AND I TOLD HER YOU WERE DYING TO MEET HER.
LUCIUS. DO YOU SEE THAT MAN ACROSS THE HALL?
THE ONE IN THE BLUE SUIT?
In public, he appears as BRUCE WAYNE...
BRUCE, YOU EITHER NEED GLASSES OR TO GET OUT MORE.
NOW REMEMBER. BE NICE.
...but in truth, the BATMAN is never far away.
MR. WAYNE, IT'S A PLEASURE.
IT'S BEEN AN HONOR WORKING WITH THE FOUNDATION.
EXCUSE ME. I HAVE TO GO.
SOMETHING'S NOT RIGHT...

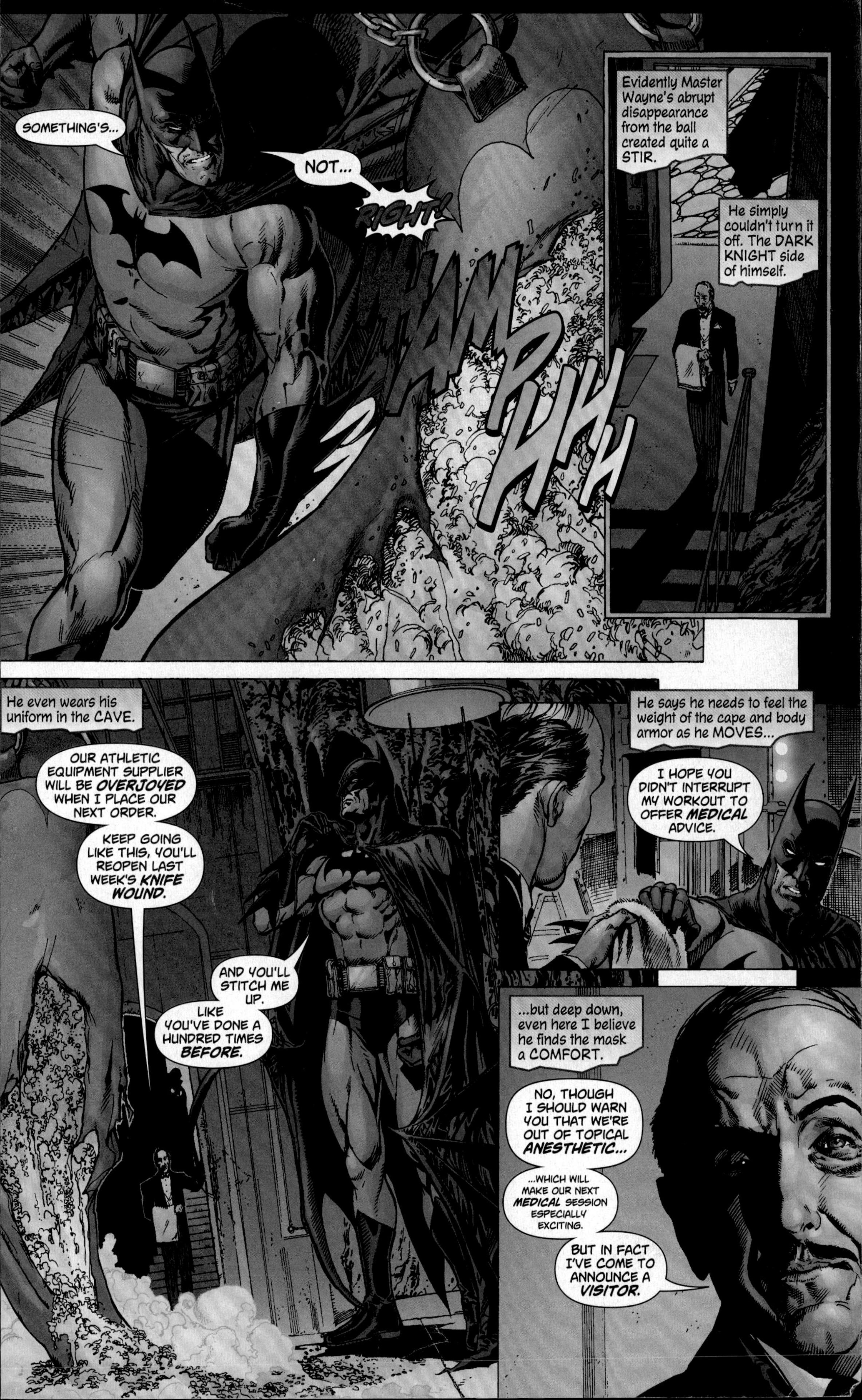
SOMETHING'S...
NOT...
RIGHT!
Evidently Master Wayne's abrupt disappearance from the ball created quite a STIR.
He simply couldn't turn it off. The DARK KNIGHT side of himself.
He even wears his uniform in the CAVE.
OUR ATHLETIC EQUIPMENT SUPPLIER WILL BE OVERJOYED WHEN I PLACE OUR NEXT ORDER.
KEEP GOING LIKE THIS, YOU'LL REOPEN LAST WEEK'S KNIFE WOUND.
AND YOU'LL STITCH ME UP.
LIKE YOU'VE DONE A HUNDRED TIMES BEFORE.
He says he needs to feel the weight of the cape and body armor as he MOVES...
I HOPE YOU DIDN'T INTERRUPT MY WORKOUT TO OFFER MEDICAL ADVICE.
...but deep down, even here I believe he finds the mask a COMFORT.
NO, THOUGH I SHOULD WARN YOU THAT WE'RE OUT OF TOPICAL ANESTHETIC...
...WHICH WILL MAKE OUR NEXT MEDICAL SESSION ESPECIALLY EXCITING.
BUT IN FACT I'VE COME TO ANNOUNCE A VISITOR.

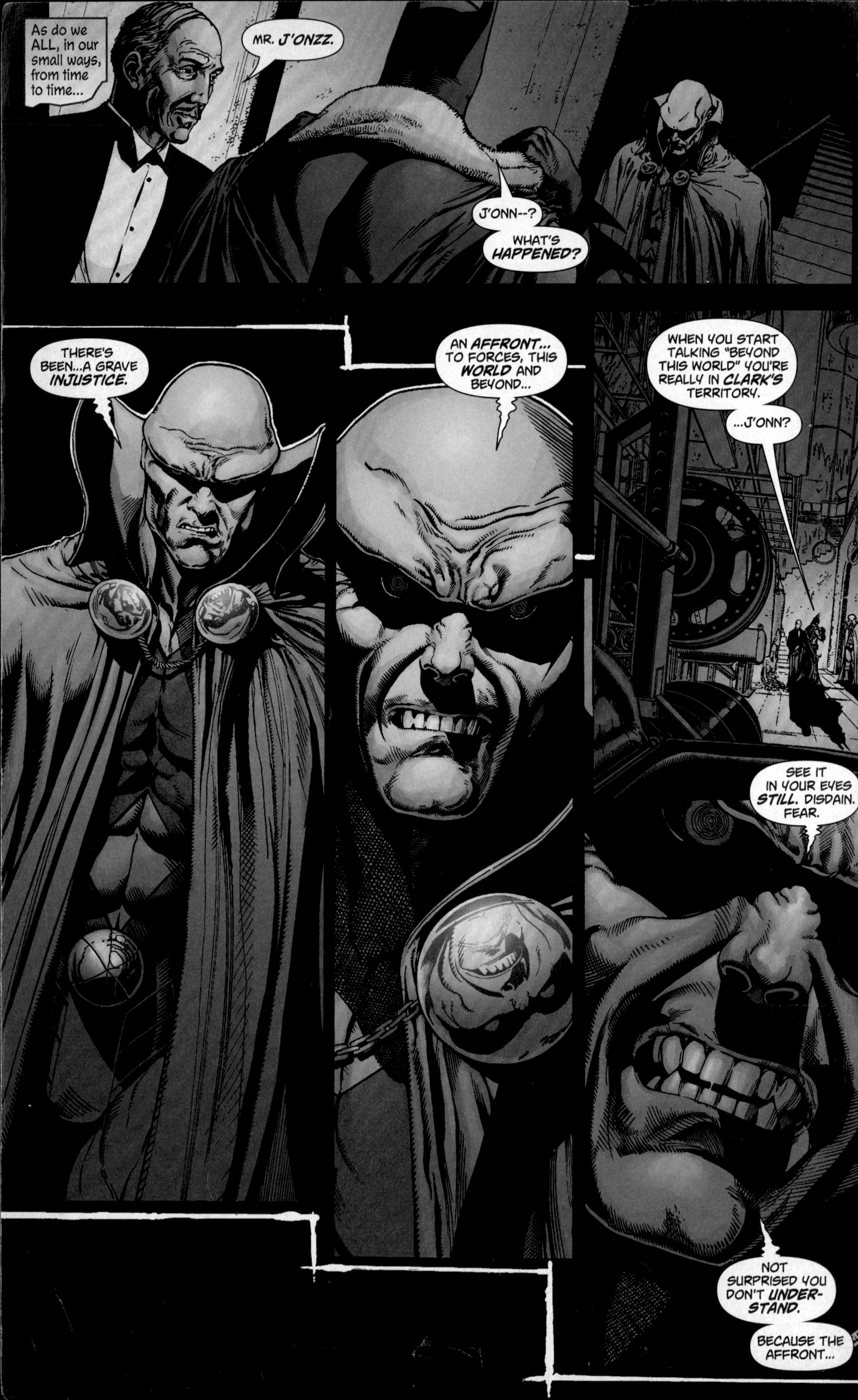

As do we ALL, in our small ways, from time to time...
MR. J'ONZZ.
J'ONN--?
WHAT'S HAPPENED?
THERE'S BEEN...A GRAVE INJUSTICE.
AN AFFRONT... TO FORCES, THIS WORLD AND BEYOND...
WHEN YOU START TALKING "BEYOND THIS WORLD" YOU'RE REALLY IN CLARK'S TERRITORY.
...J'ONN?
SEE IT IN YOUR EYES STILL. DISDAIN. FEAR.
NOT SURPRISED YOU DON'T UNDER-STAND.
BECAUSE THE AFFRONT...

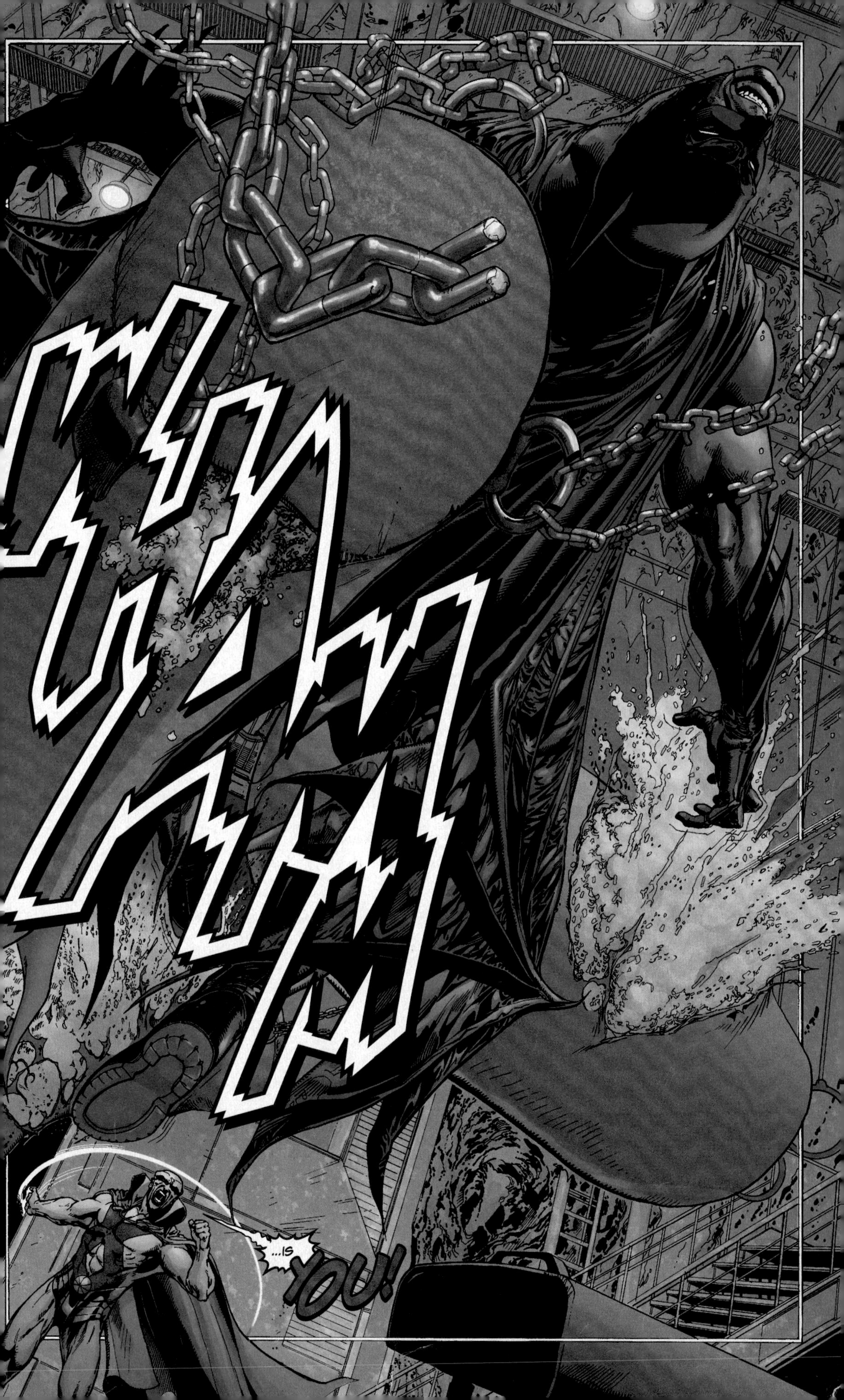
...IS
YOU!

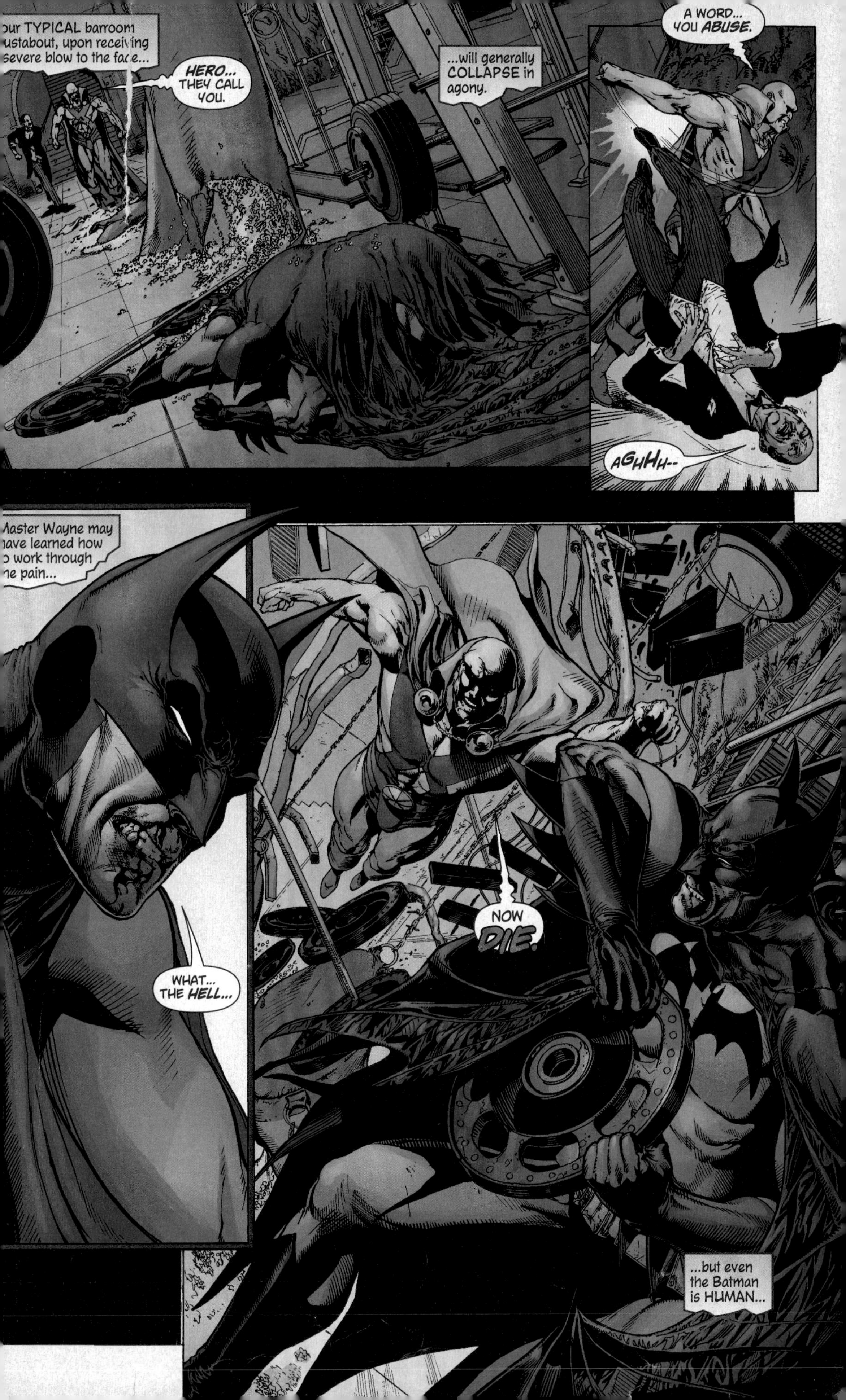
our TYPICAL barroom
ustabout, upon receiving
severe blow to the face...
HERO... THEY CALL YOU.
...will generally COLLAPSE in agony.
A WORD... YOU ABUSE.
AGHHH--
Master Wayne may
have learned how
o work through
he pain...
WHAT... THE HELL...
NOW DIE.
...but even the Batman is HUMAN...

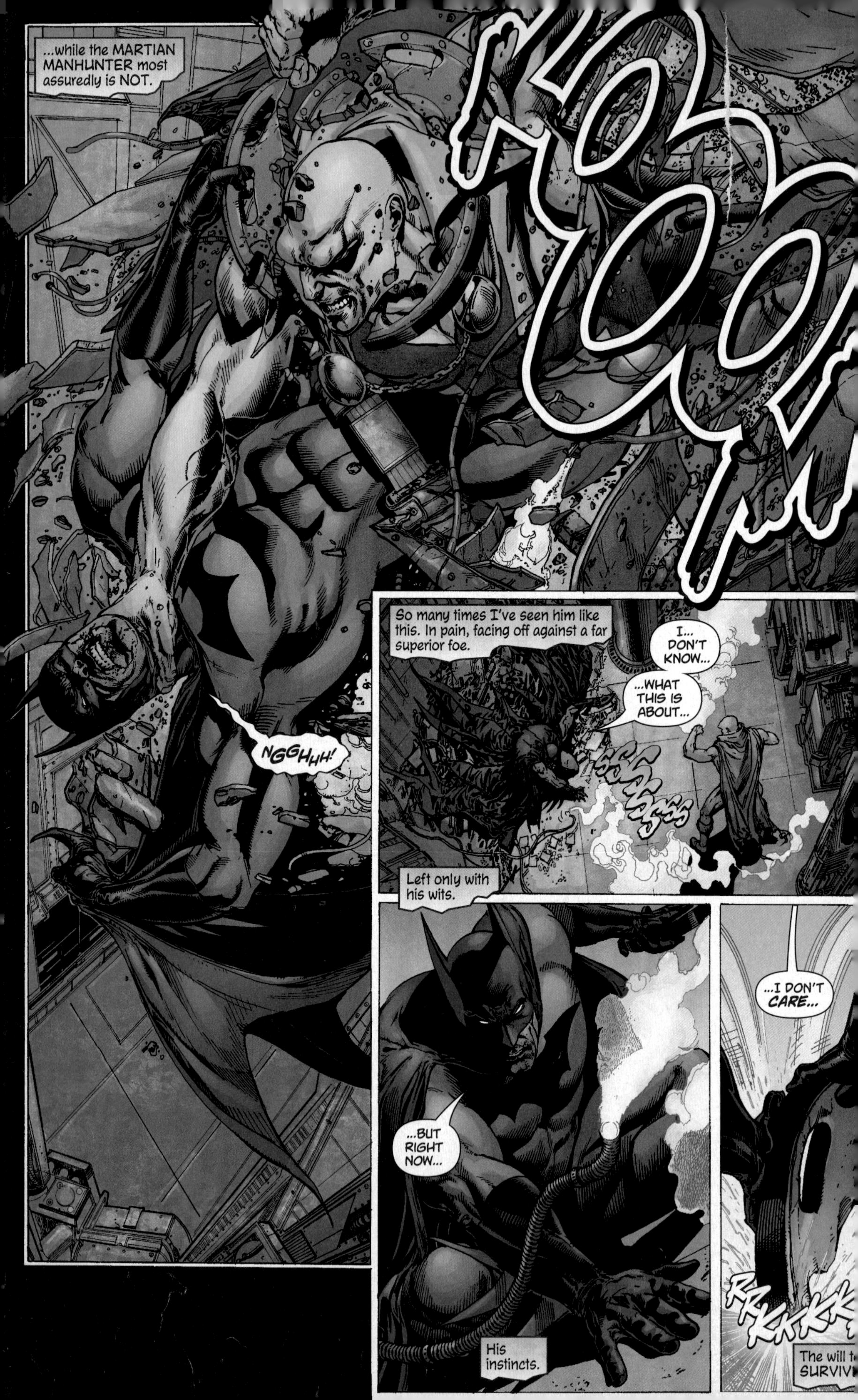
...while the MARTIAN MANHUNTER most assuredly is NOT.
NGGHHH!
So many times I've seen him like this. In pain, facing off against a far superior foe.
I... DON'T KNOW...
...WHAT THIS IS ABOUT...
Left only with his wits.
...BUT RIGHT NOW...
His instincts.
...I DON'T CARE...
The will t
SURVIV

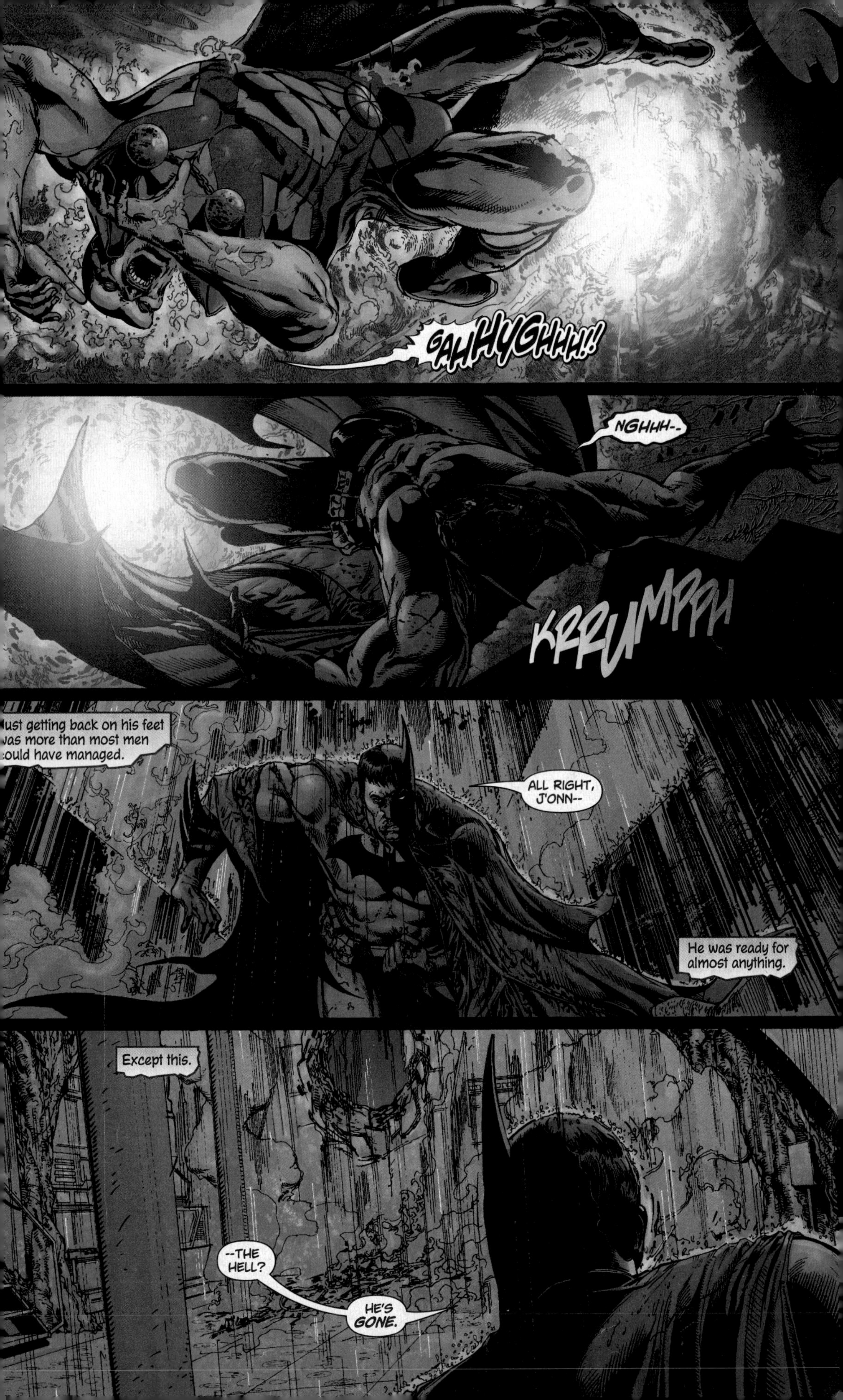

GAHHYGHHH!!
NGHHH--
KRRUMPPH
Just getting back on his feet was more than most men could have managed.
ALL RIGHT, J'ONN--
He was ready for almost anything.
Except this.
--THE HELL?
HE'S GONE.

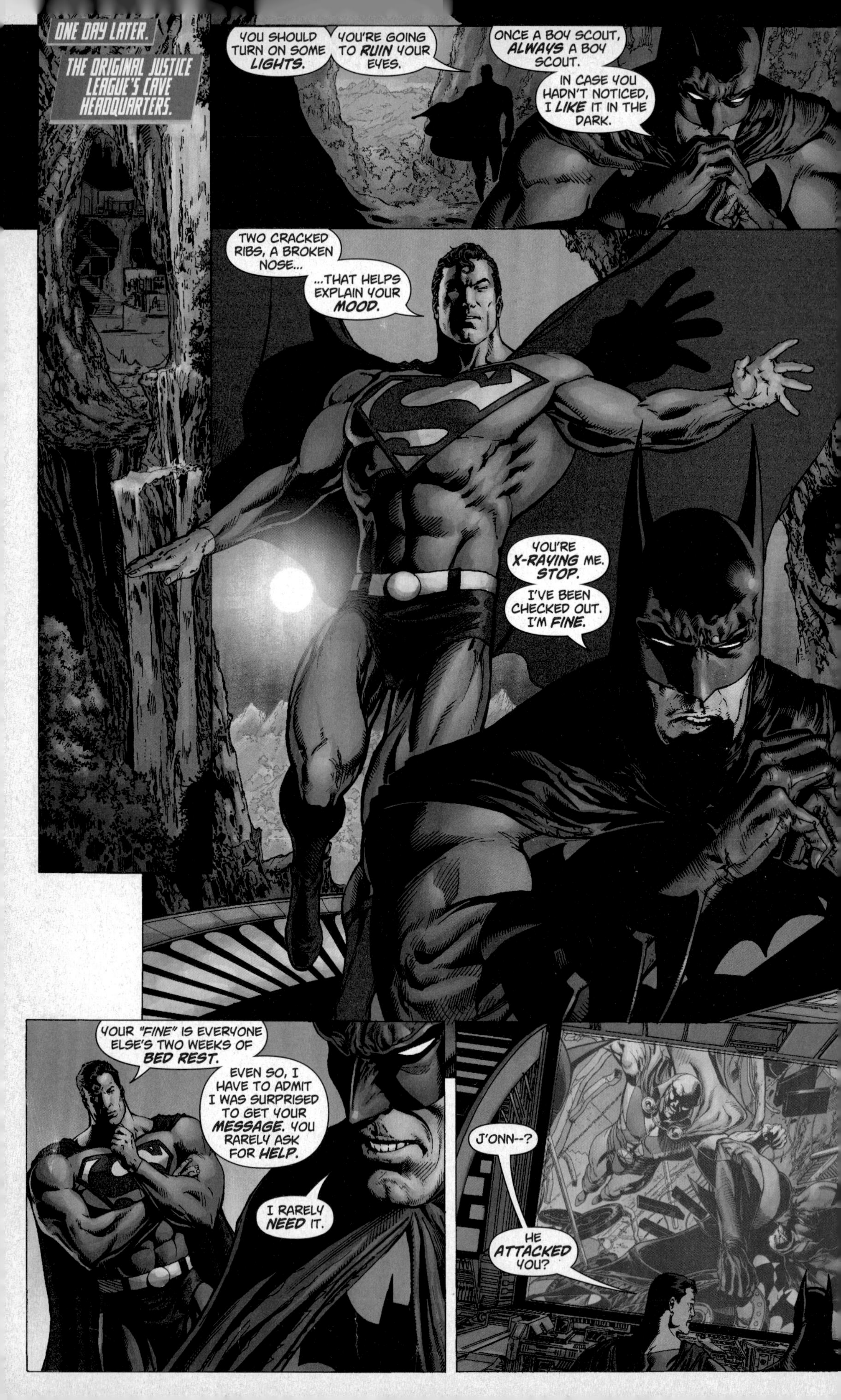
ONE DAY LATER.
THE ORIGINAL JUSTICE LEAGUE'S CAVE HEADQUARTERS.
YOU SHOULD TURN ON SOME LIGHTS.
YOU'RE GOING TO RUIN YOUR EYES.
ONCE A BOY SCOUT, ALWAYS A BOY SCOUT.
IN CASE YOU HADN'T NOTICED, I LIKE IT IN THE DARK.
TWO CRACKED RIBS, A BROKEN NOSE...
...THAT HELPS EXPLAIN YOUR MOOD.
YOU'RE X-RAYING ME. STOP.
I'VE BEEN CHECKED OUT. I'M FINE.
YOUR "FINE" IS EVERYONE ELSE'S TWO WEEKS OF BED REST.
EVEN SO, I HAVE TO ADMIT I WAS SURPRISED TO GET YOUR MESSAGE. YOU RARELY ASK FOR HELP.
I RARELY NEED IT.
J'ONN--?
HE ATTACKED YOU?

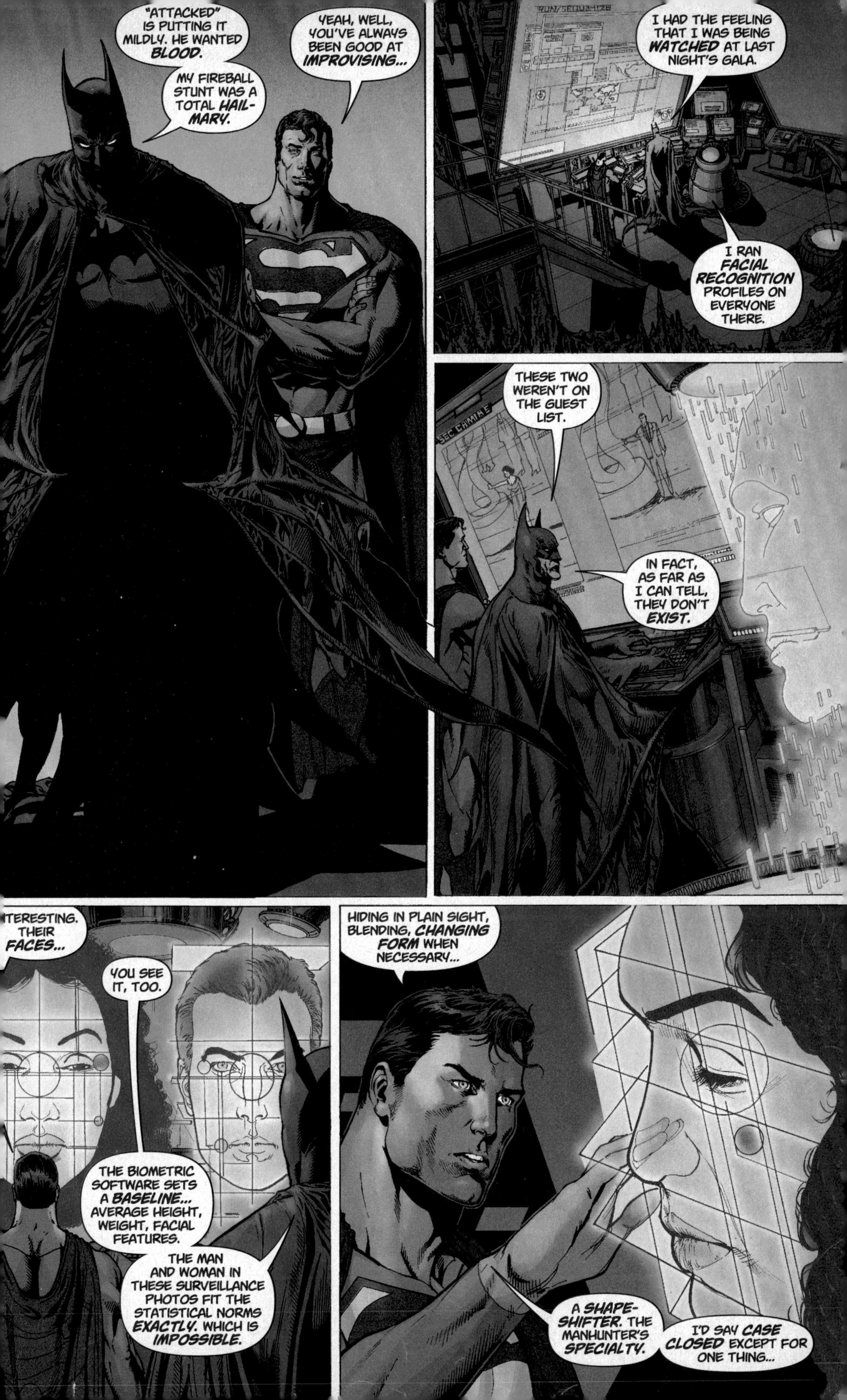
"ATTACKED" IS PUTTING IT MILDLY. HE WANTED BLOOD.
MY FIREBALL STUNT WAS A TOTAL HAIL-MARY.
YEAH, WELL, YOU'VE ALWAYS BEEN GOOD AT IMPROVISING...
I HAD THE FEELING THAT I WAS BEING WATCHED AT LAST NIGHT'S GALA.
I RAN FACIAL RECOGNITION PROFILES ON EVERYONE THERE.
THESE TWO WEREN'T ON THE GUEST LIST.
IN FACT, AS FAR AS I CAN TELL, THEY DON'T EXIST.
TERESTING. THEIR FACES...
YOU SEE IT, TOO.
THE BIOMETRIC SOFTWARE SETS A BASELINE... AVERAGE HEIGHT, WEIGHT, FACIAL FEATURES.
THE MAN AND WOMAN IN THESE SURVEILLANCE PHOTOS FIT THE STATISTICAL NORMS EXACTLY. WHICH IS IMPOSSIBLE.
HIDING IN PLAIN SIGHT, BLENDING, CHANGING FORM WHEN NECESSARY...
A SHAPE-SHIFTER. THE MANHUNTER'S SPECIALTY.
I'D SAY CASE CLOSED EXCEPT FOR ONE THING...

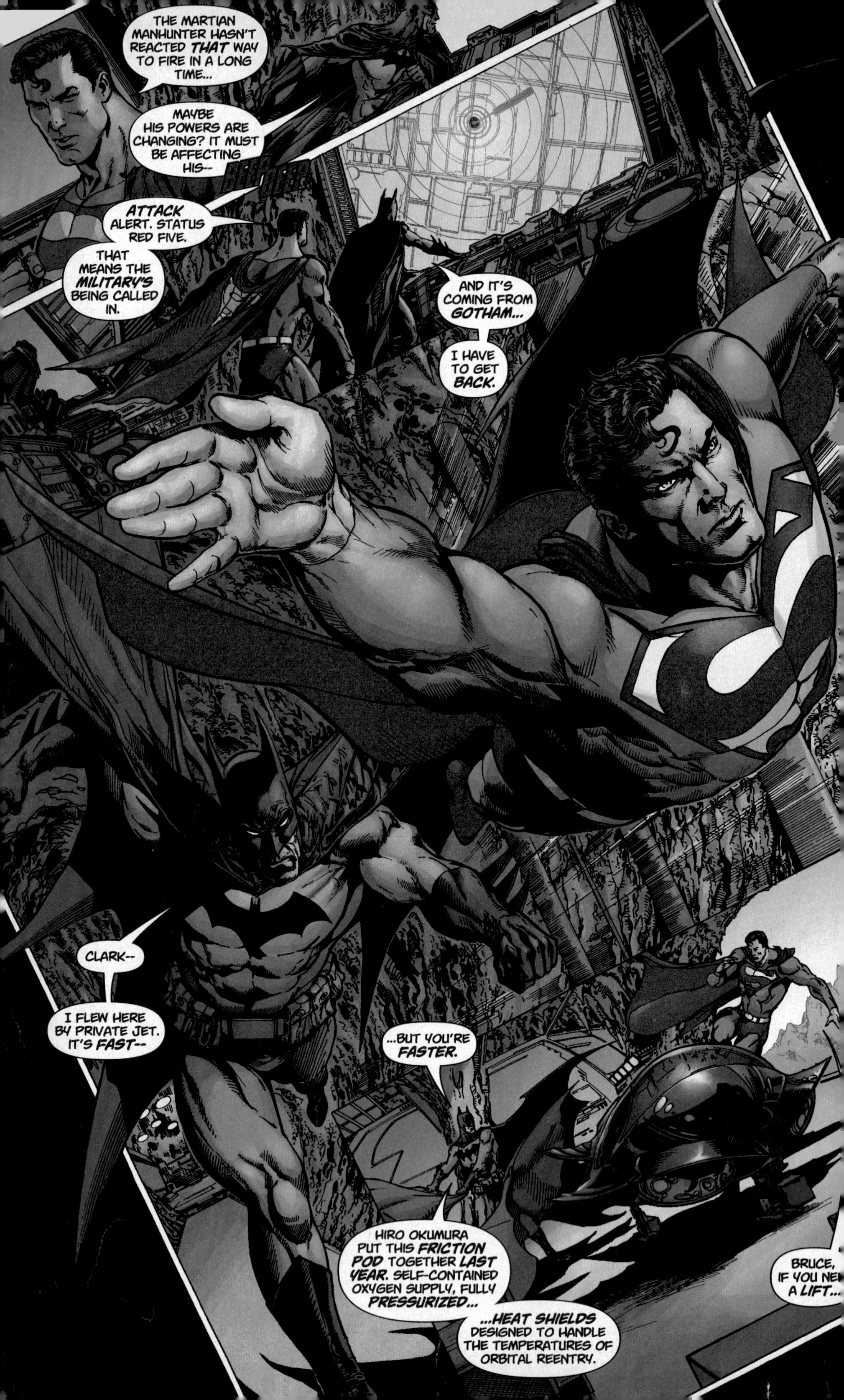
THE MARTIAN MANHUNTER HASN'T REACTED THAT WAY TO FIRE IN A LONG TIME...
MAYBE HIS POWERS ARE CHANGING? IT MUST BE AFFECTING HIS--
ATTACK ALERT. STATUS RED FIVE.
THAT MEANS THE MILITARY'S BEING CALLED IN.
AND IT'S COMING FROM GOTHAM...
I HAVE TO GET BACK.
CLARK--
I FLEW HERE BY PRIVATE JET. IT'S FAST--
...BUT YOU'RE FASTER.
HIRO OKUMURA PUT THIS FRICTION POD TOGETHER LAST YEAR. SELF-CONTAINED OXYGEN SUPPLY, FULLY PRESSURIZED...
...HEAT SHIELDS DESIGNED TO HANDLE THE TEMPERATURES OF ORBITAL REENTRY.
BRUCE, IF YOU NE
A LIFT...

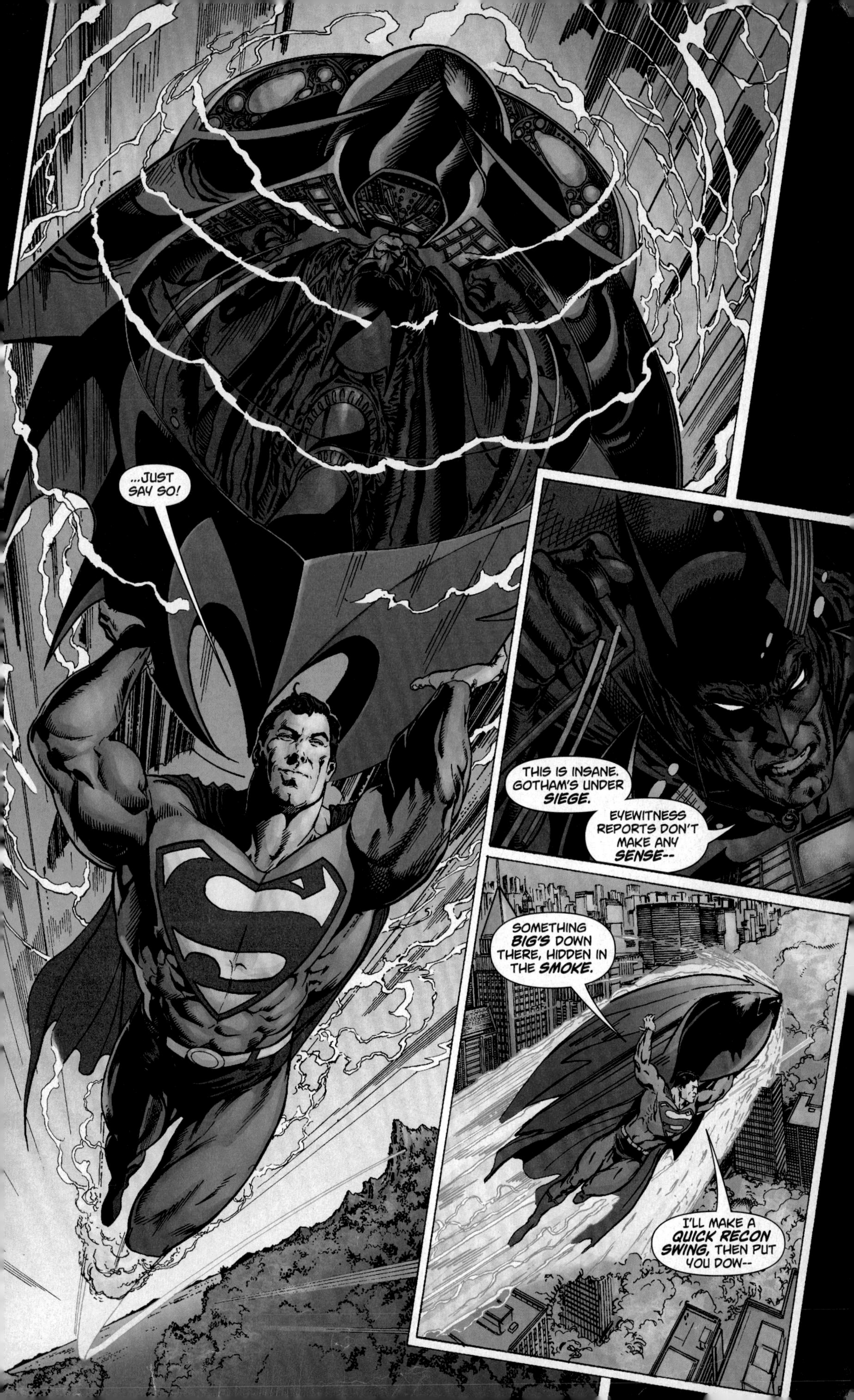
...JUST SAY SO!
THIS IS INSANE. GOTHAM'S UNDER SIEGE.
EYEWITNESS REPORTS DON'T MAKE ANY SENSE--
SOMETHING BIG'S DOWN THERE, HIDDEN IN THE SMOKE.
I'LL MAKE A QUICK RECON SWING, THEN PUT YOU DOW--

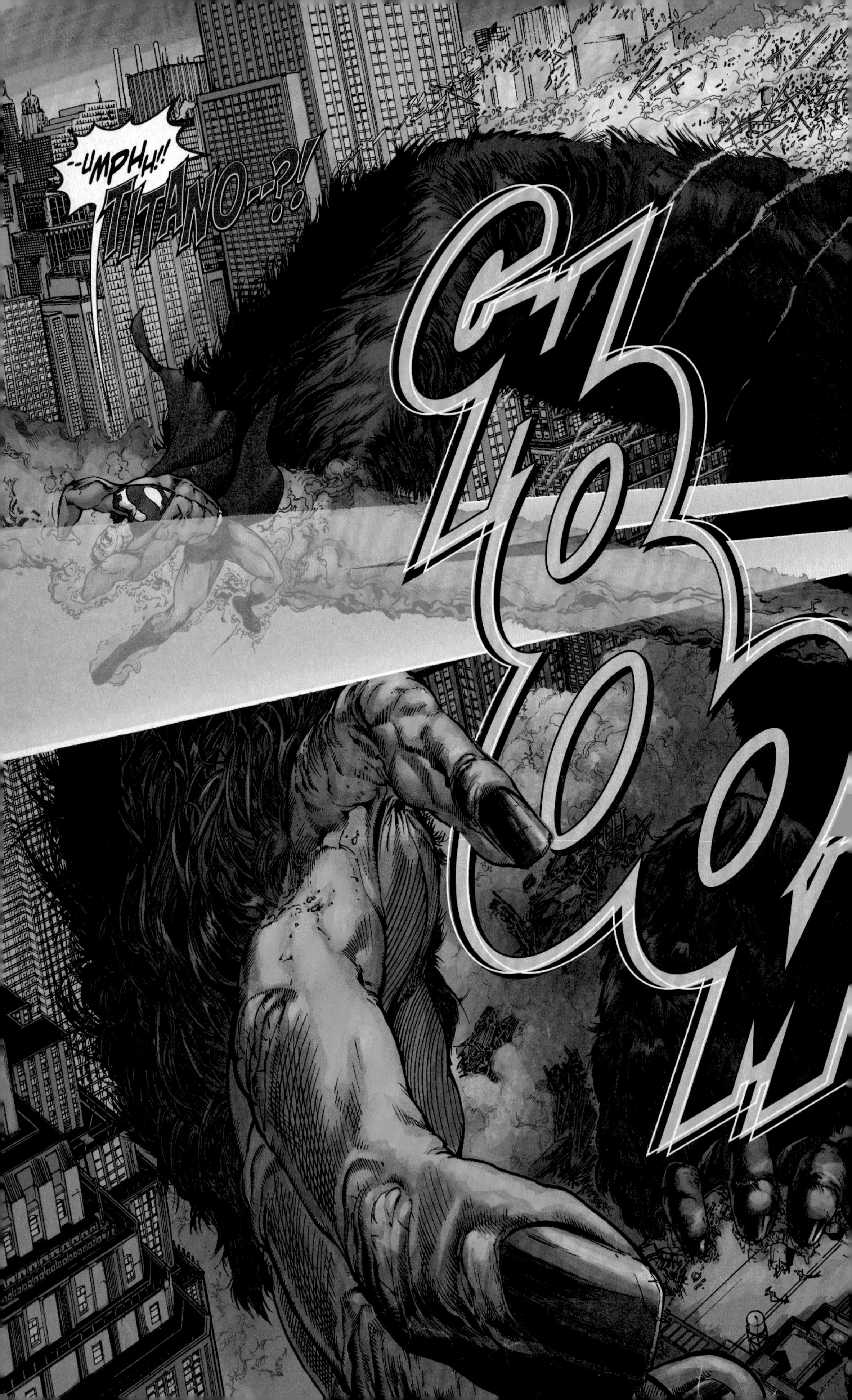
--UMPHH!!
TITANO--?!

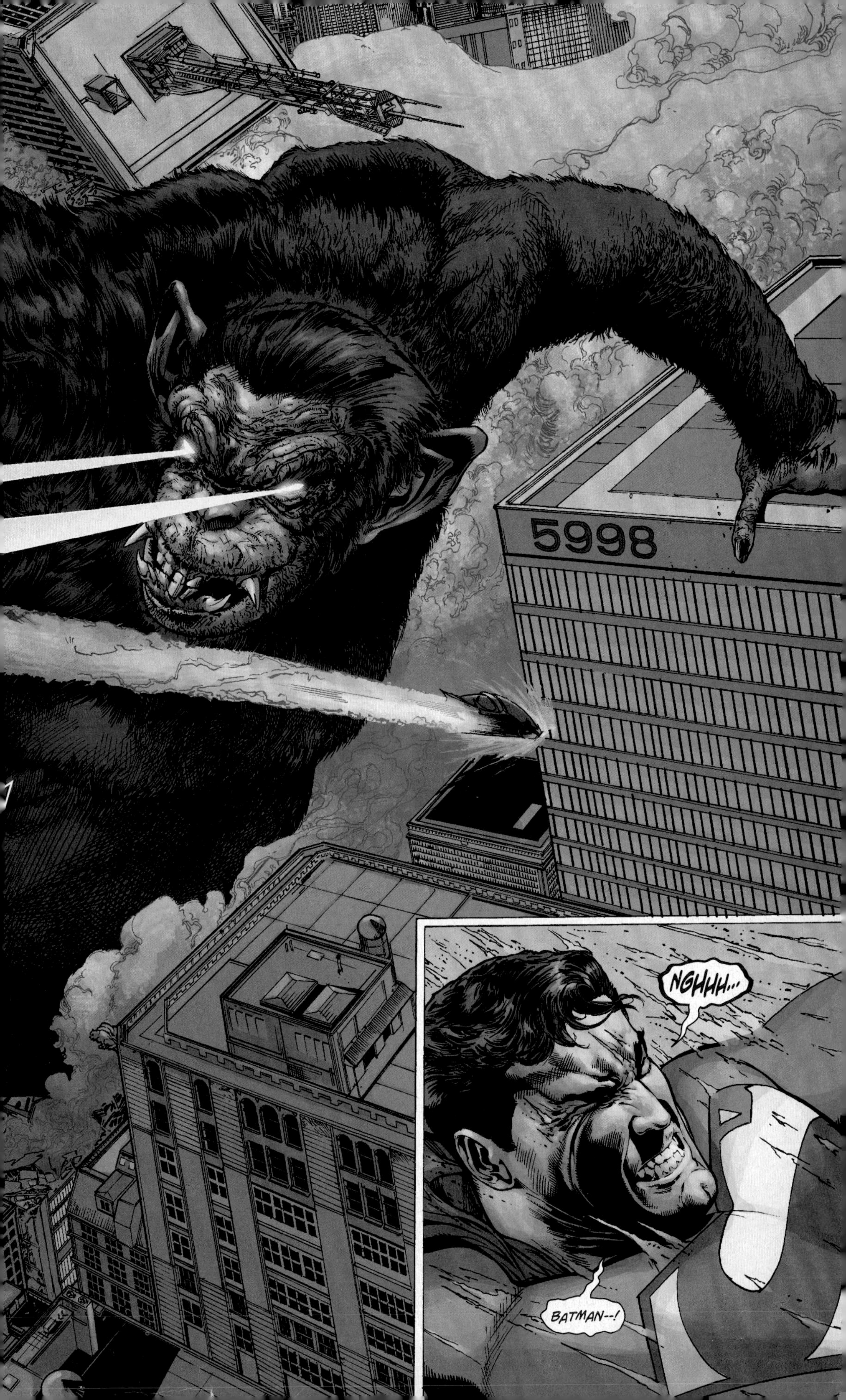
5998
NGHHH...
BATMAN--!

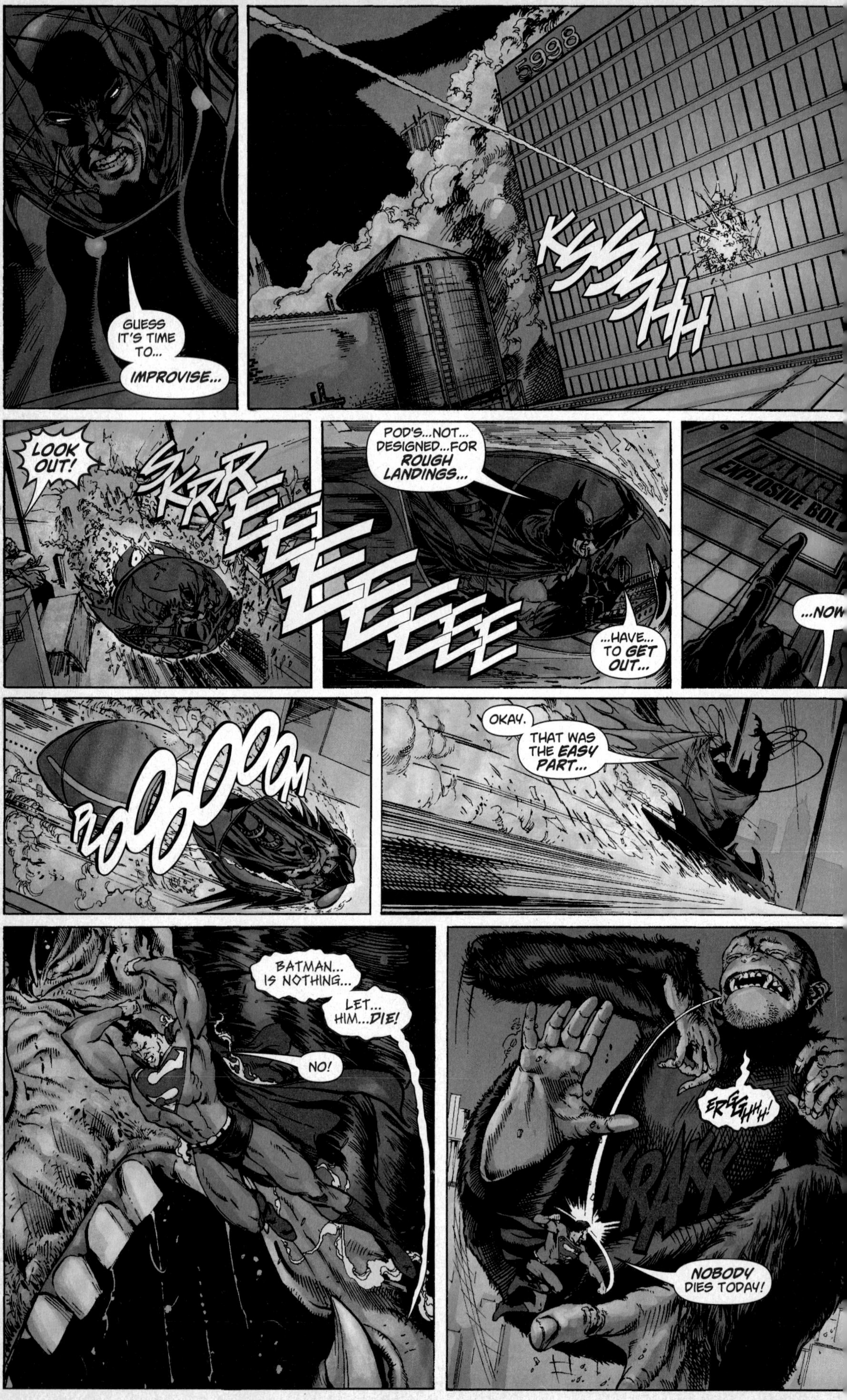
GUESS IT'S TIME TO... IMPROVISE...
5998
KSSHHH
LOOK OUT!
SKRREEEEEEEE
POD'S...NOT... DESIGNED...FOR ROUGH LANDINGS...
...HAVE... TO GET OUT...
EXPLOSIVE BOL
...NOW
FROOOOOOOM
OKAY.
THAT WAS THE EASY PART...
BATMAN... IS NOTHING...
LET... HIM...DIE!
NO!
ERGGHHH!
KRAKK
NOBODY DIES TODAY!

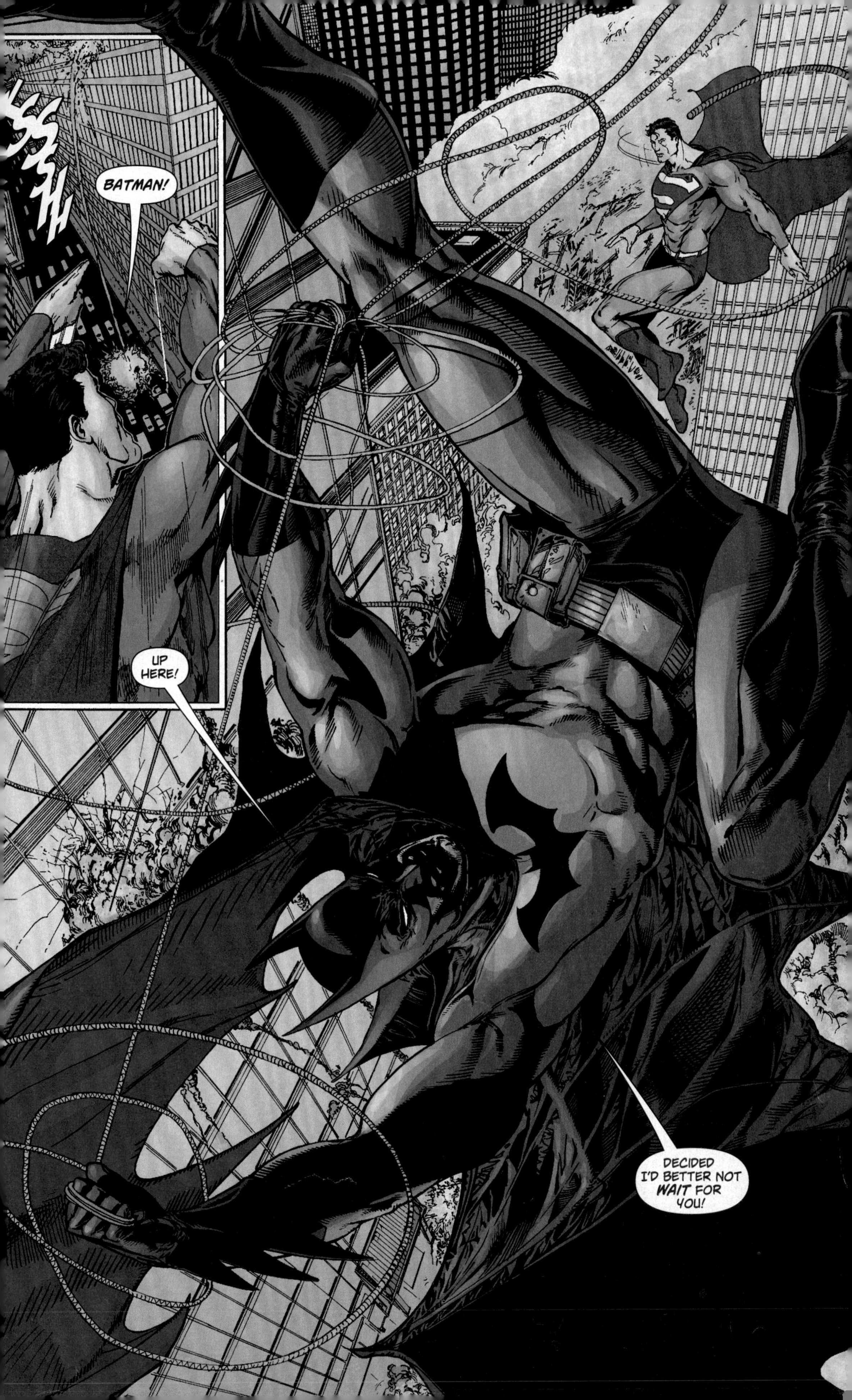
SSSHH
BATMAN!
UP HERE!
DECIDED I'D BETTER NOT WAIT FOR YOU!

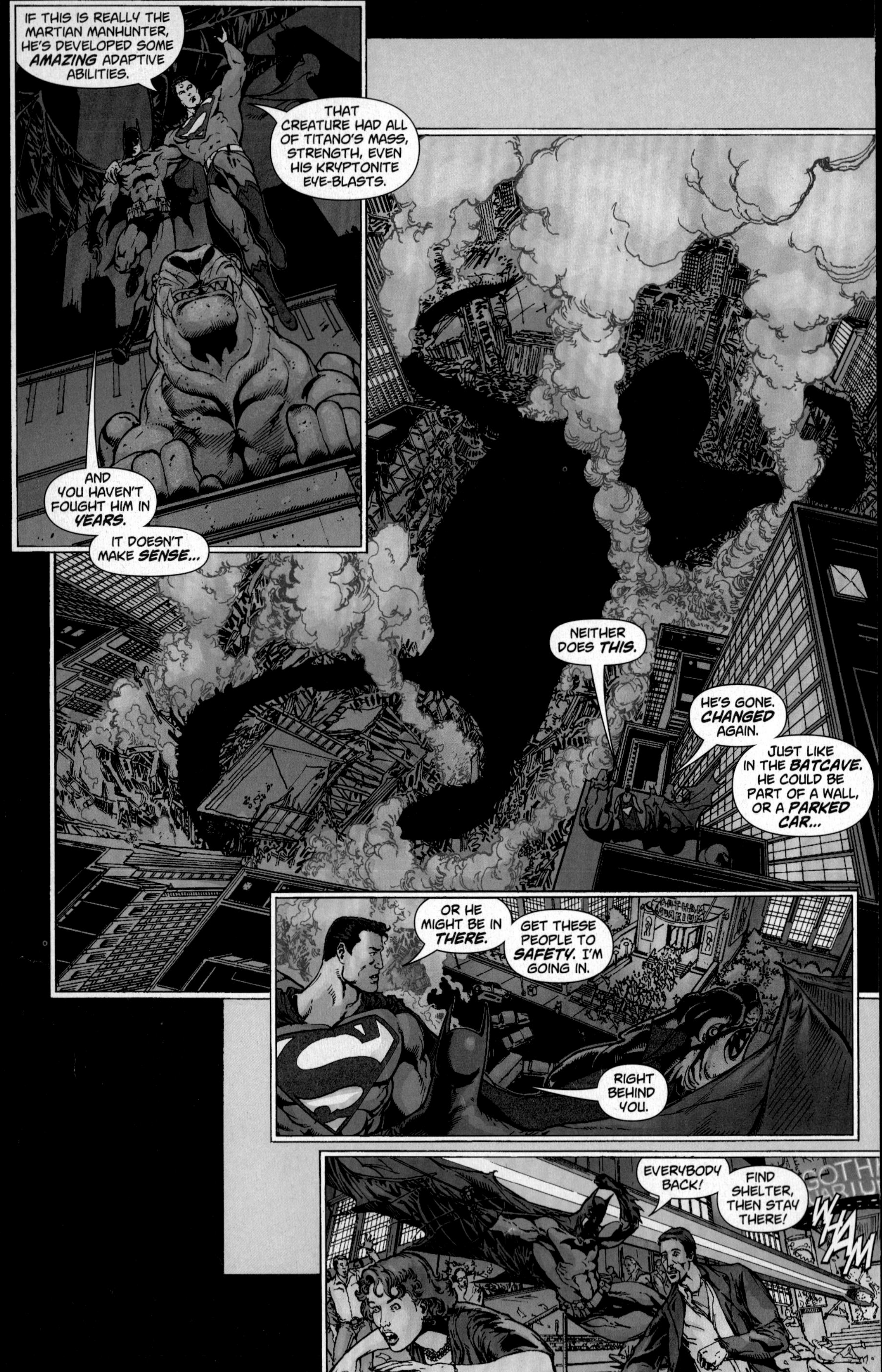
IF THIS IS REALLY THE MARTIAN MANHUNTER, HE'S DEVELOPED SOME AMAZING ADAPTIVE ABILITIES.
THAT CREATURE HAD ALL OF TITANO'S MASS, STRENGTH, EVEN HIS KRYPTONITE EYE-BLASTS.
AND YOU HAVEN'T FOUGHT HIM IN YEARS.
IT DOESN'T MAKE SENSE...
NEITHER DOES THIS.
HE'S GONE. CHANGED AGAIN.
JUST LIKE IN THE BATCAVE. HE COULD BE PART OF A WALL, OR A PARKED CAR...
OR HE MIGHT BE IN THERE.
GET THESE PEOPLE TO SAFETY. I'M GOING IN.
RIGHT BEHIND YOU.
EVERYBODY BACK!
FIND SHELTER, THEN STAY THERE!
WHAM

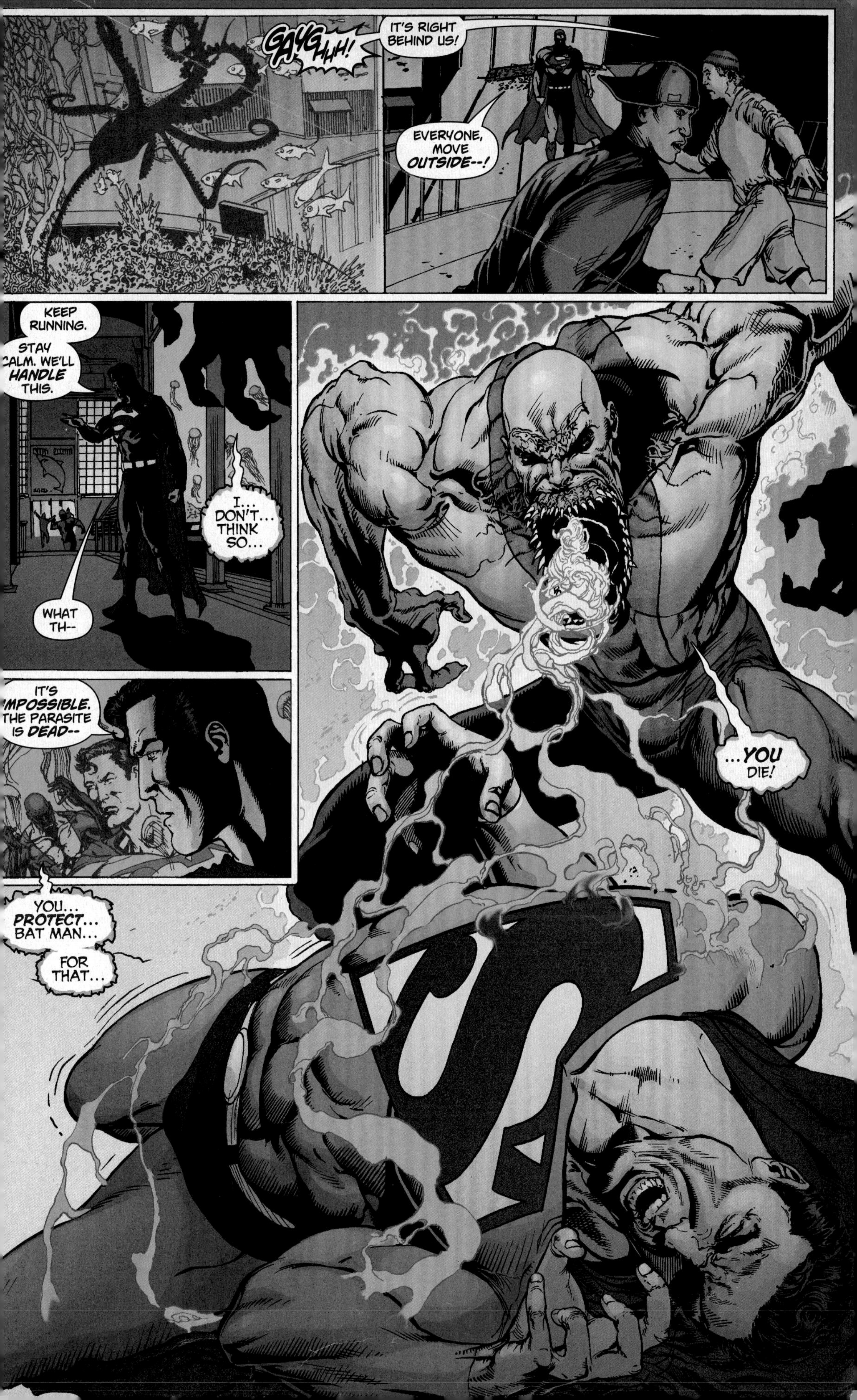
GAUGHHH!
IT'S RIGHT BEHIND US!
EVERYONE, MOVE OUTSIDE--!
KEEP RUNNING.
STAY CALM. WE'LL HANDLE THIS.
I... DON'T... THINK SO...
WHAT TH--
IT'S IMPOSSIBLE. THE PARASITE IS DEAD--
YOU... PROTECT... BAT MAN...
FOR THAT...
...YOU DIE!

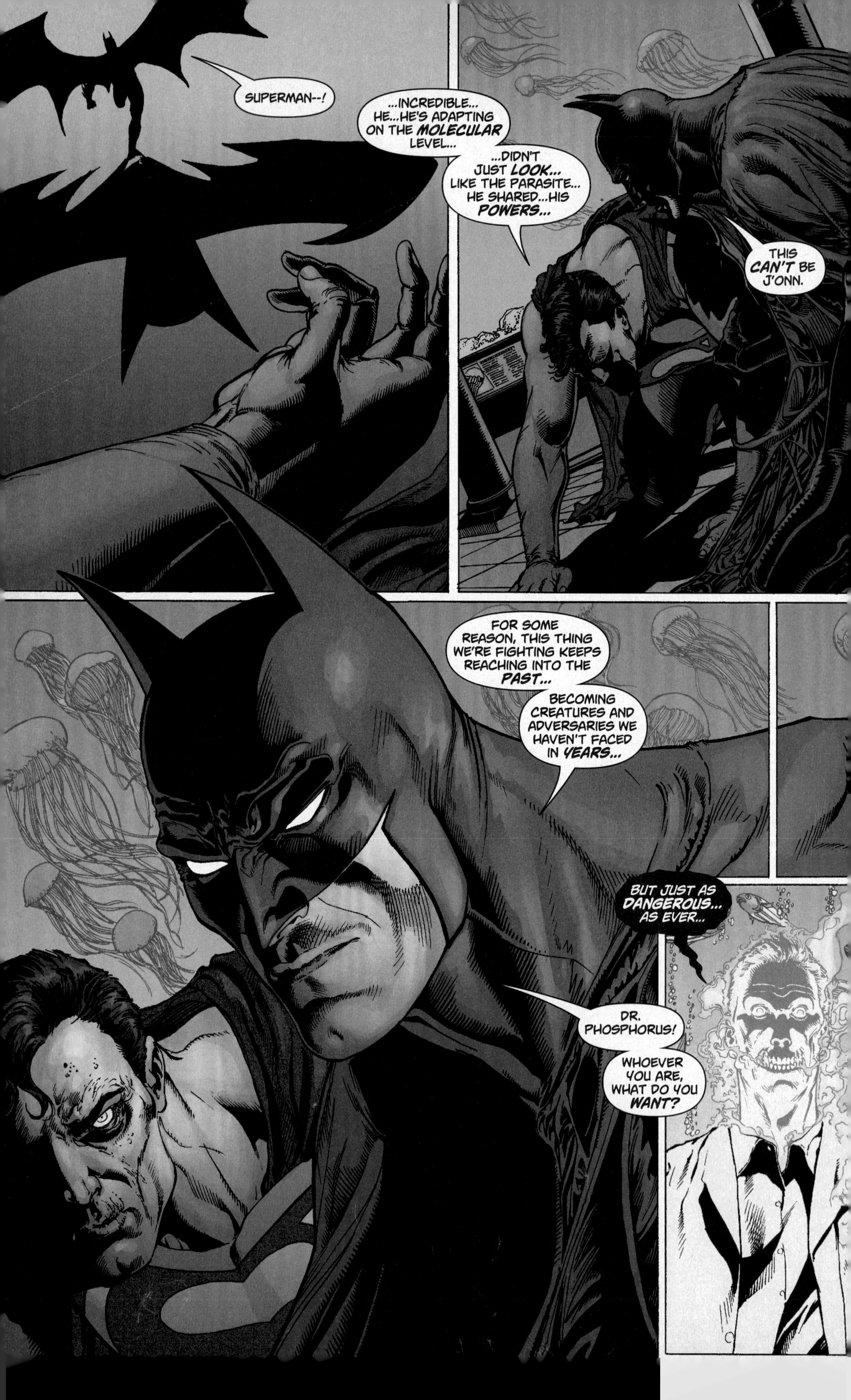
SUPERMAN--!
...INCREDIBLE... HE...HE'S ADAPTING ON THE MOLECULAR LEVEL...
...DIDN'T JUST LOOK... LIKE THE PARASITE... HE SHARED...HIS POWERS...
THIS CAN'T BE J'ONN.
FOR SOME REASON, THIS THING WE'RE FIGHTING KEEPS REACHING INTO THE PAST...
BECOMING CREATURES AND ADVERSARIES WE HAVEN'T FACED IN YEARS...
BUT JUST AS DANGEROUS... AS EVER...
DR. PHOSPHORUS!
WHOEVER YOU ARE, WHAT DO YOU WANT?

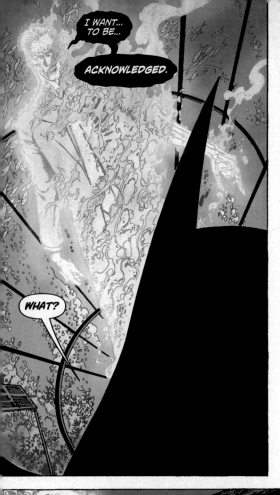

I WANT... TO BE...

ACKNOWLEDGED.

WHAT?

SO LONG... WAS I IGNORED...

...ABUSED...

...THEN FORGOTTEN...

WHICH ONE OF YOU, DAMMIT?

WHO WAS FORGOTTEN?

BATMAN--

HOLD YOUR BREATH.

CTNK

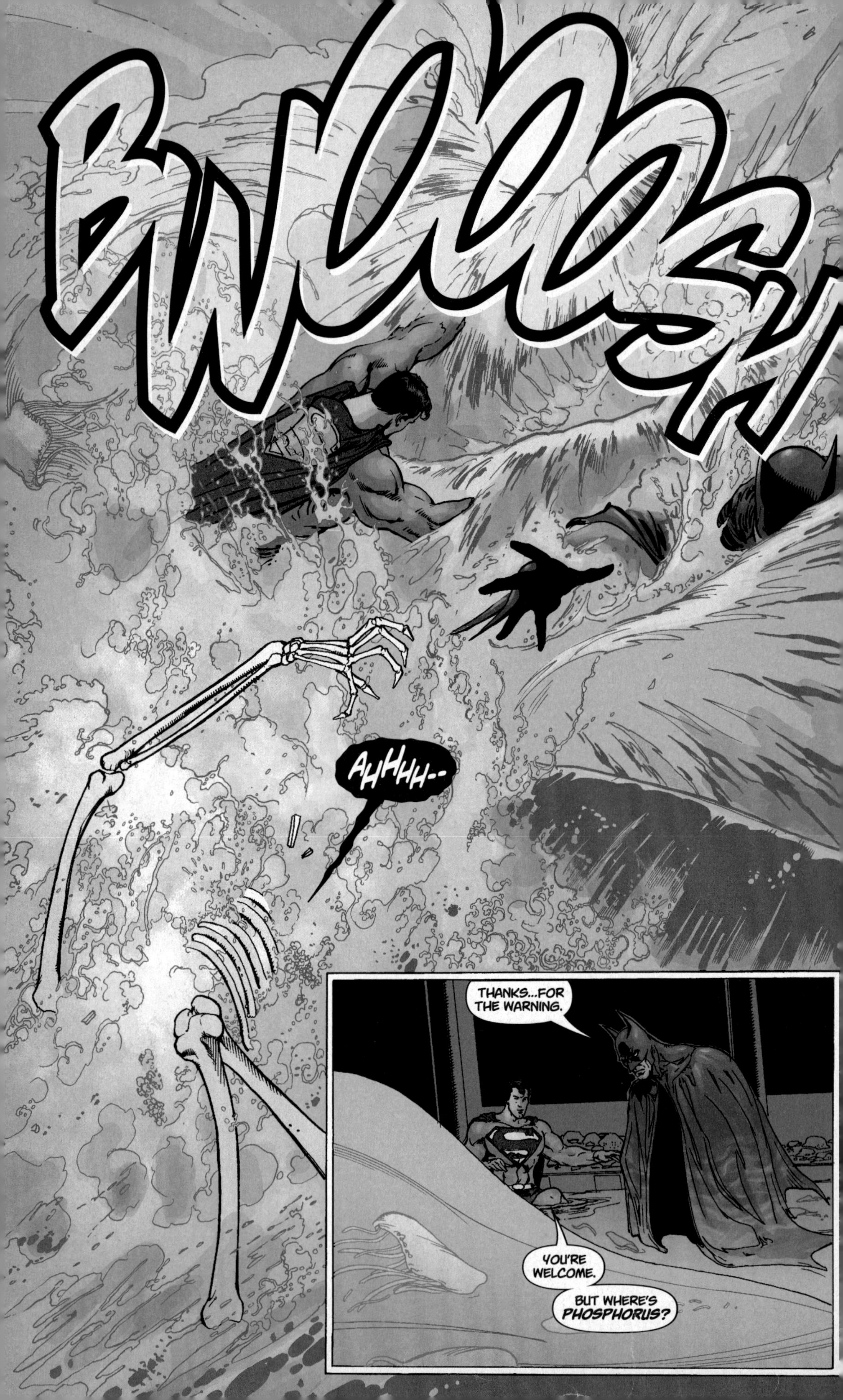
BWOOSH
AHHHH--
THANKS...FOR THE WARNING.
YOU'RE WELCOME.
BUT WHERE'S PHOSPHORUS?

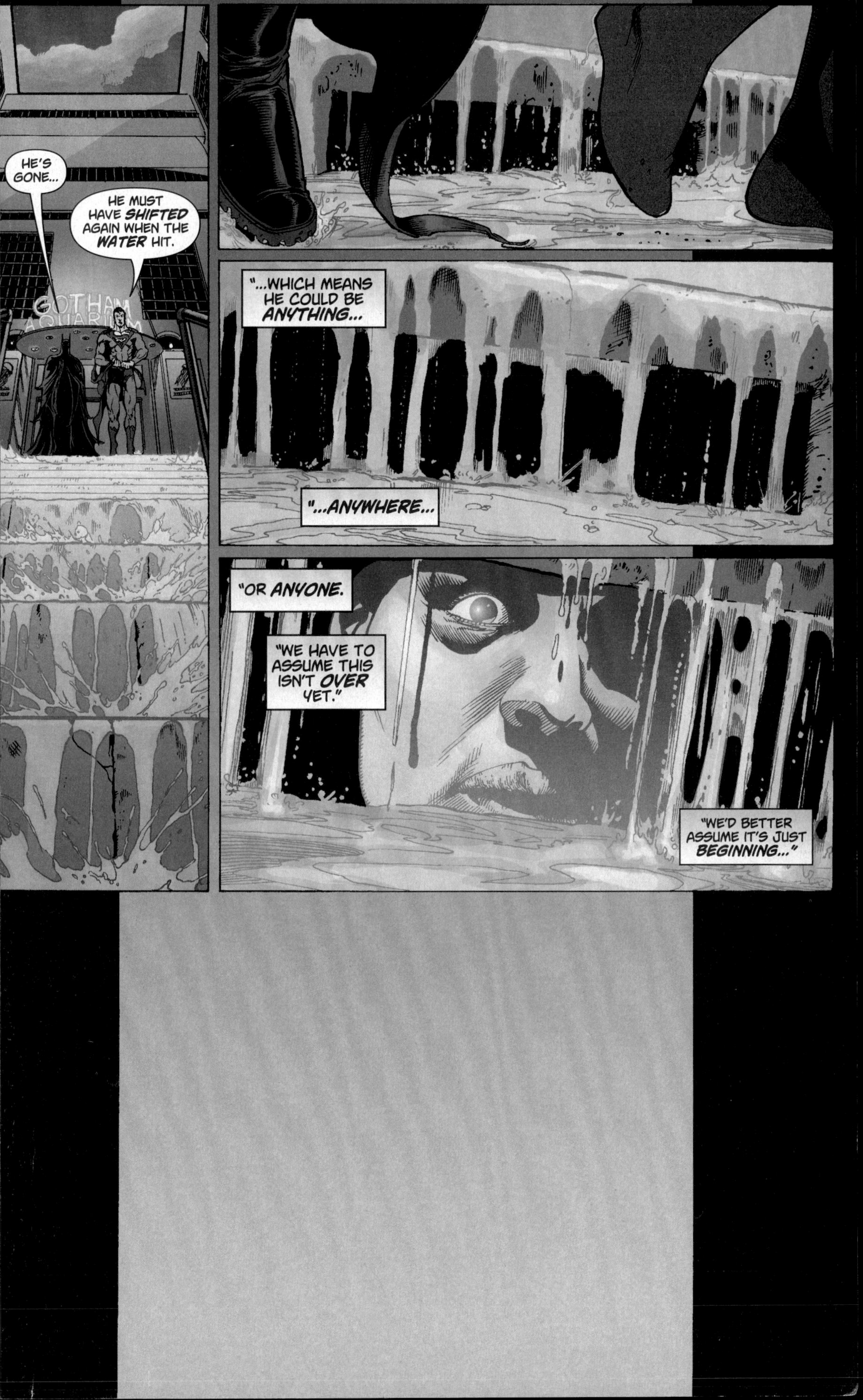
HE'S GONE...
HE MUST HAVE *SHIFTED* AGAIN WHEN THE *WATER* HIT.
"...WHICH MEANS HE COULD BE *ANYTHING*...
"...*ANYWHERE*...
"OR *ANYONE*.
"WE HAVE TO ASSUME THIS ISN'T *OVER* YET."
"WE'D BETTER ASSUME IT'S JUST *BEGINNING*..."

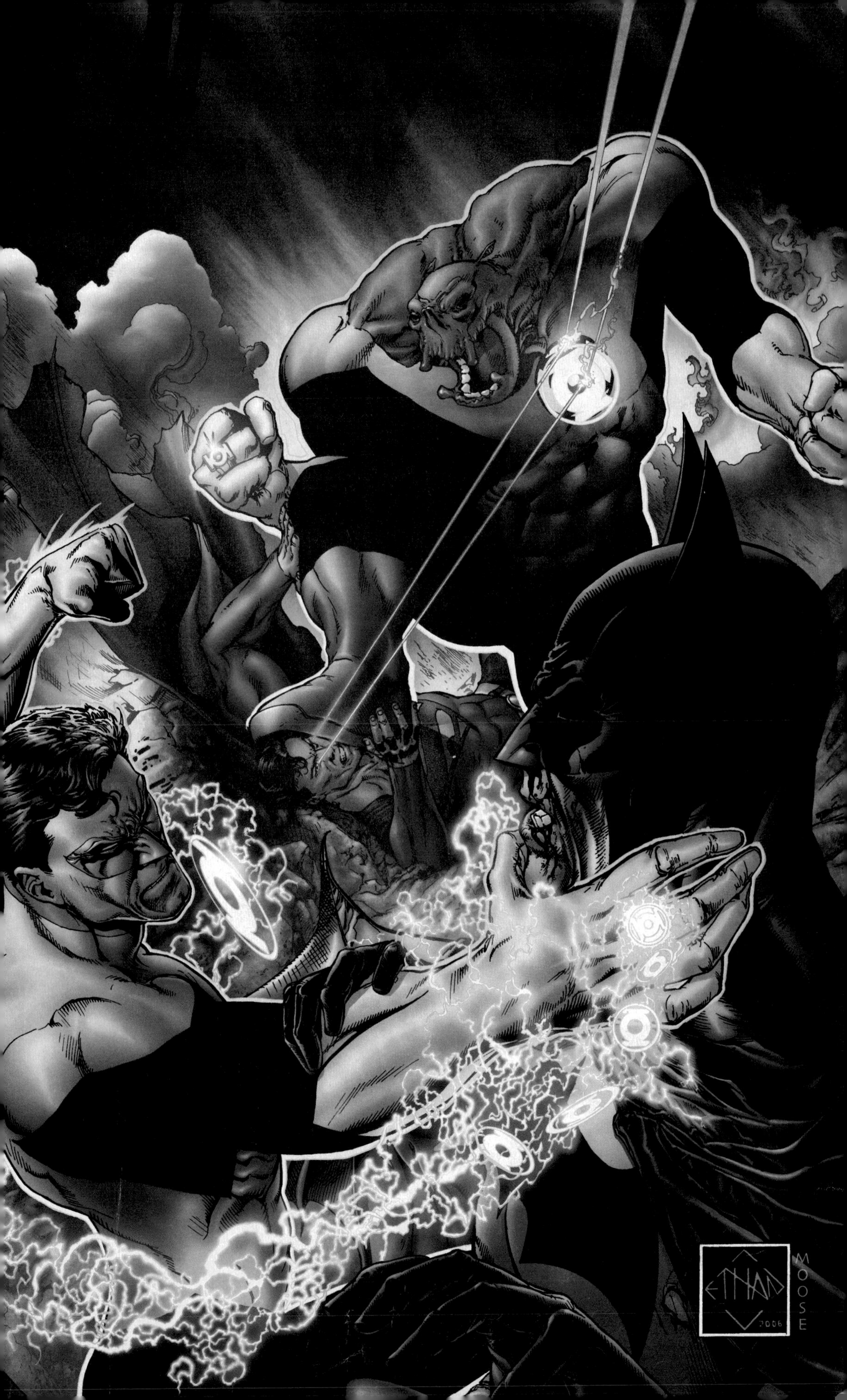
ETHAN
MOOSE
2006

THE ENEMIES AMONG US: PART TWO
From SUPERMAN/BATMAN 29
Cover by Ethan Van Sciver and Moose Baumann

Mark Verheiden
Writer

Ethan Van Sciver
Artist

Guy Major
Colors

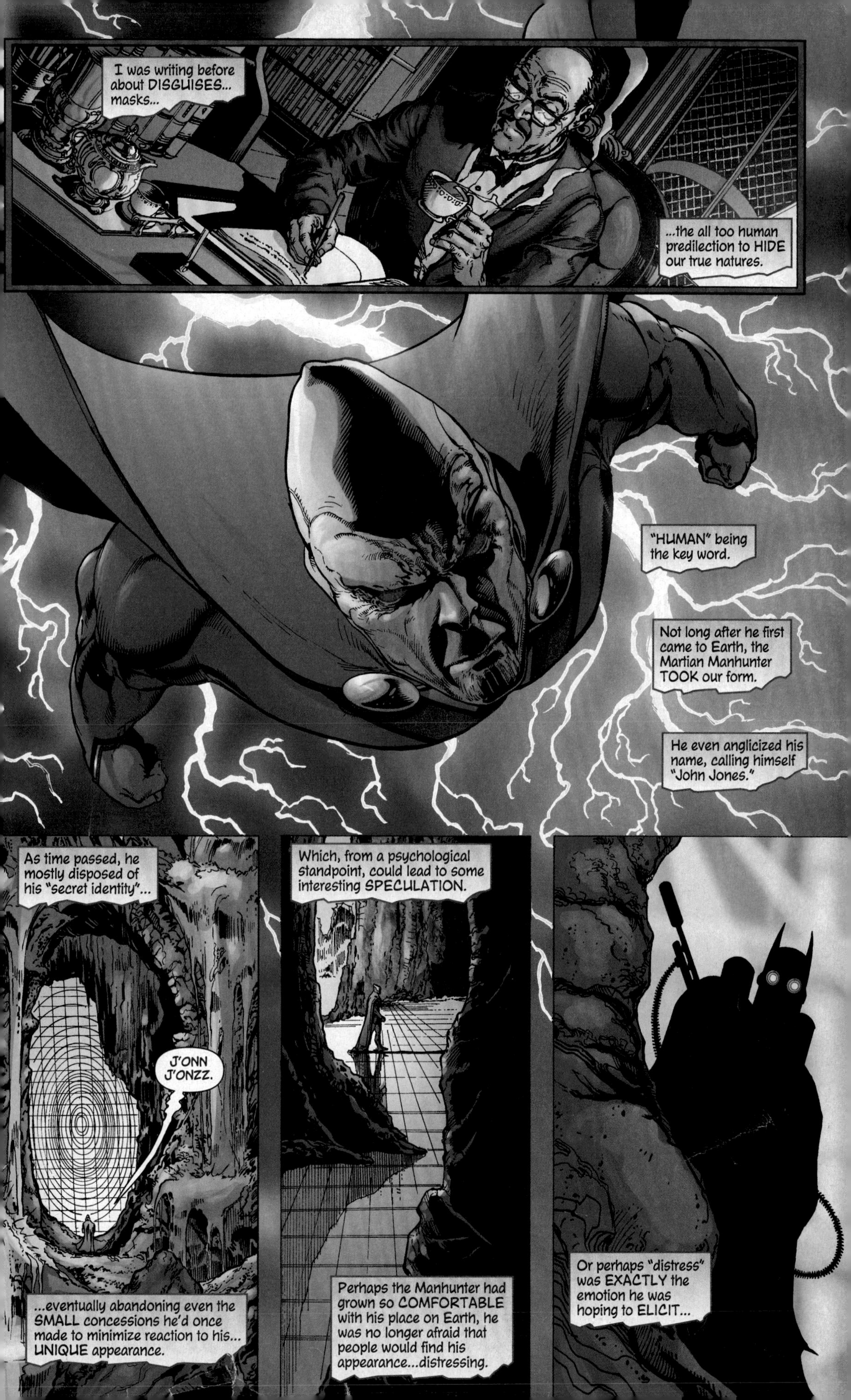
I was writing before about DISGUISES... masks...
...the all too human predilection to HIDE our true natures.
"HUMAN" being the key word.
Not long after he first came to Earth, the Martian Manhunter TOOK our form.
He even anglicized his name, calling himself "John Jones."
As time passed, he mostly disposed of his "secret identity"...
J'ONN J'ONZZ.
...eventually abandoning even the SMALL concessions he'd once made to minimize reaction to his... UNIQUE appearance.
Which, from a psychological standpoint, could lead to some interesting SPECULATION.
Perhaps the Manhunter had grown so COMFORTABLE with his place on Earth, he was no longer afraid that people would find his appearance...distressing.
Or perhaps "distress" was EXACTLY the emotion he was hoping to ELICIT...

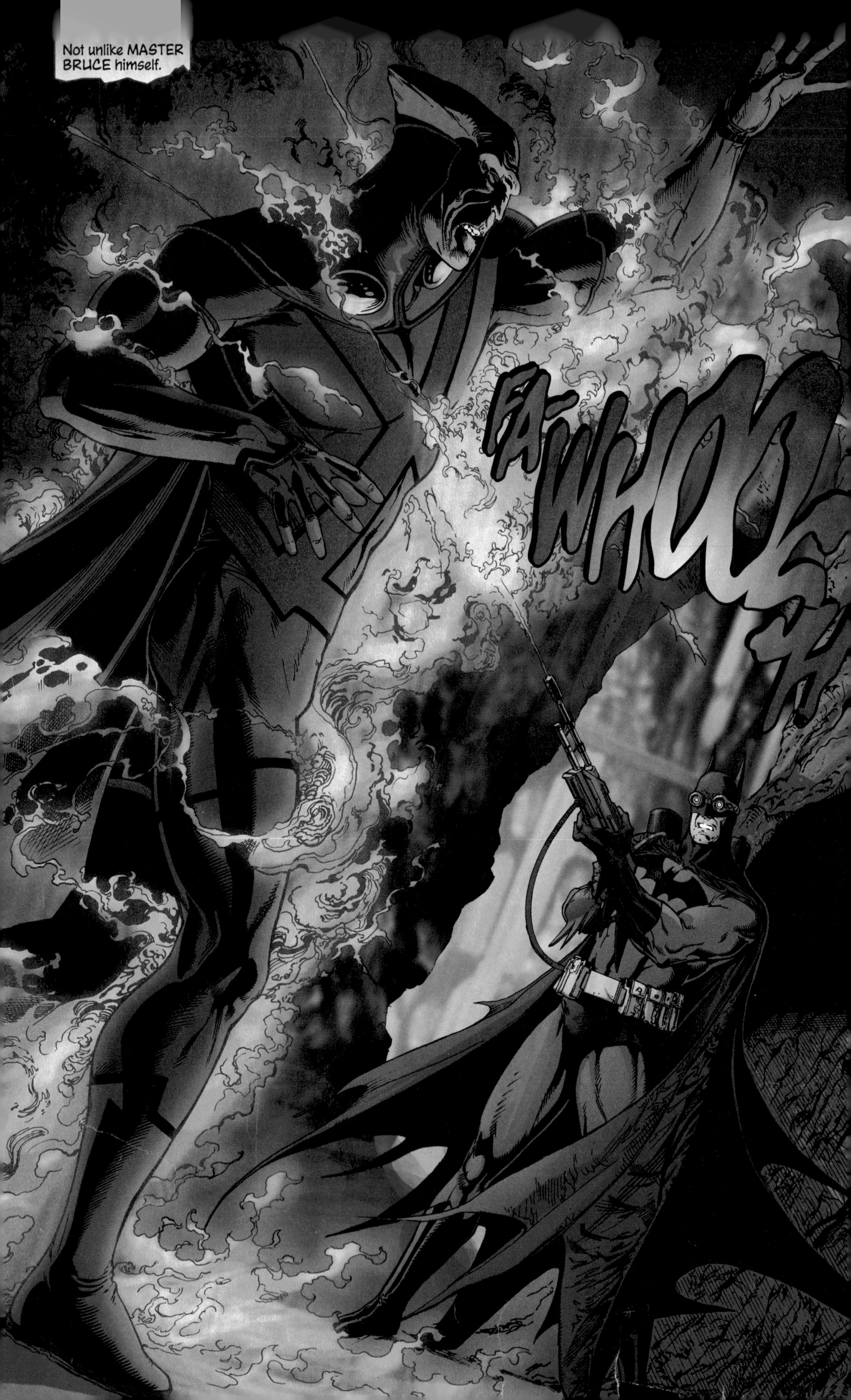
Not unlike MASTER BRUCE himself.
FA-WHOOSH

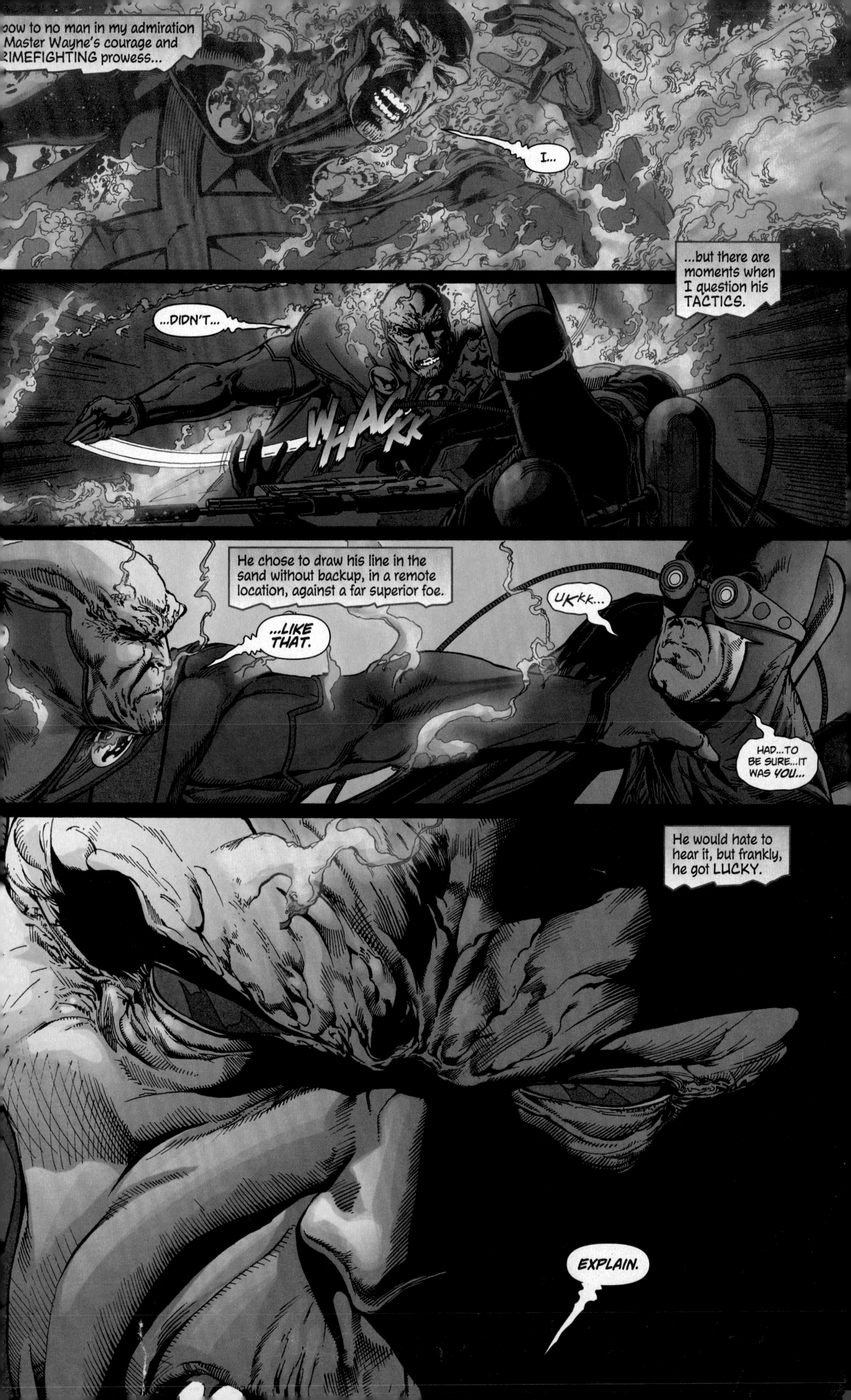
bow to no man in my admiration Master Wayne's courage and RIMEFIGHTING prowess...
I...
...but there are moments when I question his TACTICS.
...DIDN'T...
WHACKK
He chose to draw his line in the sand without backup, in a remote location, against a far superior foe.
...LIKE THAT.
UKKK...
HAD...TO BE SURE...IT WAS YOU...
He would hate to hear it, but frankly, he got LUCKY.
EXPLAIN.

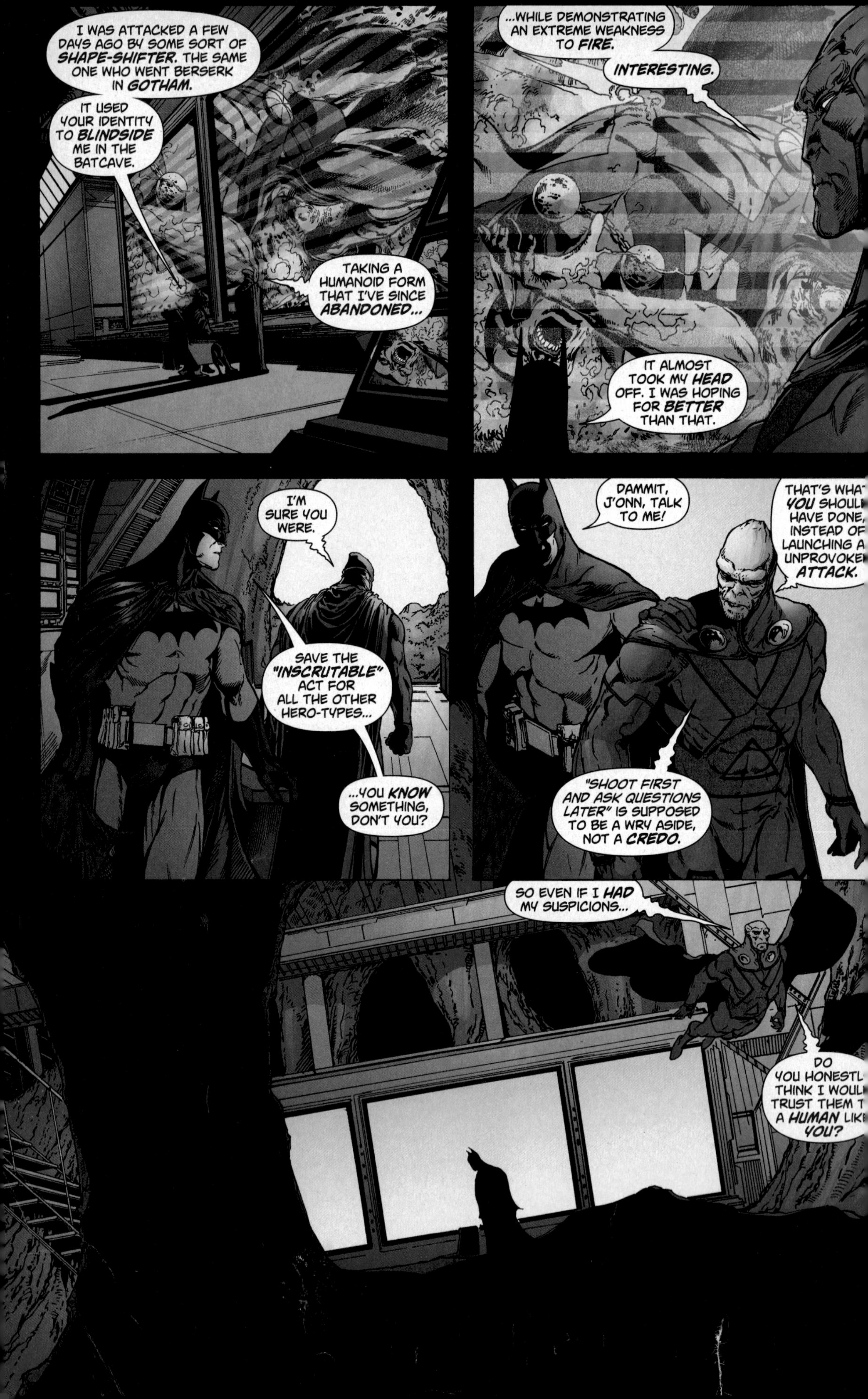
I WAS ATTACKED A FEW DAYS AGO BY SOME SORT OF SHAPE-SHIFTER. THE SAME ONE WHO WENT BERSERK IN GOTHAM.
IT USED YOUR IDENTITY TO BLINDSIDE ME IN THE BATCAVE.
TAKING A HUMANOID FORM THAT I'VE SINCE ABANDONED...
...WHILE DEMONSTRATING AN EXTREME WEAKNESS TO FIRE.
INTERESTING.
IT ALMOST TOOK MY HEAD OFF. I WAS HOPING FOR BETTER THAN THAT.
I'M SURE YOU WERE.
SAVE THE "INSCRUTABLE" ACT FOR ALL THE OTHER HERO-TYPES...
...YOU KNOW SOMETHING, DON'T YOU?
DAMMIT, J'ONN, TALK TO ME!
"SHOOT FIRST AND ASK QUESTIONS LATER" IS SUPPOSED TO BE A WRY ASIDE, NOT A CREDO.
SO EVEN IF I HAD MY SUSPICIONS...

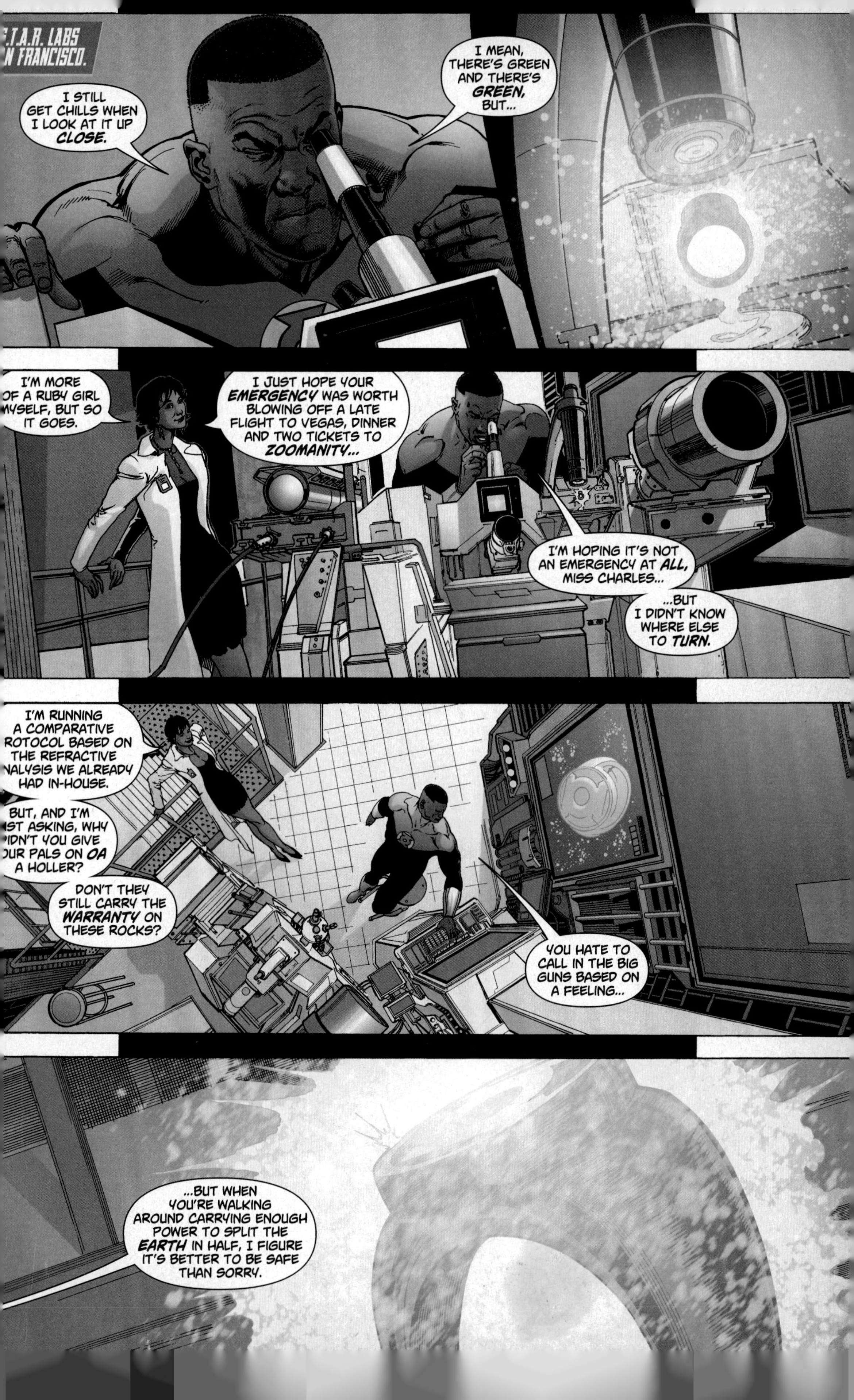
.T.A.R. LABS
N FRANCISCO.
I STILL GET CHILLS WHEN I LOOK AT IT UP CLOSE.
I MEAN, THERE'S GREEN AND THERE'S GREEN, BUT...
I'M MORE OF A RUBY GIRL MYSELF, BUT SO IT GOES.
I JUST HOPE YOUR EMERGENCY WAS WORTH BLOWING OFF A LATE FLIGHT TO VEGAS, DINNER AND TWO TICKETS TO ZOOMANITY...
I'M HOPING IT'S NOT AN EMERGENCY AT ALL, MISS CHARLES...
...BUT I DIDN'T KNOW WHERE ELSE TO TURN.
I'M RUNNING A COMPARATIVE ROTOCOL BASED ON THE REFRACTIVE NALYSIS WE ALREADY HAD IN-HOUSE.
BUT, AND I'M ST ASKING, WHY DIDN'T YOU GIVE UR PALS ON OA A HOLLER?
DON'T THEY STILL CARRY THE WARRANTY ON THESE ROCKS?
YOU HATE TO CALL IN THE BIG GUNS BASED ON A FEELING...
...BUT WHEN YOU'RE WALKING AROUND CARRYING ENOUGH POWER TO SPLIT THE EARTH IN HALF, I FIGURE IT'S BETTER TO BE SAFE THAN SORRY.

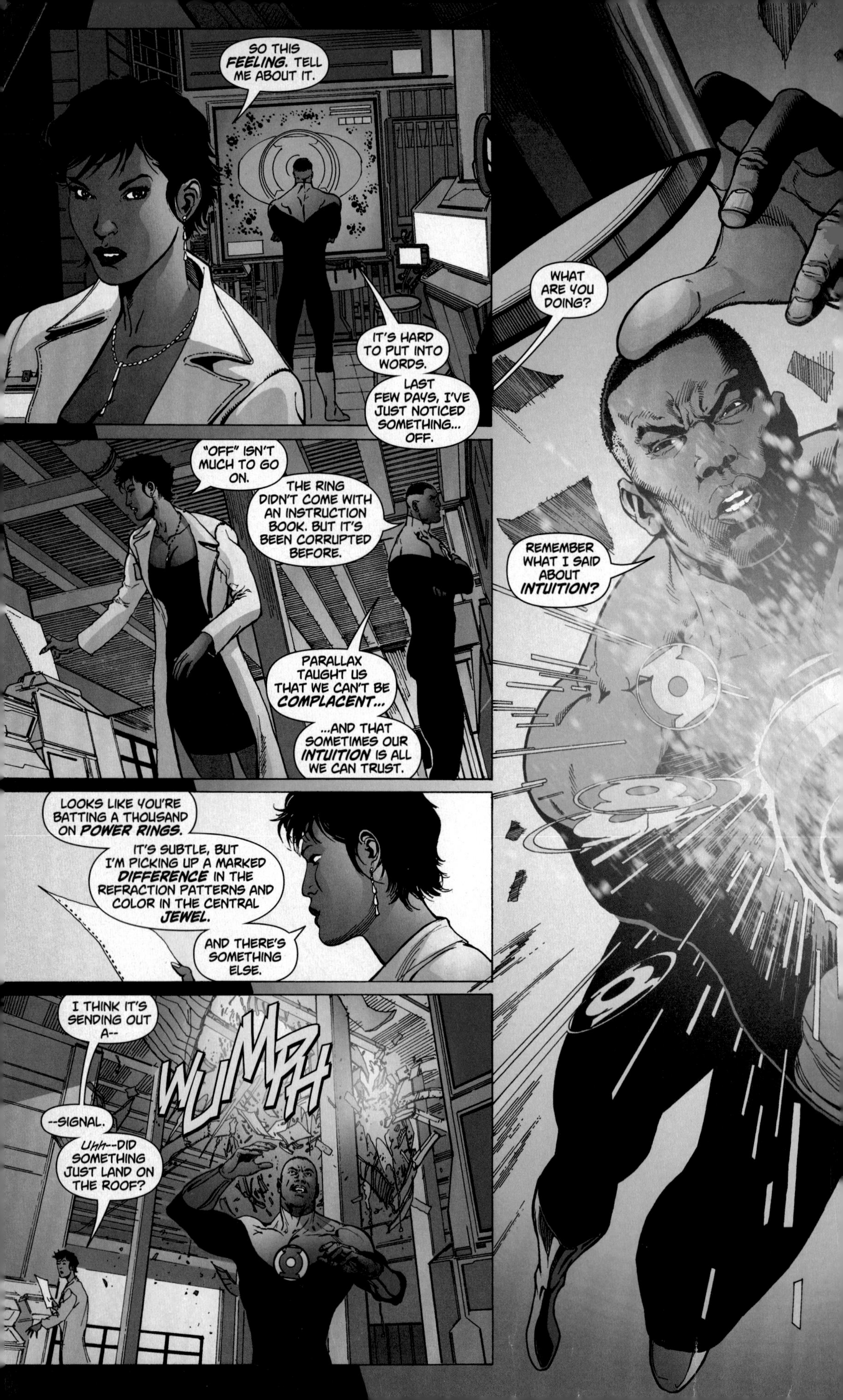
SO THIS FEELING. TELL ME ABOUT IT.
IT'S HARD TO PUT INTO WORDS.
LAST FEW DAYS, I'VE JUST NOTICED SOMETHING... OFF.
"OFF" ISN'T MUCH TO GO ON.
THE RING DIDN'T COME WITH AN INSTRUCTION BOOK. BUT IT'S BEEN CORRUPTED BEFORE.
PARALLAX TAUGHT US THAT WE CAN'T BE COMPLACENT...
...AND THAT SOMETIMES OUR INTUITION IS ALL WE CAN TRUST.
LOOKS LIKE YOU'RE BATTING A THOUSAND ON POWER RINGS.
IT'S SUBTLE, BUT I'M PICKING UP A MARKED DIFFERENCE IN THE REFRACTION PATTERNS AND COLOR IN THE CENTRAL JEWEL.
AND THERE'S SOMETHING ELSE.
I THINK IT'S SENDING OUT A--
WUMPH
--SIGNAL.
Uhh--DID SOMETHING JUST LAND ON THE ROOF?
WHAT ARE YOU DOING?
REMEMBER WHAT I SAID ABOUT INTUITION?

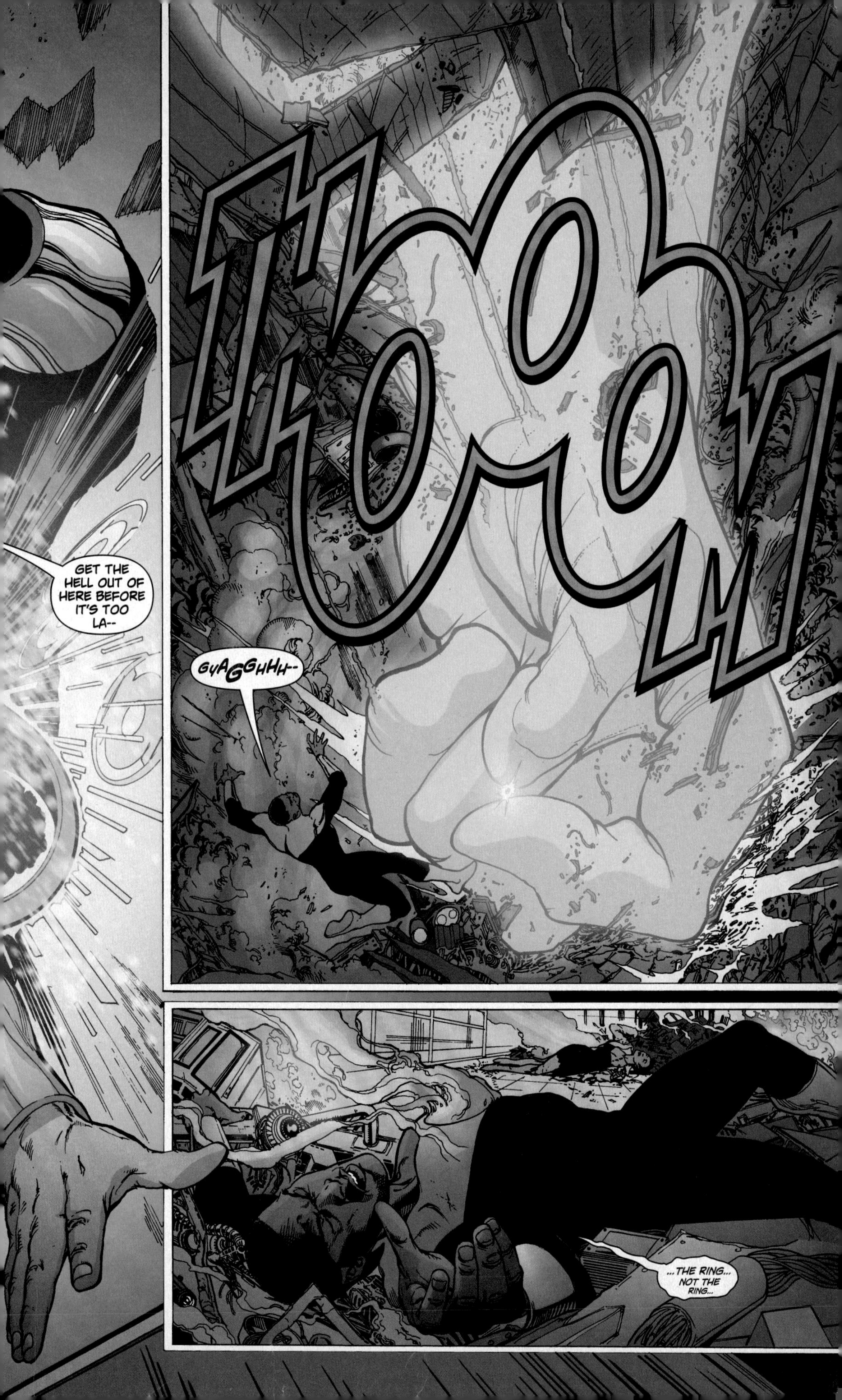

THOOOM
GET THE HELL OUT OF HERE BEFORE IT'S TOO LA--
GYAGGHHH--
...THE RING... NOT THE RING...

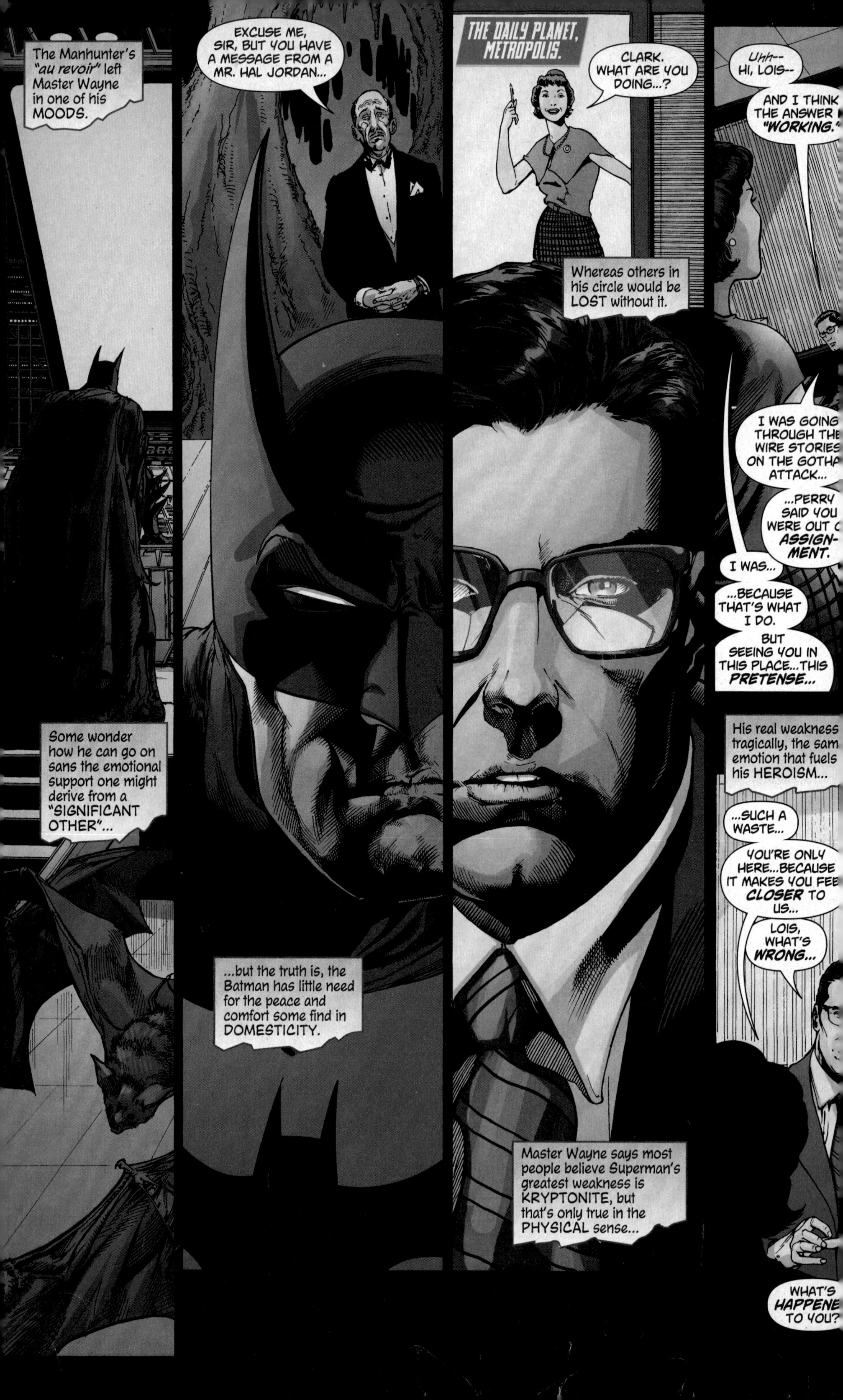

The Manhunter's "au revoir" left Master Wayne in one of his MOODS.
EXCUSE ME, SIR, BUT YOU HAVE A MESSAGE FROM A MR. HAL JORDAN...
Some wonder how he can go on sans the emotional support one might derive from a "SIGNIFICANT OTHER"...
...but the truth is, the Batman has little need for the peace and comfort some find in DOMESTICITY.
THE DAILY PLANET, METROPOLIS.
CLARK. WHAT ARE YOU DOING...?
Whereas others in his circle would be LOST without it.
Master Wayne says most people believe Superman's greatest weakness is KRYPTONITE, but that's only true in the PHYSICAL sense...
Uhh-- HI, LOIS--
AND I THINK THE ANSWER "WORKING."
I WAS GOING THROUGH THE WIRE STORIES ON THE GOTHA ATTACK...
...PERRY SAID YOU WERE OUT ASSIGN-MENT.
I WAS...
...BECAUSE THAT'S WHAT I DO.
BUT SEEING YOU IN THIS PLACE...THIS PRETENSE...
His real weakness tragically, the sam emotion that fuels his HEROISM...
...SUCH A WASTE...
YOU'RE ONLY HERE...BECAUSE IT MAKES YOU FEE CLOSER TO US...
LOIS, WHAT'S WRONG...
WHAT'S HAPPENE TO YOU?

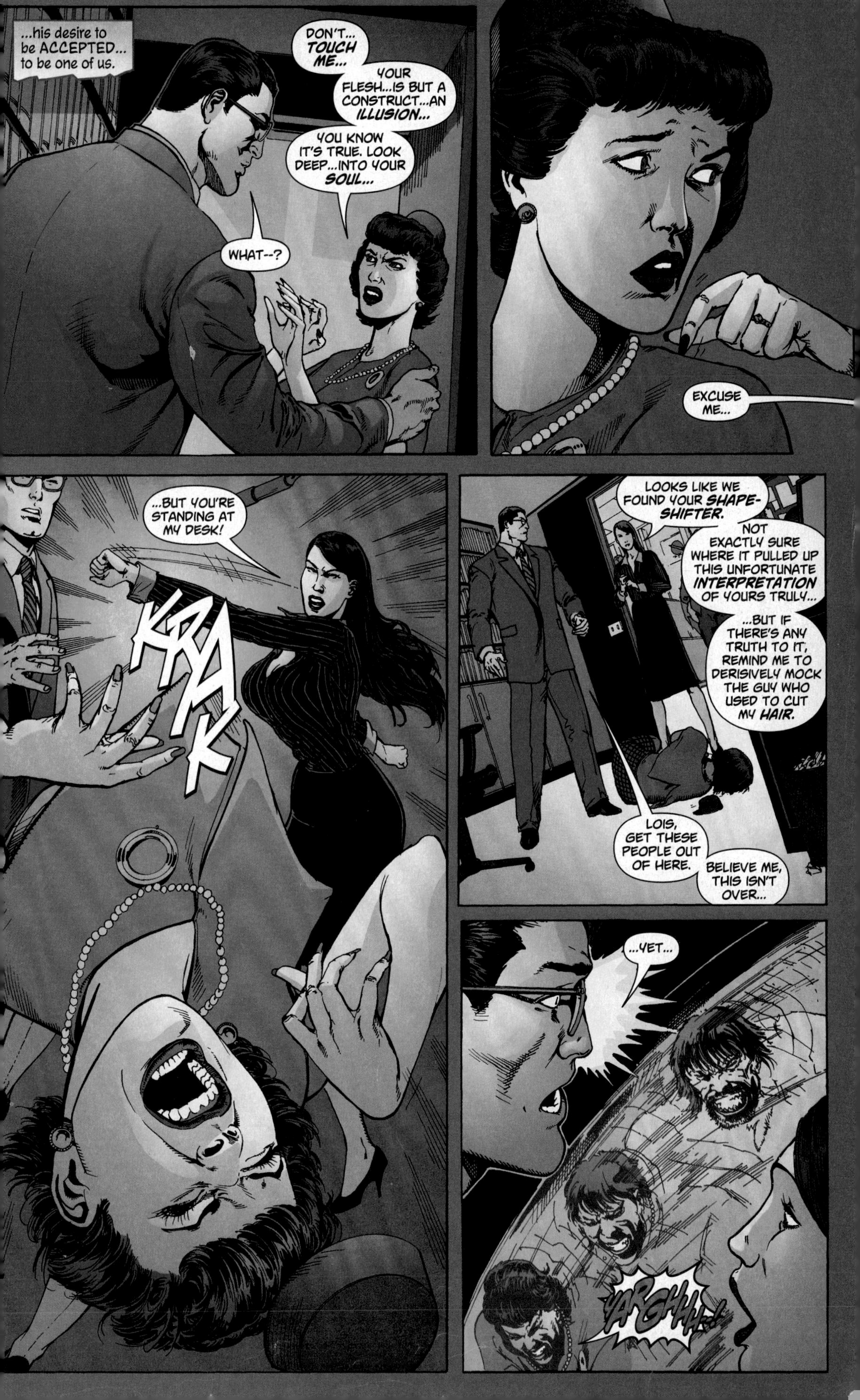

...his desire to be ACCEPTED... to be one of us.
DON'T... TOUCH ME...
YOUR FLESH...IS BUT A CONSTRUCT...AN ILLUSION...
YOU KNOW IT'S TRUE. LOOK DEEP...INTO YOUR SOUL...
WHAT--?
EXCUSE ME...
...BUT YOU'RE STANDING AT MY DESK!
KRAK
LOOKS LIKE WE FOUND YOUR SHAPE-SHIFTER.
NOT EXACTLY SURE WHERE IT PULLED UP THIS UNFORTUNATE INTERPRETATION OF YOURS TRULY...
...BUT IF THERE'S ANY TRUTH TO IT, REMIND ME TO DERISIVELY MOCK THE GUY WHO USED TO CUT MY HAIR.
LOIS, GET THESE PEOPLE OUT OF HERE.
BELIEVE ME, THIS ISN'T OVER...
...YET...
YARGHHH--!

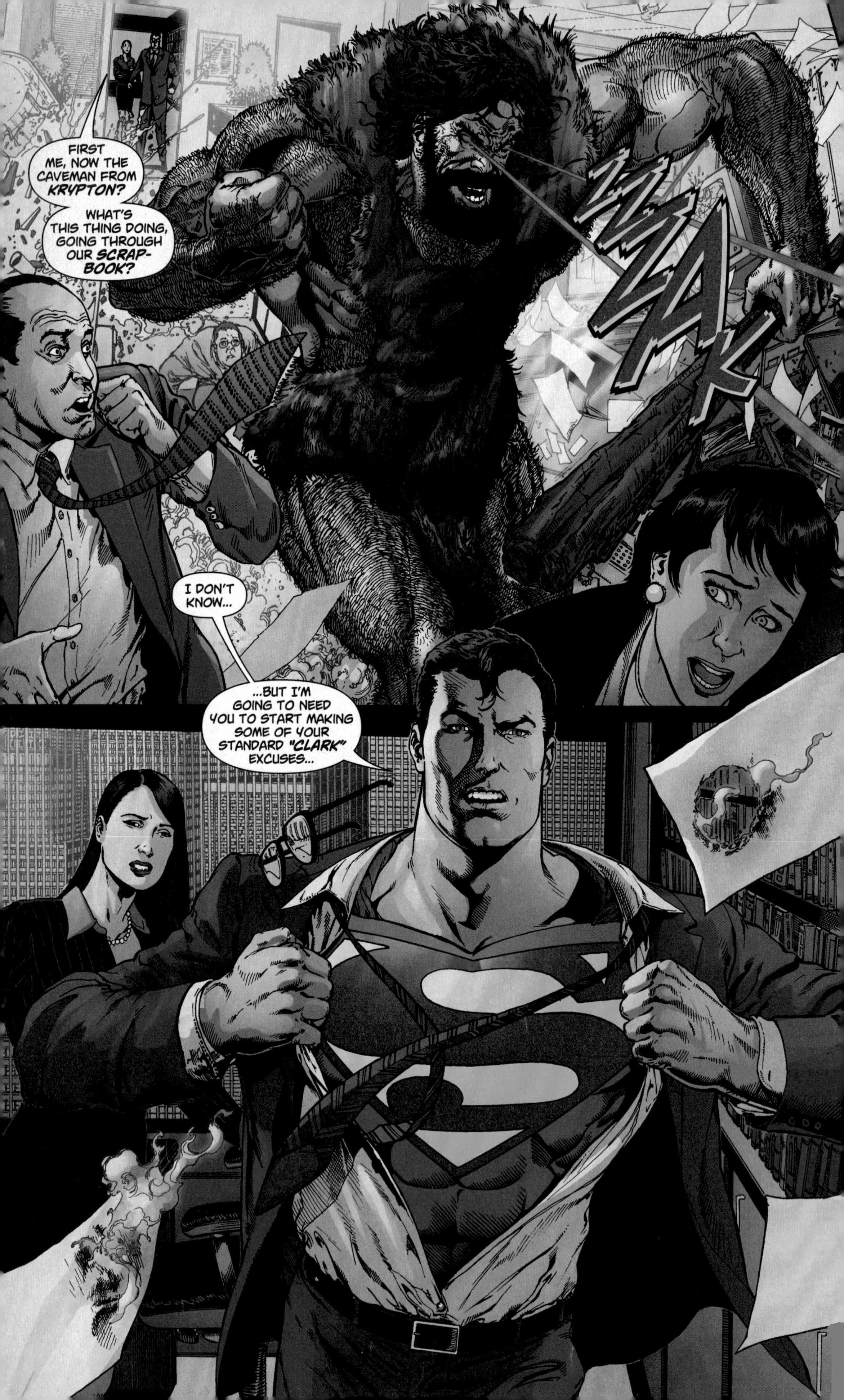

FIRST ME, NOW THE CAVEMAN FROM KRYPTON?
WHAT'S THIS THING DOING, GOING THROUGH OUR SCRAP-BOOK?
WHAK
I DON'T KNOW...
...BUT I'M GOING TO NEED YOU TO START MAKING SOME OF YOUR STANDARD "CLARK" EXCUSES...

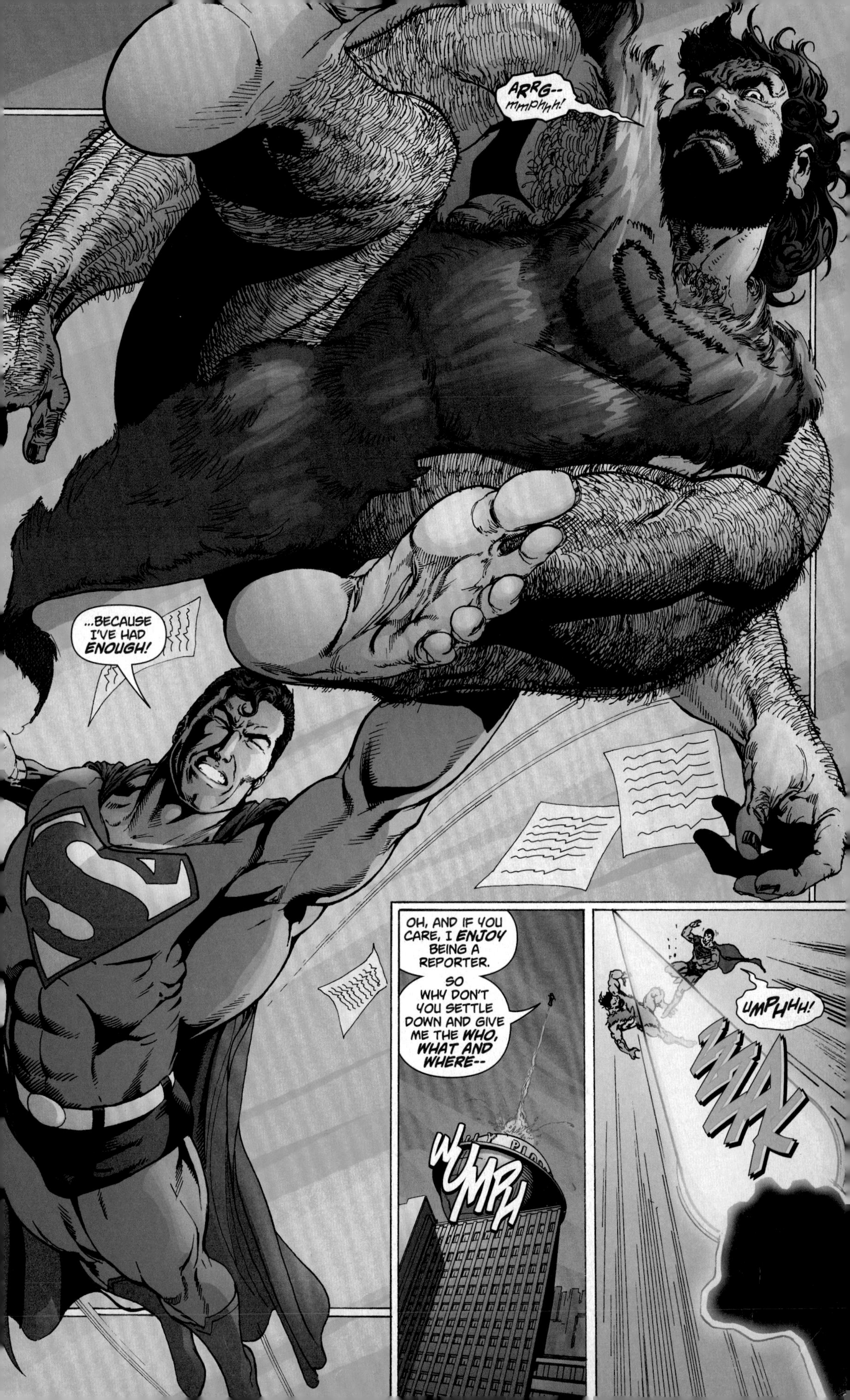
ARRG-- mmphhh!
...BECAUSE I'VE HAD ENOUGH!
OH, AND IF YOU CARE, I ENJOY BEING A REPORTER.
SO WHY DON'T YOU SETTLE DOWN AND GIVE ME THE WHO, WHAT AND WHERE--
WUMPH
UMPHHH!
WAK

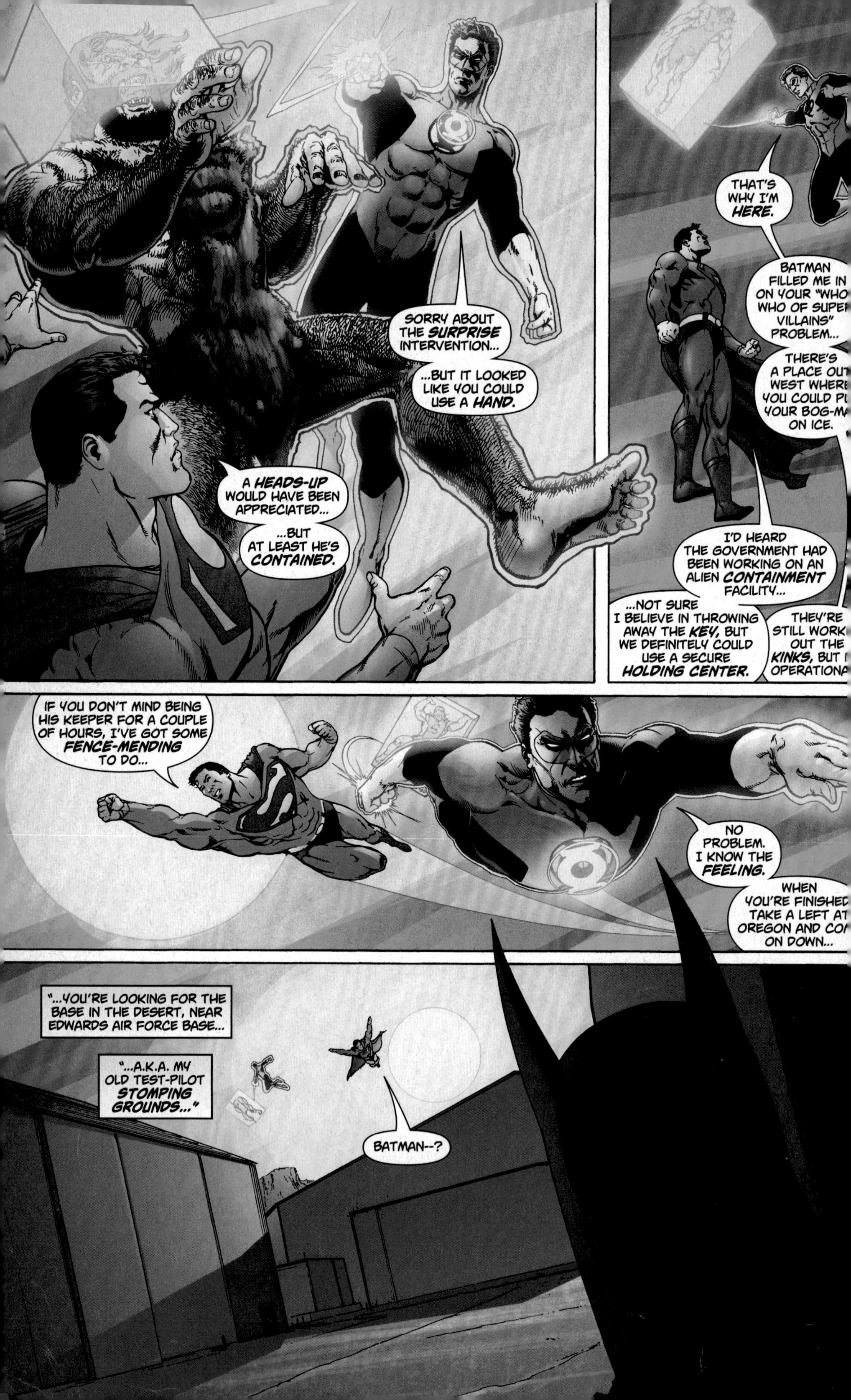
SORRY ABOUT THE SURPRISE INTERVENTION...
...BUT IT LOOKED LIKE YOU COULD USE A HAND.
A HEADS-UP WOULD HAVE BEEN APPRECIATED...
...BUT AT LEAST HE'S CONTAINED.
THAT'S WHY I'M HERE.
BATMAN FILLED ME IN ON YOUR "WHO'S WHO OF SUPER VILLAINS" PROBLEM...
THERE'S A PLACE OUT WEST WHERE YOU COULD PU YOUR BOG-MA ON ICE.
I'D HEARD THE GOVERNMENT HAD BEEN WORKING ON AN ALIEN CONTAINMENT FACILITY...
...NOT SURE I BELIEVE IN THROWING AWAY THE KEY, BUT WE DEFINITELY COULD USE A SECURE HOLDING CENTER.
THEY'RE STILL WORK OUT THE KINKS, BUT I OPERATIONA
IF YOU DON'T MIND BEING HIS KEEPER FOR A COUPLE OF HOURS, I'VE GOT SOME FENCE-MENDING TO DO...
NO PROBLEM. I KNOW THE FEELING.
WHEN YOU'RE FINISHED TAKE A LEFT AT OREGON AND CO ON DOWN...
"...YOU'RE LOOKING FOR THE BASE IN THE DESERT, NEAR EDWARDS AIR FORCE BASE...
"...A.K.A. MY OLD TEST-PILOT STOMPING GROUNDS..."
BATMAN--?

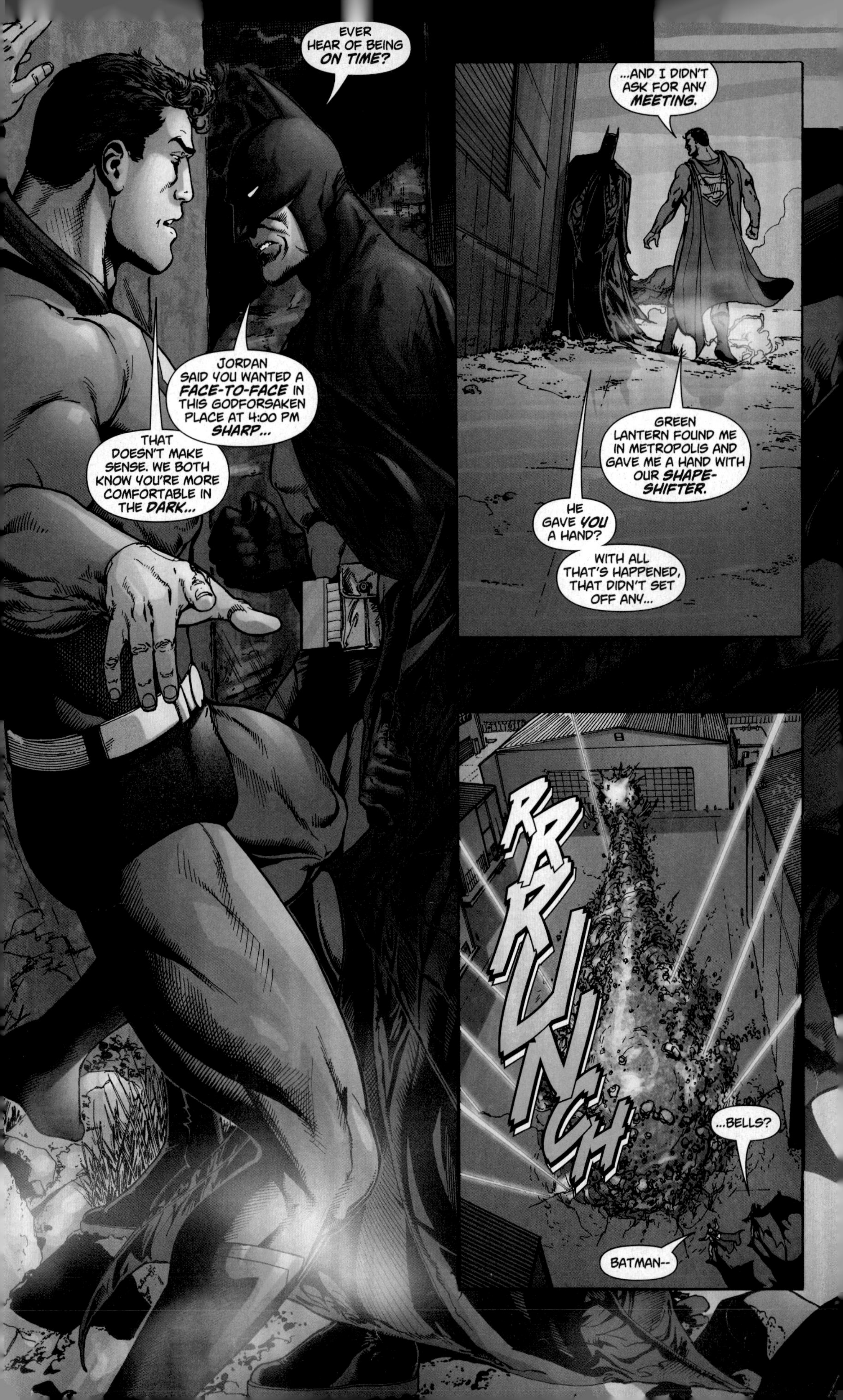

EVER HEAR OF BEING ON TIME?
JORDAN SAID YOU WANTED A FACE-TO-FACE IN THIS GODFORSAKEN PLACE AT 4:00 PM SHARP...
THAT DOESN'T MAKE SENSE. WE BOTH KNOW YOU'RE MORE COMFORTABLE IN THE DARK...
...AND I DIDN'T ASK FOR ANY MEETING.
GREEN LANTERN FOUND ME IN METROPOLIS AND GAVE ME A HAND WITH OUR SHAPE-SHIFTER.
HE GAVE YOU A HAND?
WITH ALL THAT'S HAPPENED, THAT DIDN'T SET OFF ANY...
RRRUNCH
...BELLS?
BATMAN--

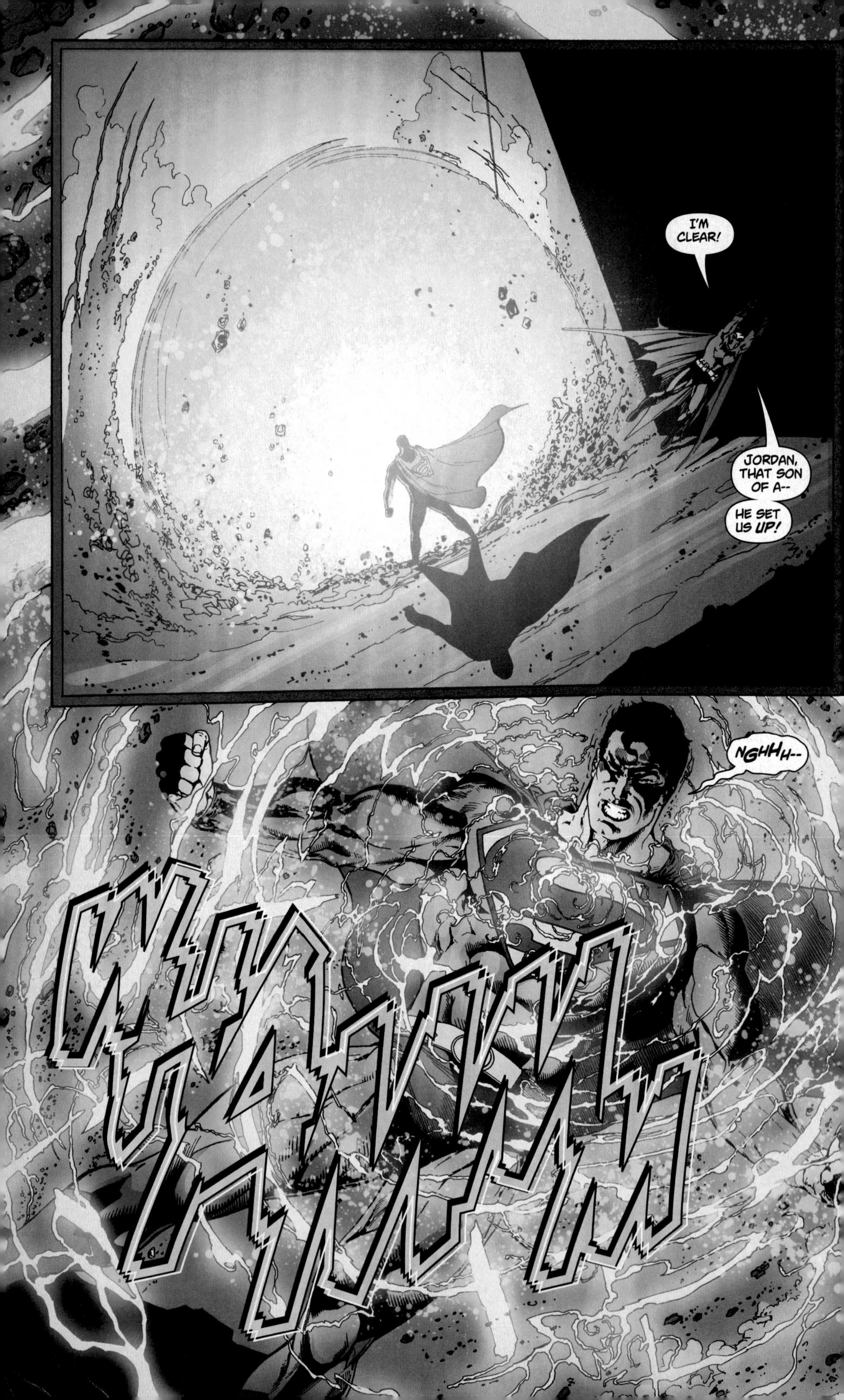
I'M CLEAR!
JORDAN, THAT SON OF A--
HE SET US UP!
NGHHH--
WHAMM

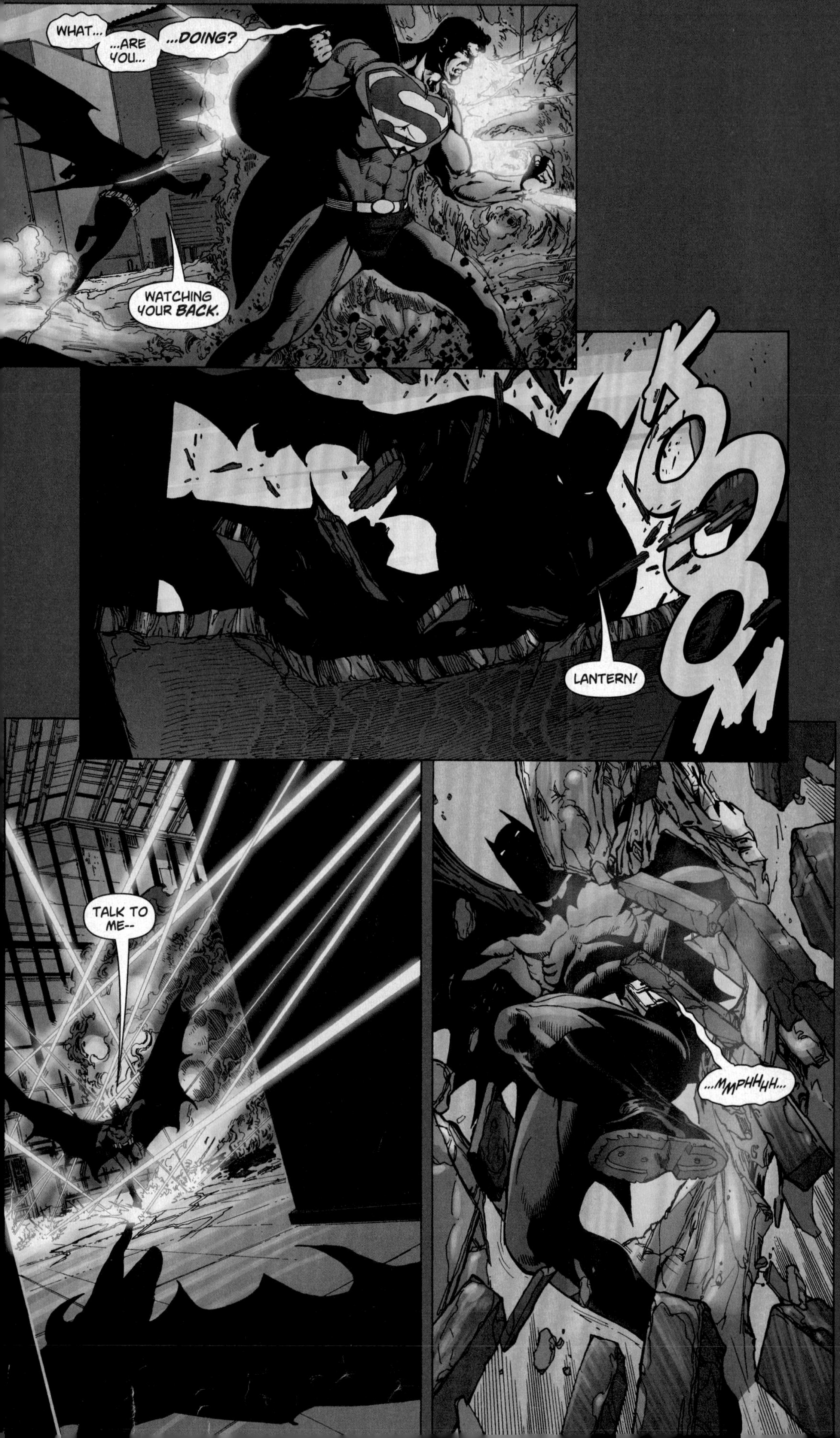
WHAT...
...ARE YOU...
...DOING?
WATCHING YOUR BACK.
KOOOM
LANTERN!
TALK TO ME--
...MMPHHHH...

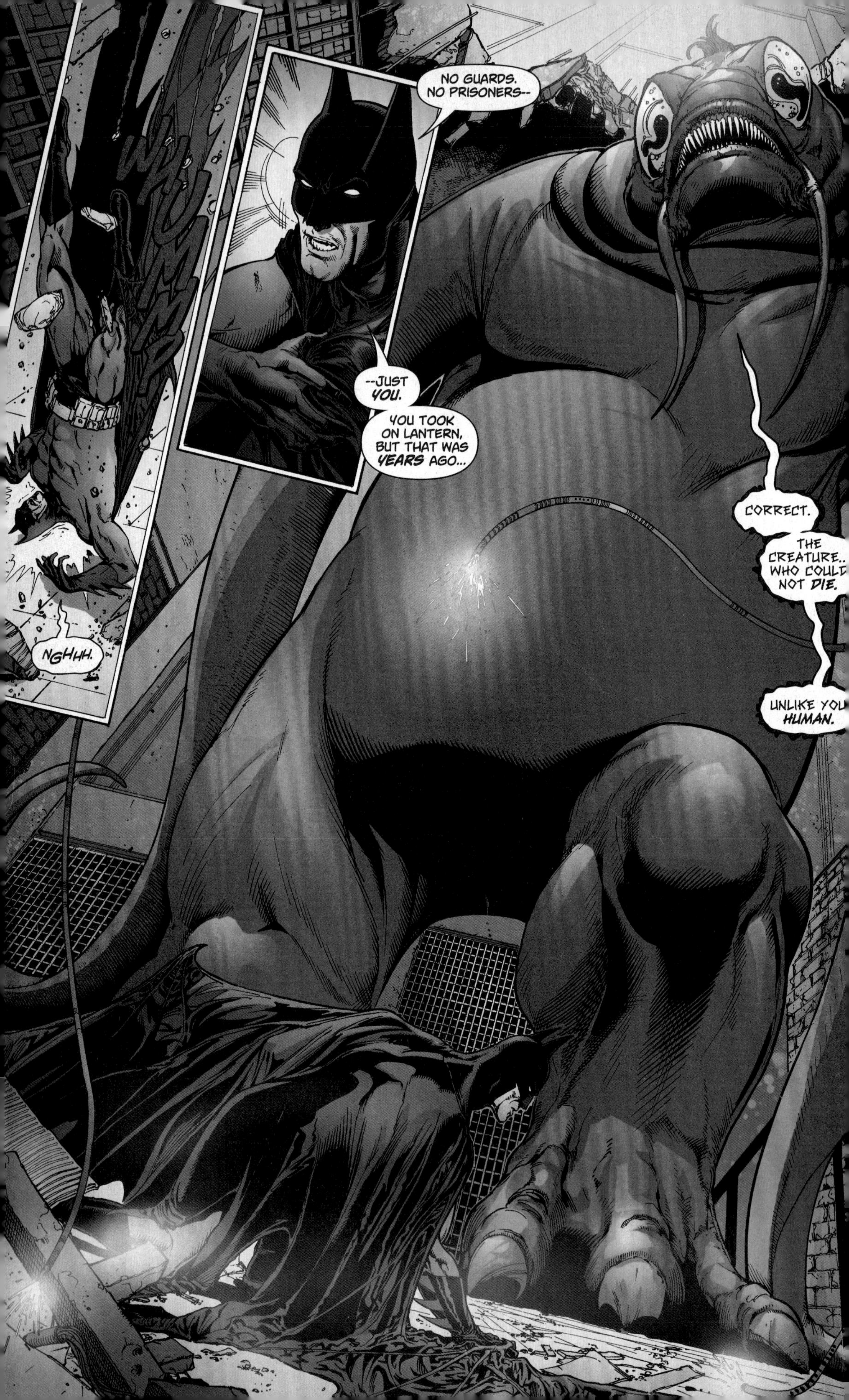
NGHHH.
NO GUARDS. NO PRISONERS--
--JUST YOU.
YOU TOOK ON LANTERN, BUT THAT WAS YEARS AGO...
CORRECT.
THE CREATURE.. WHO COULD NOT DIE.
UNLIKE YOU HUMAN.

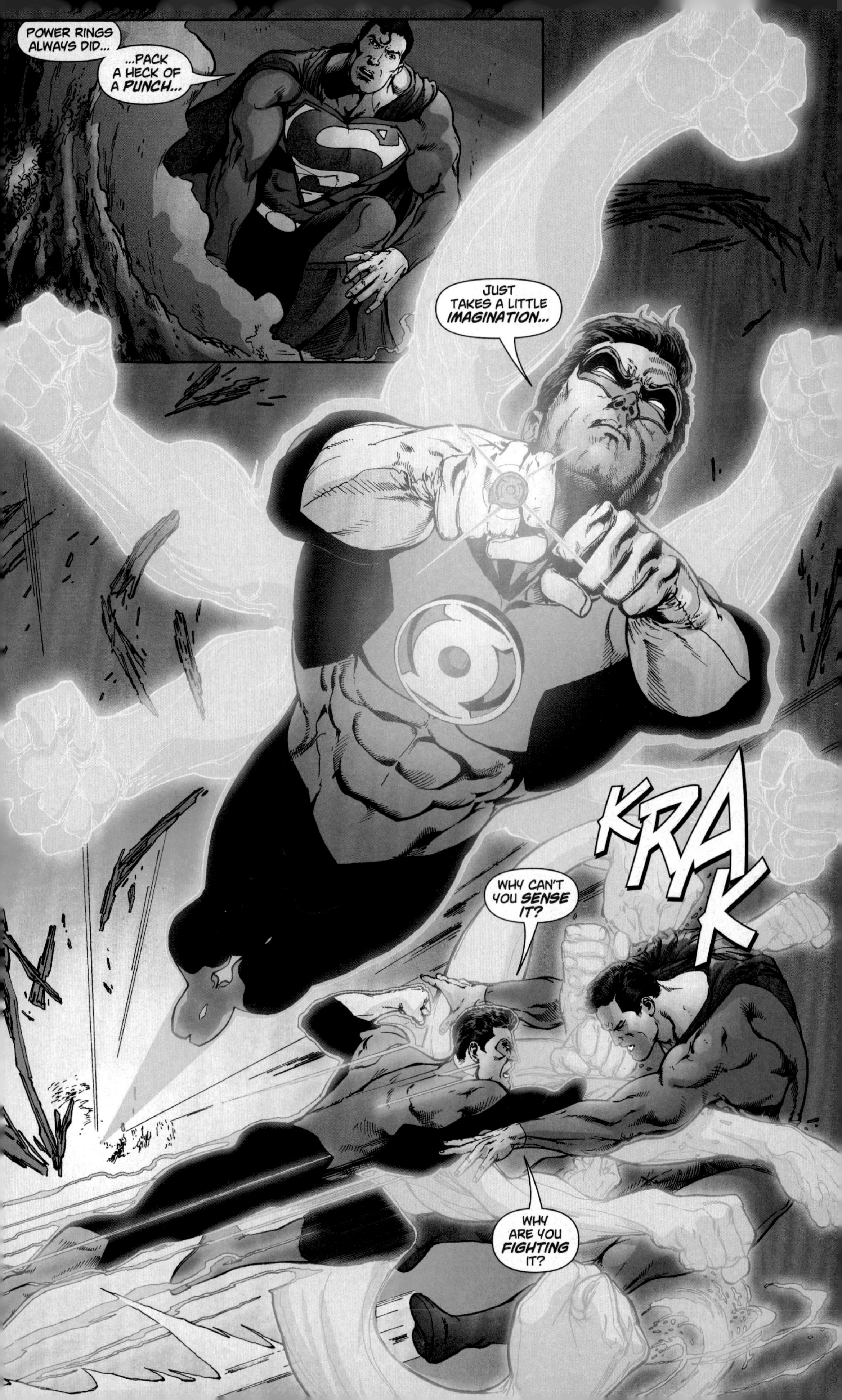
POWER RINGS ALWAYS DID...
...PACK A HECK OF A PUNCH...
JUST TAKES A LITTLE IMAGINATION...
KRAK
WHY CAN'T YOU SENSE IT?
WHY ARE YOU FIGHTING IT?

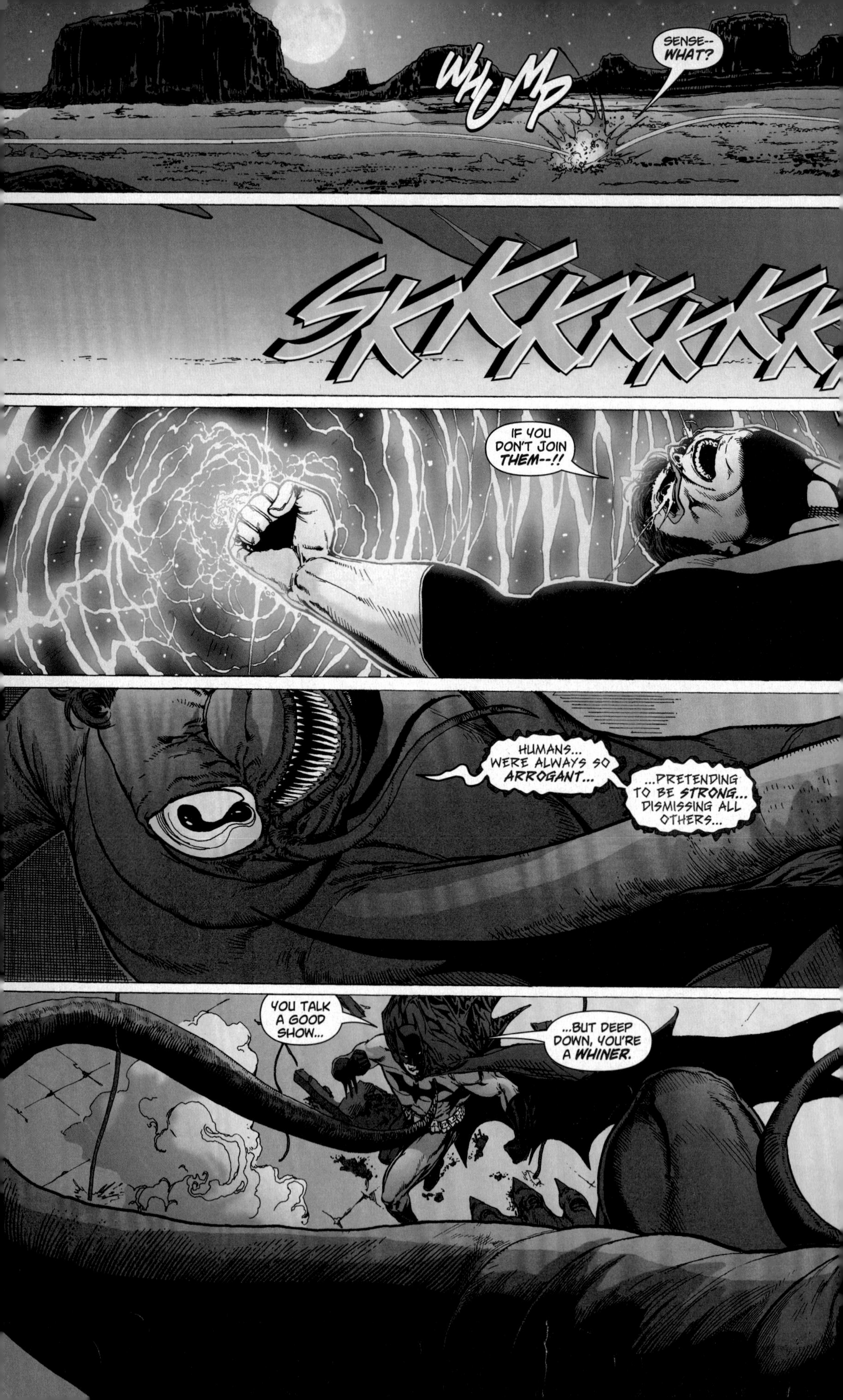
WHUMP
SENSE-- WHAT?
SKKKKKKK
IF YOU DON'T JOIN THEM--!!
HUMANS... WERE ALWAYS SO ARROGANT...
...PRETENDING TO BE STRONG... DISMISSING ALL OTHERS...
YOU TALK A GOOD SHOW...
...BUT DEEP DOWN, YOU'RE A WHINER.

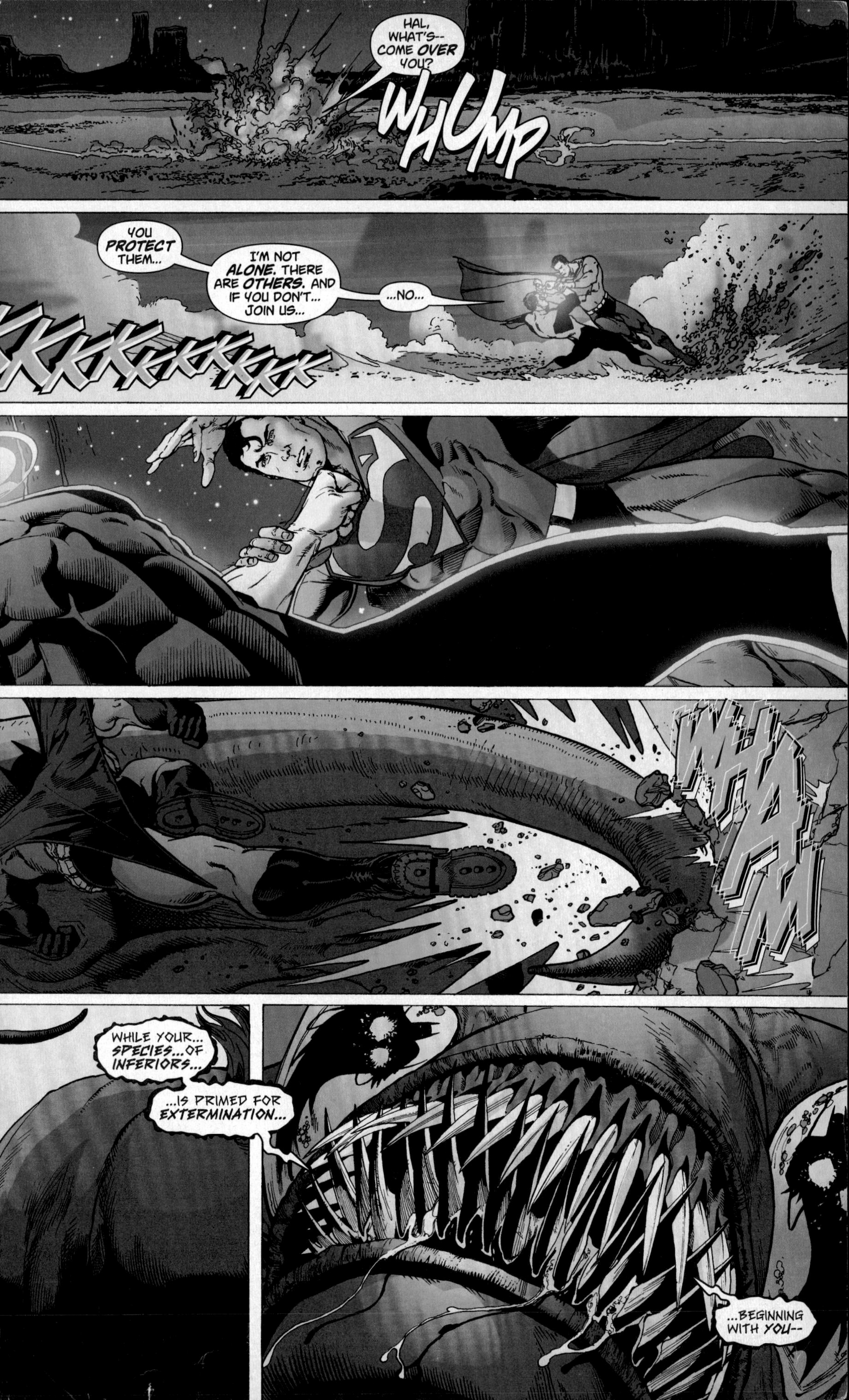

HAL, WHAT'S-- COME OVER YOU?
WHUMP
YOU PROTECT THEM...
I'M NOT ALONE. THERE ARE OTHERS. AND IF YOU DON'T... JOIN US...
...NO...
KKKKKKKKKKKKK
WHAM
WHILE YOUR... SPECIES...OF INFERIORS...
...IS PRIMED FOR EXTERMINATION...
...BEGINNING WITH YOU--

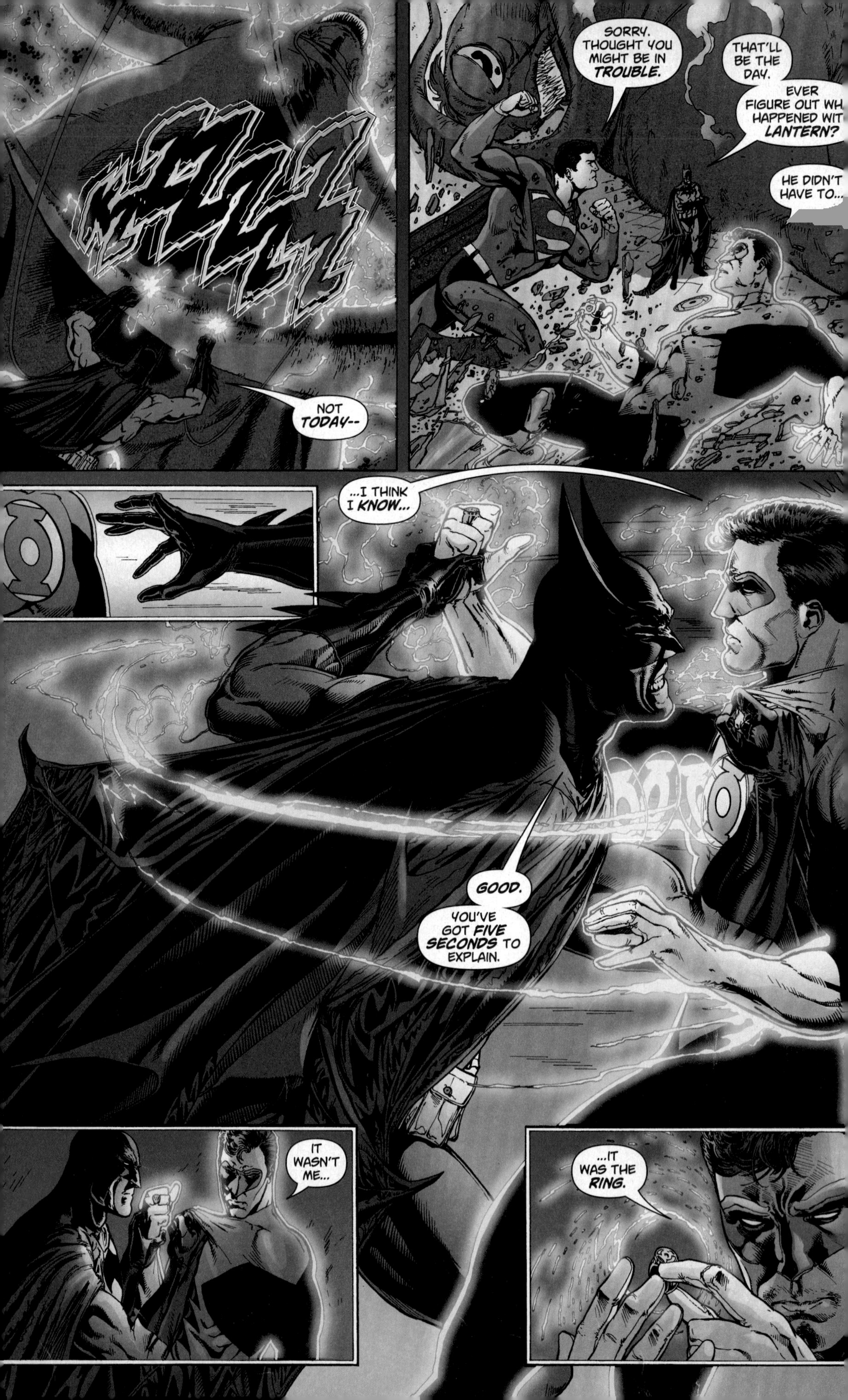

NOT TODAY--
SORRY. THOUGHT YOU MIGHT BE IN TROUBLE.
THAT'LL BE THE DAY.
EVER FIGURE OUT WH HAPPENED WIT LANTERN?
HE DIDN'T HAVE TO...
...I THINK I KNOW...
GOOD.
YOU'VE GOT FIVE SECONDS TO EXPLAIN.
IT WASN'T ME...
...IT WAS THE RING.

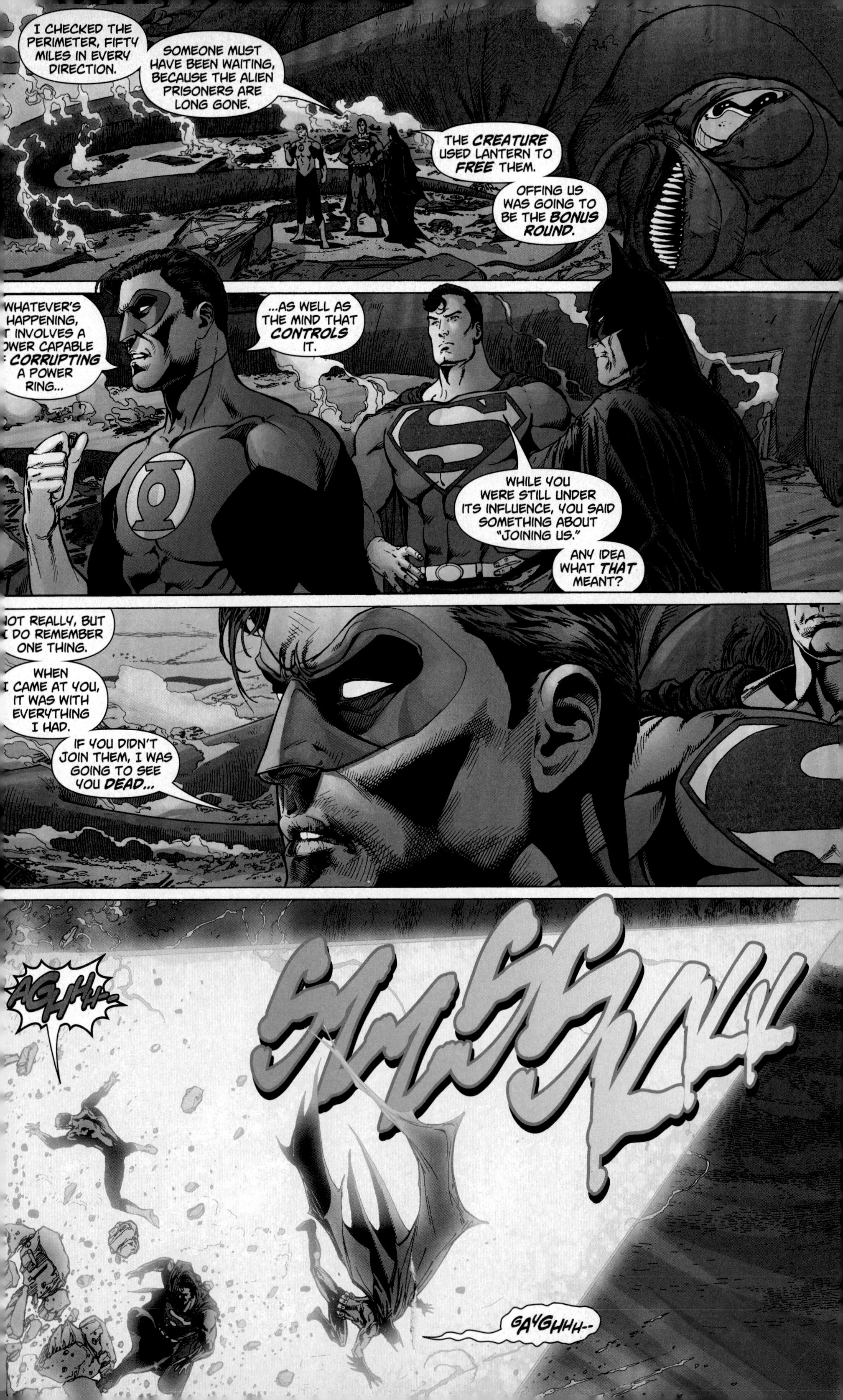
I CHECKED THE PERIMETER, FIFTY MILES IN EVERY DIRECTION.
SOMEONE MUST HAVE BEEN WAITING, BECAUSE THE ALIEN PRISONERS ARE LONG GONE.
THE CREATURE USED LANTERN TO FREE THEM.
OFFING US WAS GOING TO BE THE BONUS ROUND.
WHATEVER'S HAPPENING, IT INVOLVES A POWER CAPABLE OF CORRUPTING A POWER RING...
...AS WELL AS THE MIND THAT CONTROLS IT.
WHILE YOU WERE STILL UNDER ITS INFLUENCE, YOU SAID SOMETHING ABOUT "JOINING US."
ANY IDEA WHAT THAT MEANT?
NOT REALLY, BUT I DO REMEMBER ONE THING.
WHEN I CAME AT YOU, IT WAS WITH EVERYTHING I HAD.
IF YOU DIDN'T JOIN THEM, I WAS GOING TO SEE YOU DEAD...
AGUHH--
SMASSHHK
GAYGHHH--

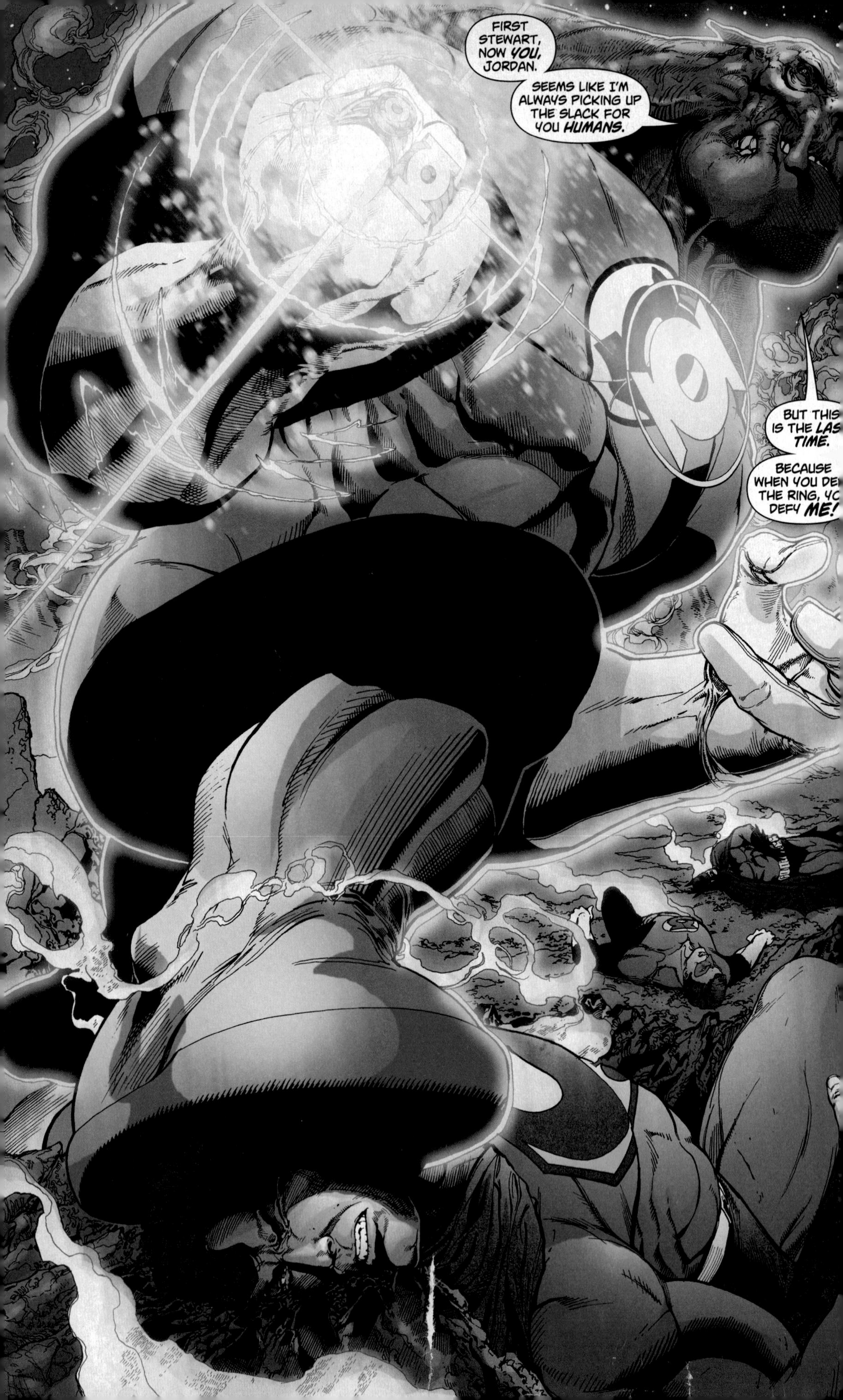

FIRST STEWART, NOW YOU, JORDAN.
SEEMS LIKE I'M ALWAYS PICKING UP THE SLACK FOR YOU HUMANS.
BUT THIS IS THE LAS TIME.
BECAUSE WHEN YOU DE THE RING, YO DEFY ME!

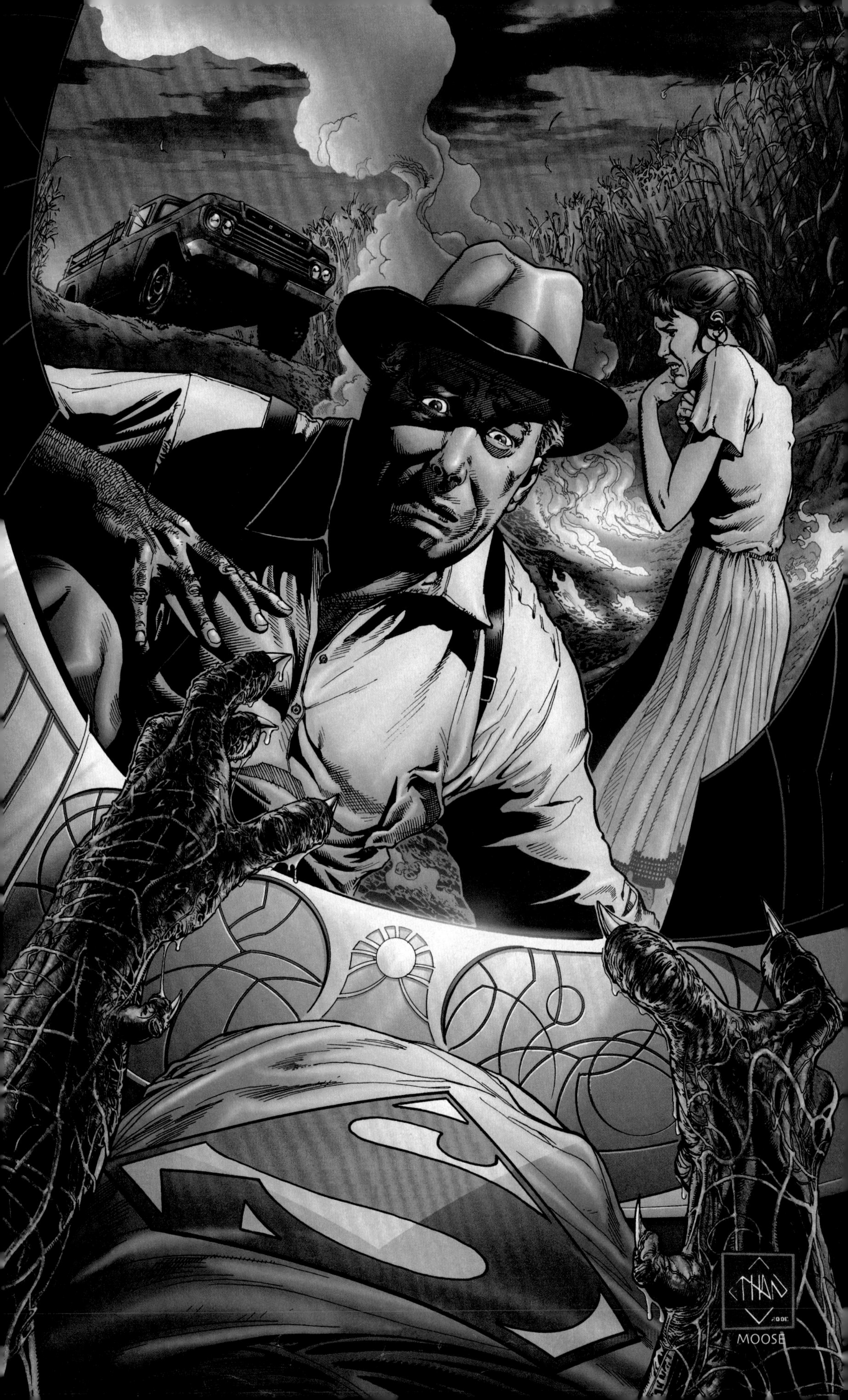
MOOSE

THE ENEMIES AMONG US: PART THREE
From SUPERMAN/BATMAN 30
Cover by Ethan Van Sciver and Moose Baumann

Mark Verheiden
Writer

Ethan Van Sciver
Pencils

Marlo Alquiza
Inks

Guy Major
Colors

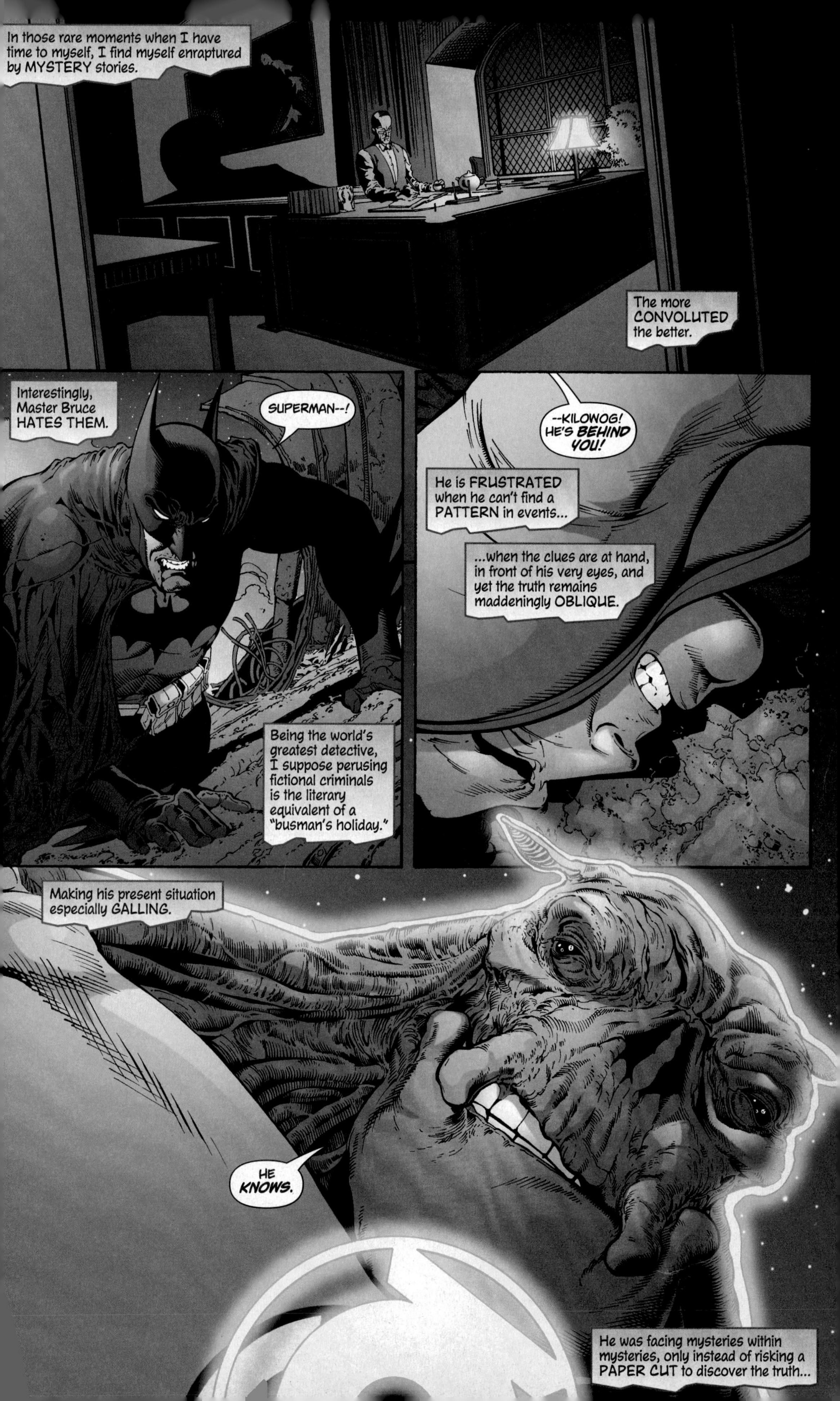
In those rare moments when I have time to myself, I find myself enraptured by MYSTERY stories.
The more CONVOLUTED the better.
Interestingly, Master Bruce HATES THEM.
SUPERMAN--!
Being the world's greatest detective, I suppose perusing fictional criminals is the literary equivalent of a "busman's holiday."
--KILOWOG! HE'S BEHIND YOU!
He is FRUSTRATED when he can't find a PATTERN in events...
...when the clues are at hand, in front of his very eyes, and yet the truth remains maddeningly OBLIQUE.
Making his present situation especially GALLING.
HE KNOWS.
He was facing mysteries within mysteries, only instead of risking a PAPER CUT to discover the truth...

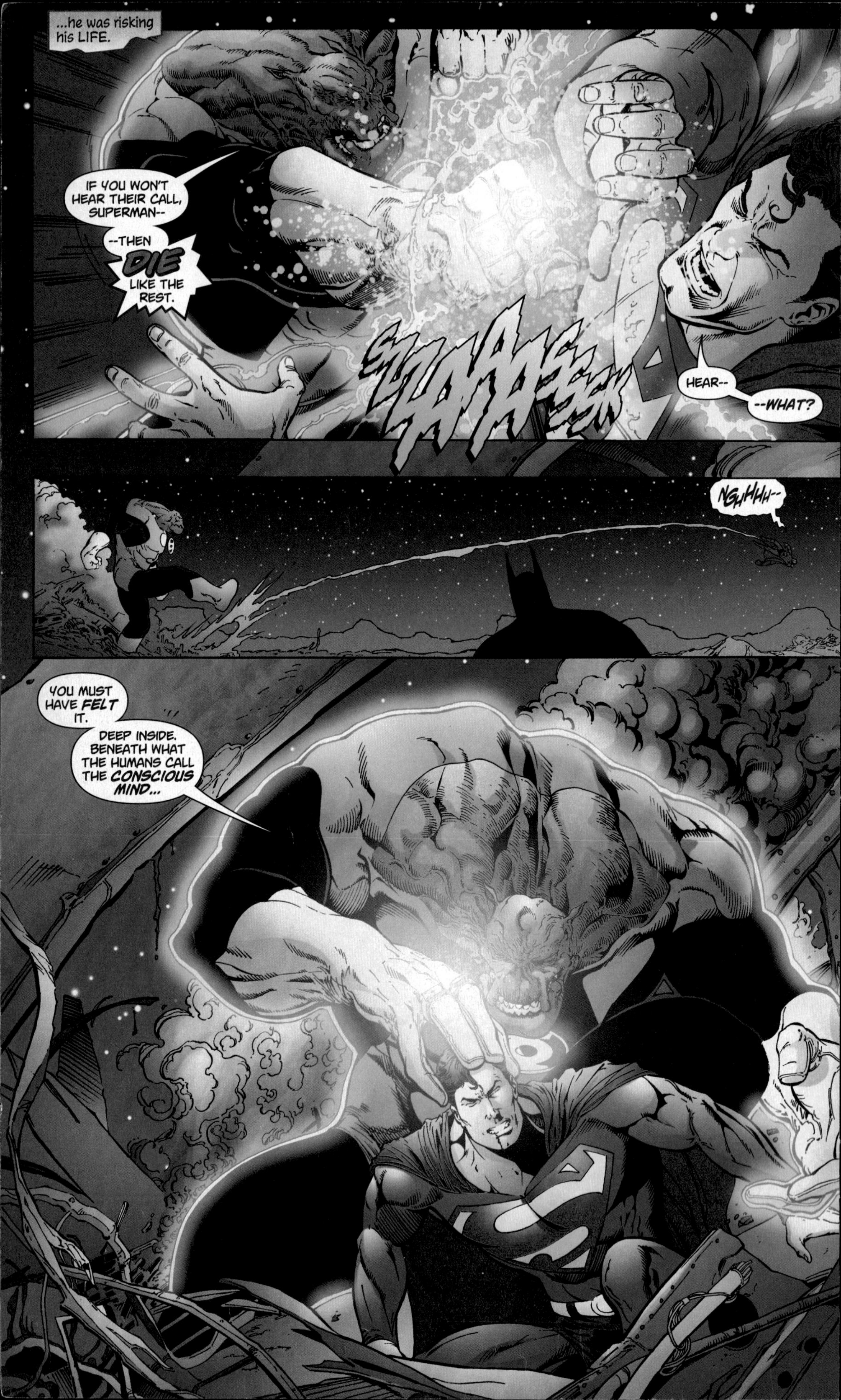
...he was risking his LIFE.
IF YOU WON'T HEAR THEIR CALL, SUPERMAN--
--THEN DIE LIKE THE REST.
HEAR--
--WHAT?
NGUHHH--
YOU MUST HAVE FELT IT.
DEEP INSIDE. BENEATH WHAT THE HUMANS CALL THE CONSCIOUS MIND...

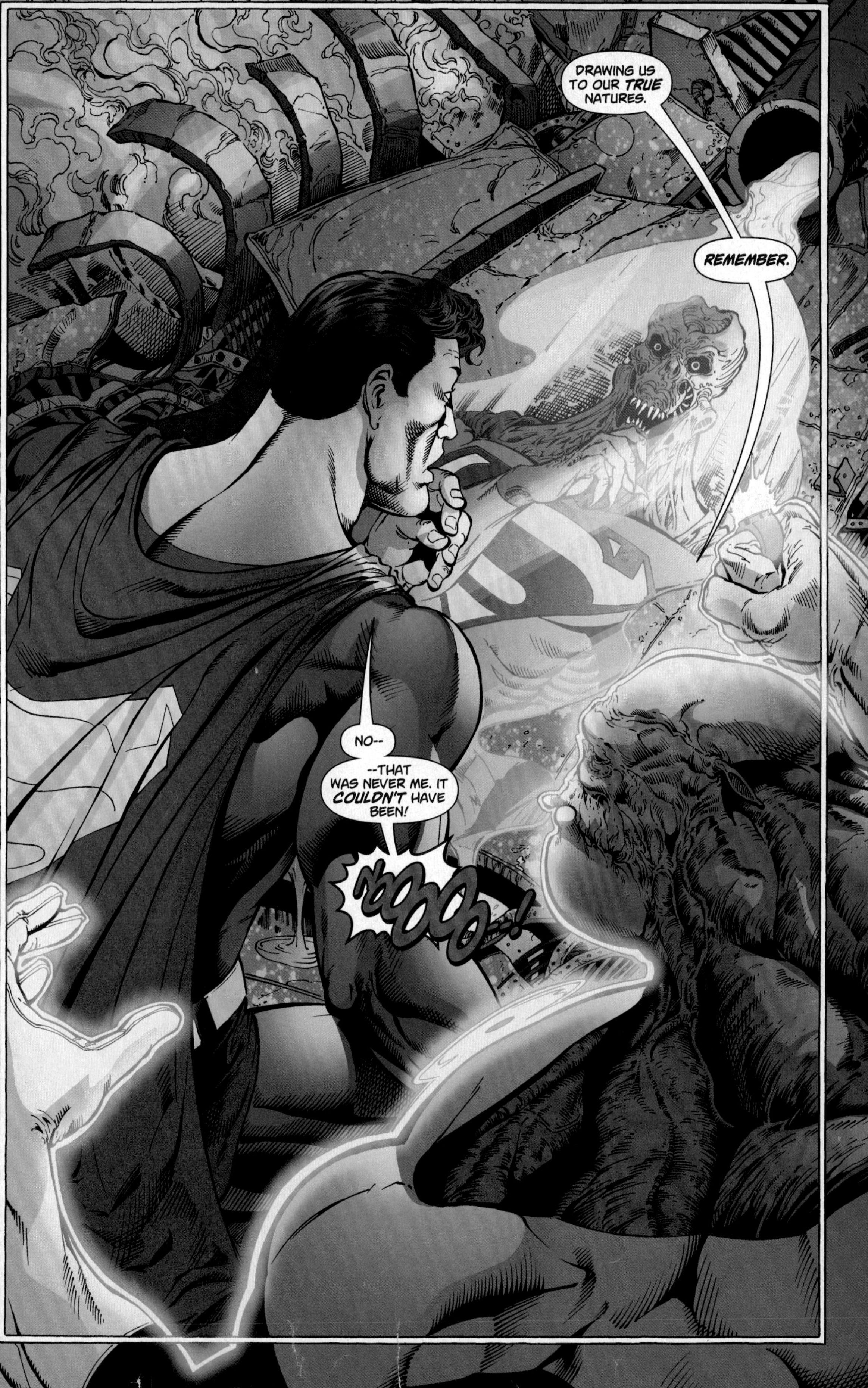
DRAWING US TO OUR TRUE NATURES.
REMEMBER.
NO--
--THAT WAS NEVER ME. IT COULDN'T HAVE BEEN!
NOOOOO--!

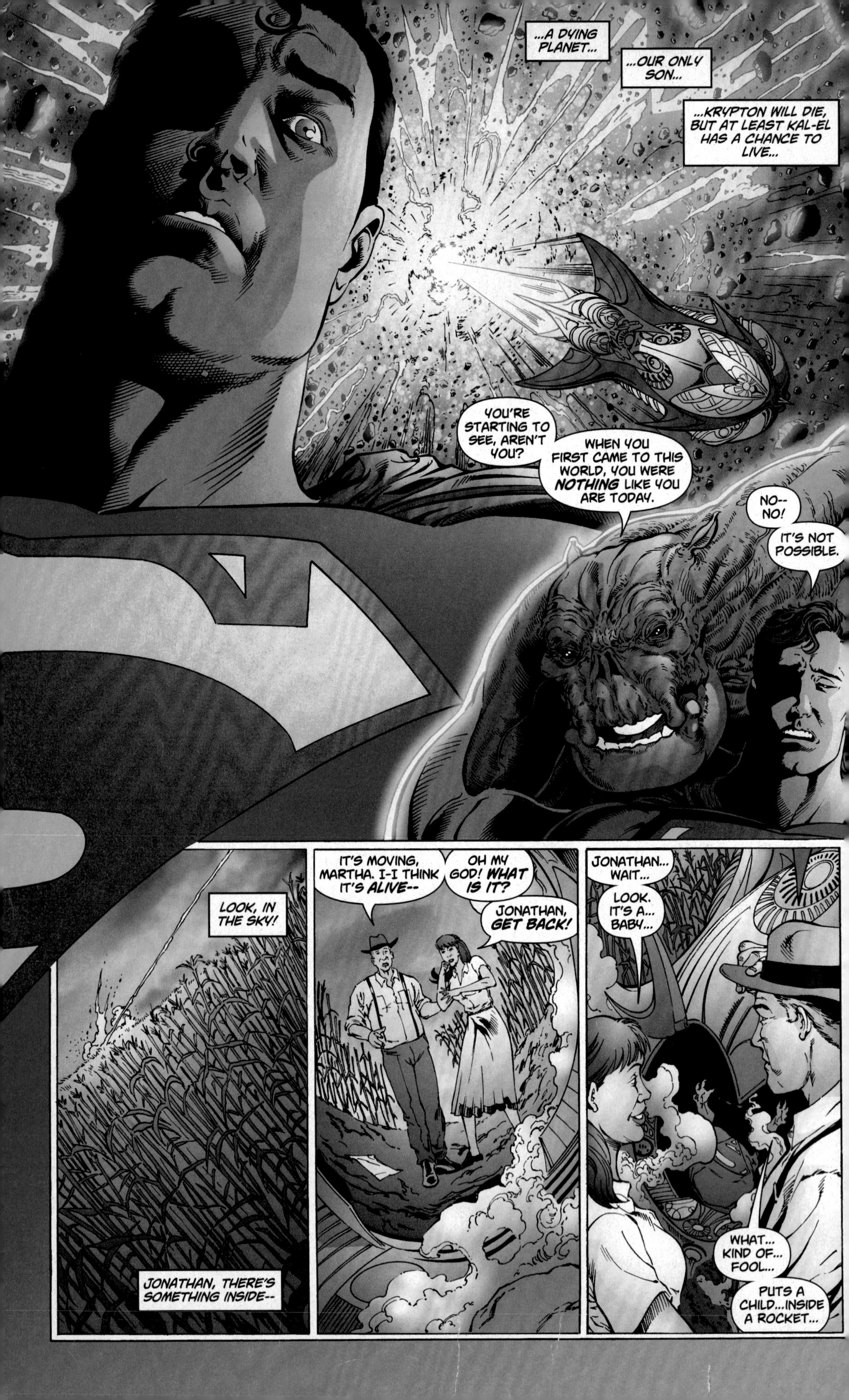

...A DYING PLANET...
...OUR ONLY SON...
...KRYPTON WILL DIE, BUT AT LEAST KAL-EL HAS A CHANCE TO LIVE...
YOU'RE STARTING TO SEE, AREN'T YOU?
WHEN YOU FIRST CAME TO THIS WORLD, YOU WERE NOTHING LIKE YOU ARE TODAY.
NO-- NO!
IT'S NOT POSSIBLE.
LOOK, IN THE SKY!
JONATHAN, THERE'S SOMETHING INSIDE--
IT'S MOVING, MARTHA. I-I THINK IT'S ALIVE--
OH MY GOD! WHAT IS IT?
JONATHAN, GET BACK!
JONATHAN... WAIT...
LOOK. IT'S A... BABY...
WHAT... KIND OF... FOOL...
PUTS A CHILD...INSIDE A ROCKET...

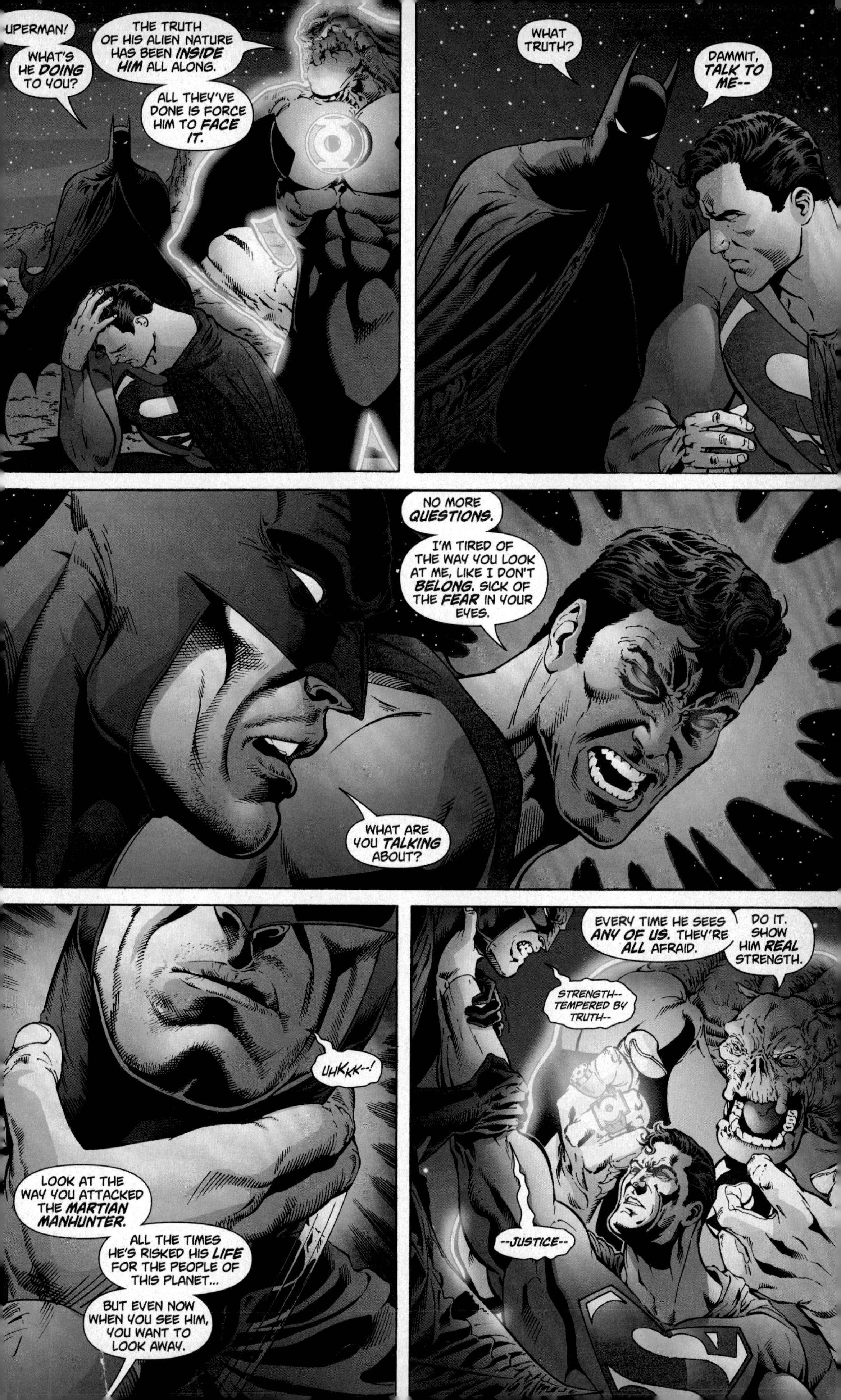

UPERMAN!
WHAT'S HE DOING TO YOU?
THE TRUTH OF HIS ALIEN NATURE HAS BEEN INSIDE HIM ALL ALONG.
ALL THEY'VE DONE IS FORCE HIM TO FACE IT.
WHAT TRUTH?
DAMMIT, TALK TO ME--
NO MORE QUESTIONS.
I'M TIRED OF THE WAY YOU LOOK AT ME, LIKE I DON'T BELONG. SICK OF THE FEAR IN YOUR EYES.
WHAT ARE YOU TALKING ABOUT?
UHKKK--!
LOOK AT THE WAY YOU ATTACKED THE MARTIAN MANHUNTER.
ALL THE TIMES HE'S RISKED HIS LIFE FOR THE PEOPLE OF THIS PLANET...
BUT EVEN NOW WHEN YOU SEE HIM, YOU WANT TO LOOK AWAY.
EVERY TIME HE SEES ANY OF US. THEY'RE ALL AFRAID.
DO IT. SHOW HIM REAL STRENGTH.
STRENGTH-- TEMPERED BY TRUTH--
--JUSTICE--

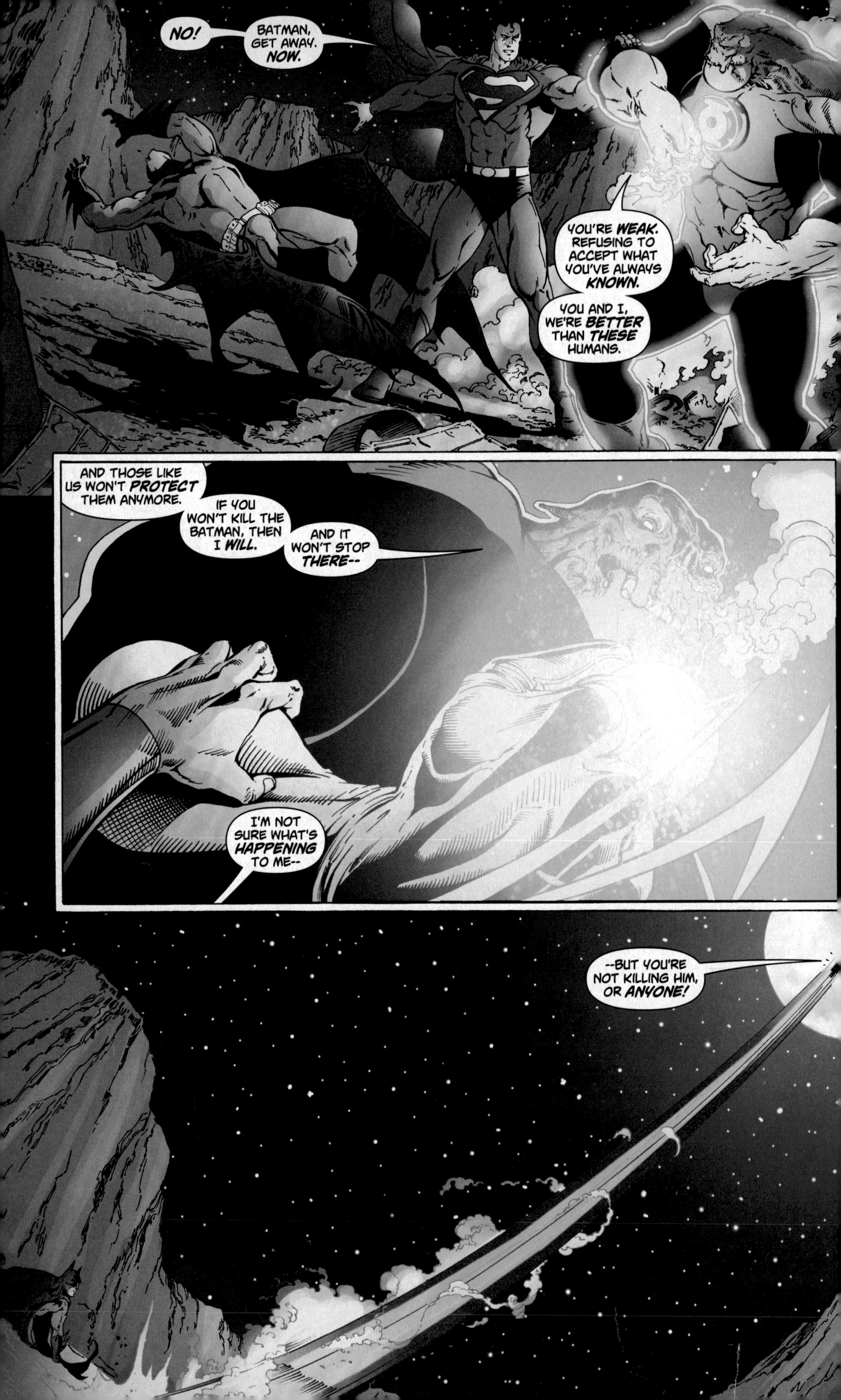

NO!
BATMAN, GET AWAY. NOW.
YOU'RE WEAK. REFUSING TO ACCEPT WHAT YOU'VE ALWAYS KNOWN.
YOU AND I, WE'RE BETTER THAN THESE HUMANS.
AND THOSE LIKE US WON'T PROTECT THEM ANYMORE.
IF YOU WON'T KILL THE BATMAN, THEN I WILL.
AND IT WON'T STOP THERE--
I'M NOT SURE WHAT'S HAPPENING TO ME--
--BUT YOU'RE NOT KILLING HIM, OR ANYONE!

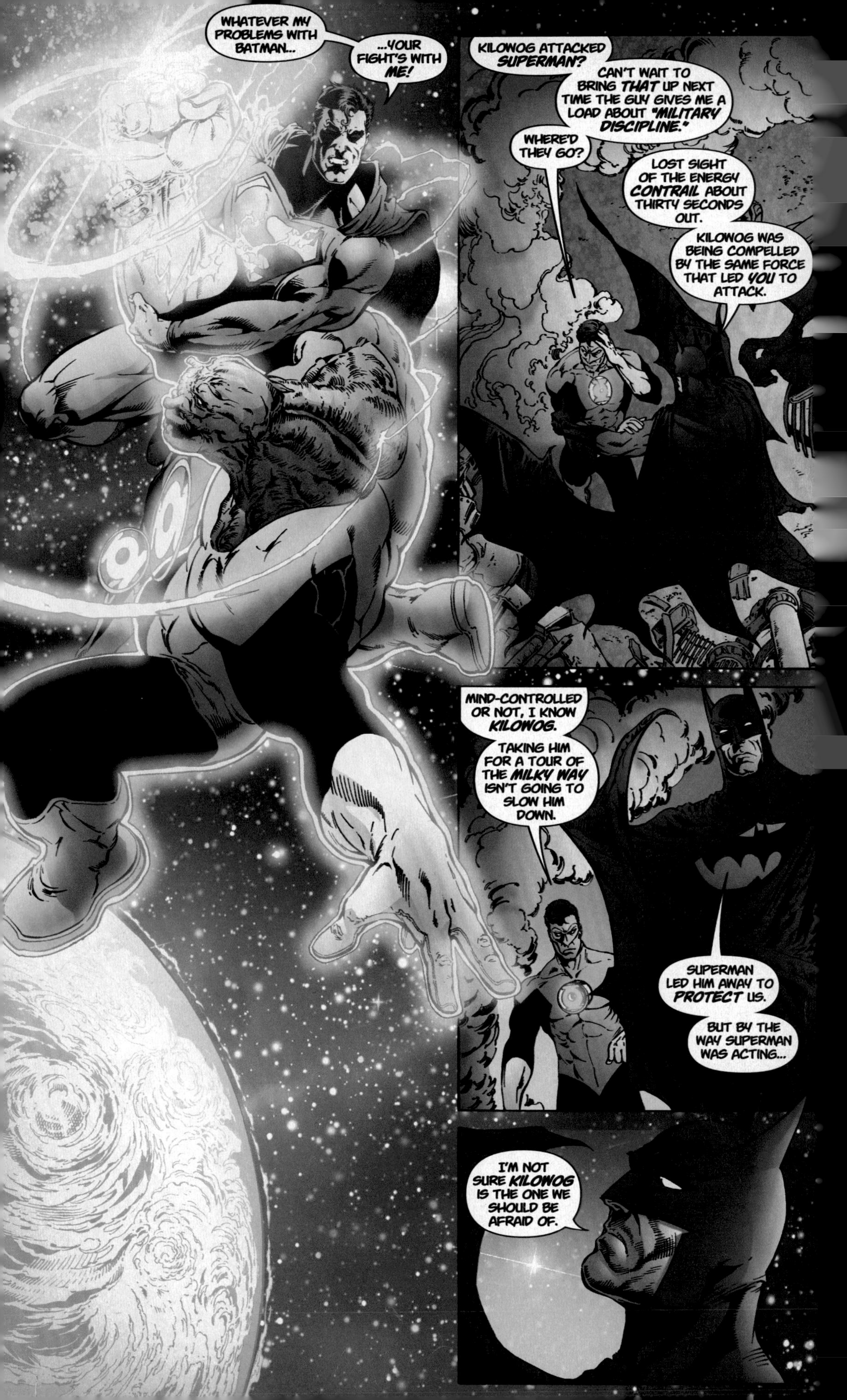
WHATEVER MY PROBLEMS WITH BATMAN...
...YOUR FIGHT'S WITH ME!
KILOWOG ATTACKED SUPERMAN?
CAN'T WAIT TO BRING THAT UP NEXT TIME THE GUY GIVES ME A LOAD ABOUT "MILITARY DISCIPLINE."
WHERE'D THEY GO?
LOST SIGHT OF THE ENERGY CONTRAIL ABOUT THIRTY SECONDS OUT.
KILOWOG WAS BEING COMPELLED BY THE SAME FORCE THAT LED YOU TO ATTACK.
MIND-CONTROLLED OR NOT, I KNOW KILOWOG.
TAKING HIM FOR A TOUR OF THE MILKY WAY ISN'T GOING TO SLOW HIM DOWN.
SUPERMAN LED HIM AWAY TO PROTECT US.
BUT BY THE WAY SUPERMAN WAS ACTING...
I'M NOT SURE KILOWOG IS THE ONE WE SHOULD BE AFRAID OF.

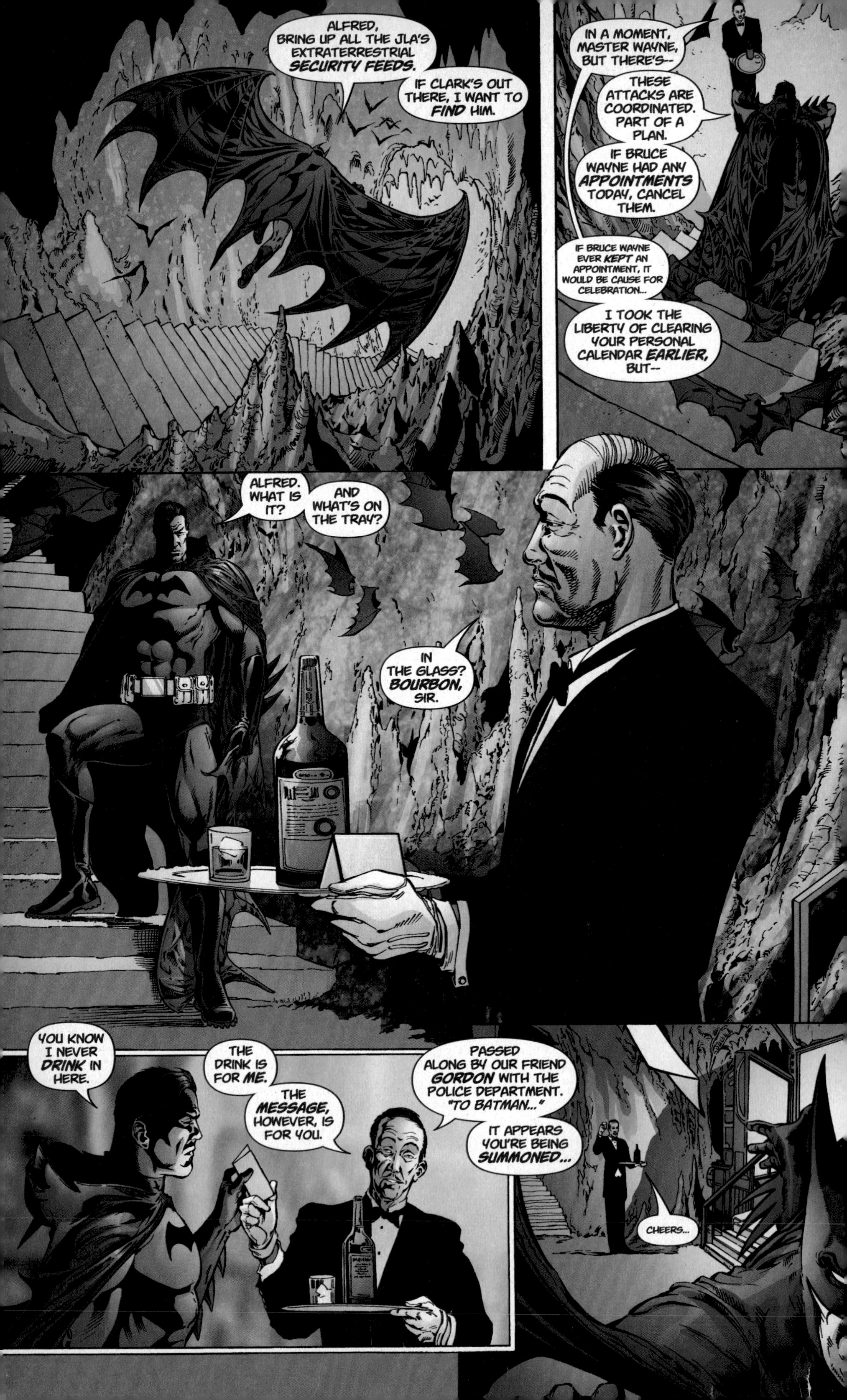
ALFRED, BRING UP ALL THE JLA'S EXTRATERRESTRIAL SECURITY FEEDS.
IF CLARK'S OUT THERE, I WANT TO FIND HIM.
IN A MOMENT, MASTER WAYNE, BUT THERE'S--
THESE ATTACKS ARE COORDINATED. PART OF A PLAN.
IF BRUCE WAYNE HAD ANY APPOINTMENTS TODAY, CANCEL THEM.
IF BRUCE WAYNE EVER KEPT AN APPOINTMENT, IT WOULD BE CAUSE FOR CELEBRATION...
I TOOK THE LIBERTY OF CLEARING YOUR PERSONAL CALENDAR EARLIER, BUT--
ALFRED. WHAT IS IT?
AND WHAT'S ON THE TRAY?
IN THE GLASS? BOURBON, SIR.
YOU KNOW I NEVER DRINK IN HERE.
THE DRINK IS FOR ME.
THE MESSAGE, HOWEVER, IS FOR YOU.
PASSED ALONG BY OUR FRIEND GORDON WITH THE POLICE DEPARTMENT. "TO BATMAN..."
IT APPEARS YOU'RE BEING SUMMONED...
CHEERS...

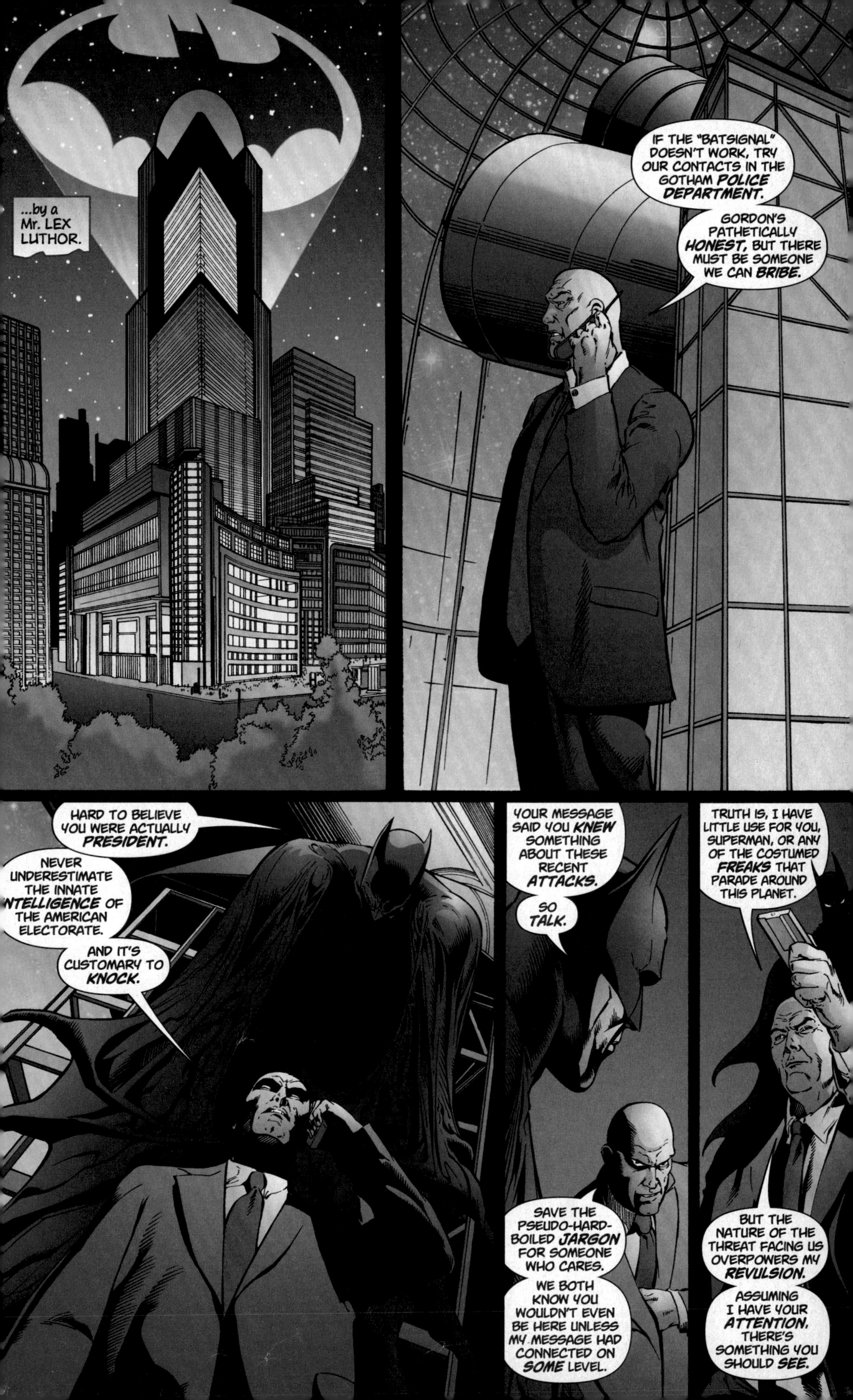
...by a Mr. LEX LUTHOR.
IF THE "BATSIGNAL" DOESN'T WORK, TRY OUR CONTACTS IN THE GOTHAM POLICE DEPARTMENT.
GORDON'S PATHETICALLY HONEST, BUT THERE MUST BE SOMEONE WE CAN BRIBE.
HARD TO BELIEVE YOU WERE ACTUALLY PRESIDENT.
NEVER UNDERESTIMATE THE INNATE INTELLIGENCE OF THE AMERICAN ELECTORATE.
AND IT'S CUSTOMARY TO KNOCK.
YOUR MESSAGE SAID YOU KNEW SOMETHING ABOUT THESE RECENT ATTACKS.
SO TALK.
SAVE THE PSEUDO-HARD-BOILED JARGON FOR SOMEONE WHO CARES.
WE BOTH KNOW YOU WOULDN'T EVEN BE HERE UNLESS MY MESSAGE HAD CONNECTED ON SOME LEVEL.
TRUTH IS, I HAVE LITTLE USE FOR YOU, SUPERMAN, OR ANY OF THE COSTUMED FREAKS THAT PARADE AROUND THIS PLANET.
BUT THE NATURE OF THE THREAT FACING US OVERPOWERS MY REVULSION.
ASSUMING I HAVE YOUR ATTENTION, THERE'S SOMETHING YOU SHOULD SEE.

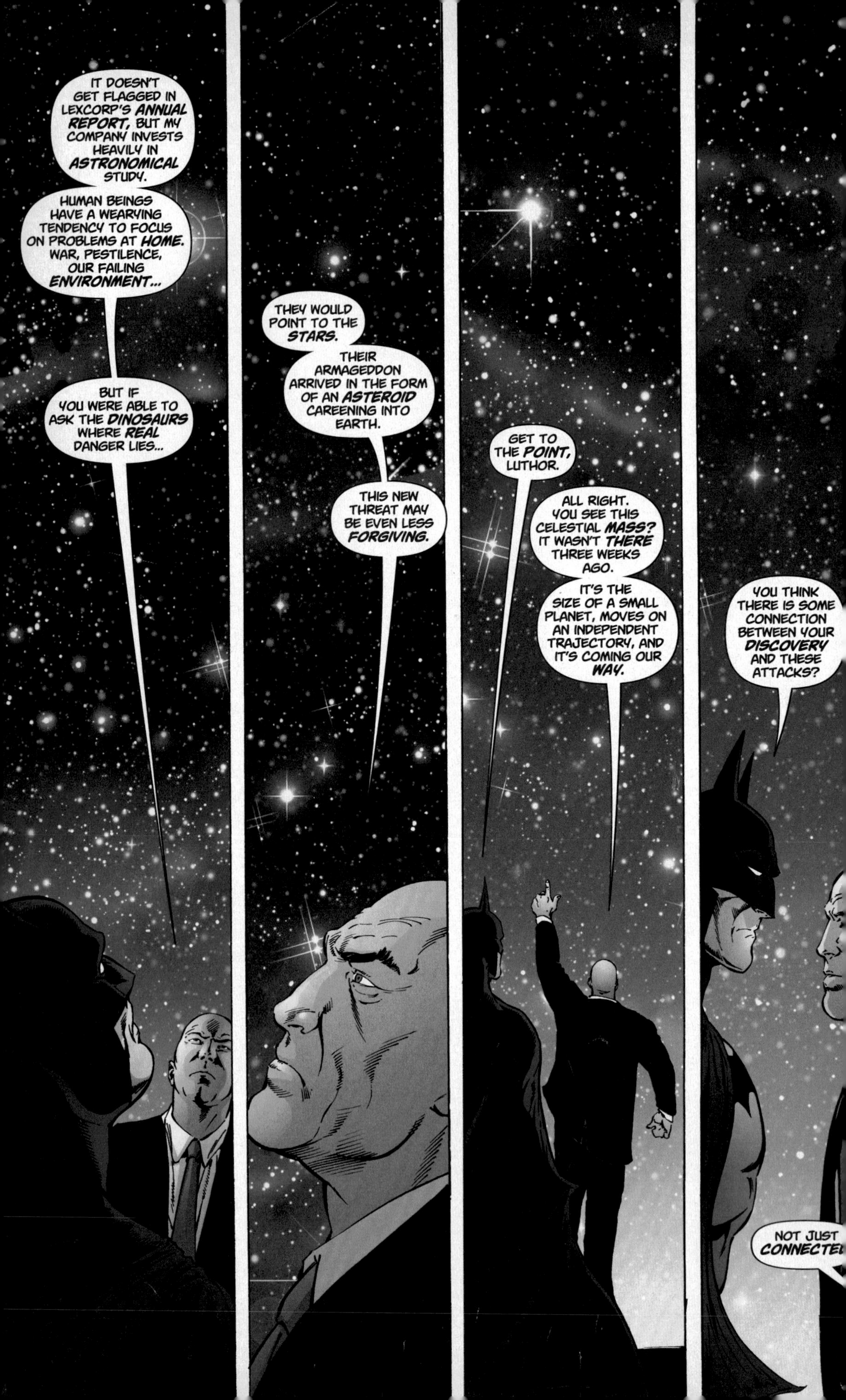
IT DOESN'T GET FLAGGED IN LEXCORP'S ANNUAL REPORT, BUT MY COMPANY INVESTS HEAVILY IN ASTRONOMICAL STUDY.
HUMAN BEINGS HAVE A WEARYING TENDENCY TO FOCUS ON PROBLEMS AT HOME. WAR, PESTILENCE, OUR FAILING ENVIRONMENT...
BUT IF YOU WERE ABLE TO ASK THE DINOSAURS WHERE REAL DANGER LIES...
THEY WOULD POINT TO THE STARS.
THEIR ARMAGEDDON ARRIVED IN THE FORM OF AN ASTEROID CAREENING INTO EARTH.
THIS NEW THREAT MAY BE EVEN LESS FORGIVING.
GET TO THE POINT, LUTHOR.
ALL RIGHT. YOU SEE THIS CELESTIAL MASS? IT WASN'T THERE THREE WEEKS AGO.
IT'S THE SIZE OF A SMALL PLANET, MOVES ON AN INDEPENDENT TRAJECTORY, AND IT'S COMING OUR WAY.
YOU THINK THERE IS SOME CONNECTION BETWEEN YOUR DISCOVERY AND THESE ATTACKS?
NOT JUST CONNECTE

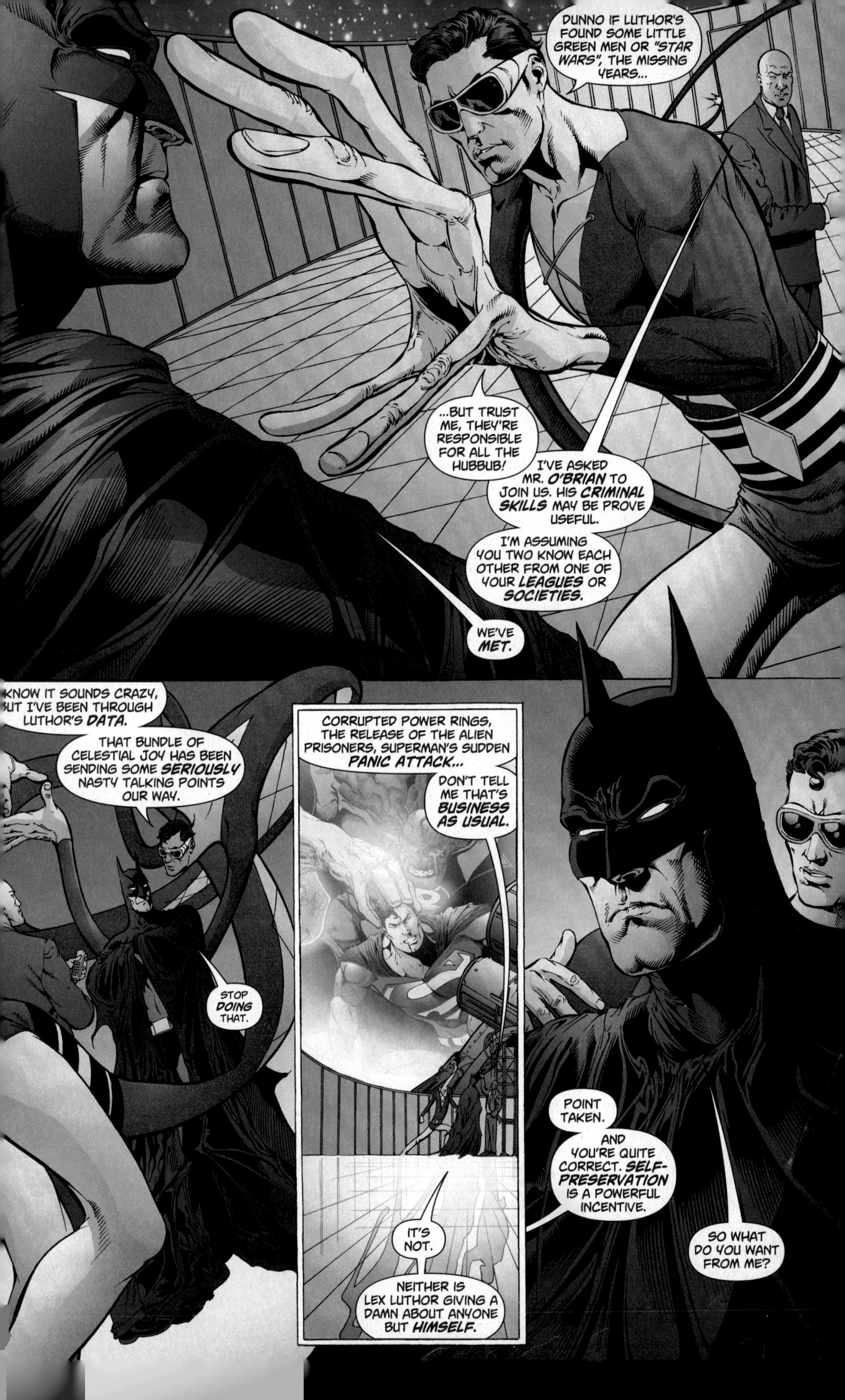
DUNNO IF LUTHOR'S FOUND SOME LITTLE GREEN MEN OR "STAR WARS", THE MISSING YEARS...
...BUT TRUST ME, THEY'RE RESPONSIBLE FOR ALL THE HUBBUB!
I'VE ASKED MR. O'BRIAN TO JOIN US. HIS CRIMINAL SKILLS MAY BE PROVE USEFUL.
I'M ASSUMING YOU TWO KNOW EACH OTHER FROM ONE OF YOUR LEAGUES OR SOCIETIES.
WE'VE MET.
KNOW IT SOUNDS CRAZY, BUT I'VE BEEN THROUGH LUTHOR'S DATA.
THAT BUNDLE OF CELESTIAL JOY HAS BEEN SENDING SOME SERIOUSLY NASTY TALKING POINTS OUR WAY.
STOP DOING THAT.
CORRUPTED POWER RINGS, THE RELEASE OF THE ALIEN PRISONERS, SUPERMAN'S SUDDEN PANIC ATTACK...
DON'T TELL ME THAT'S BUSINESS AS USUAL.
IT'S NOT.
NEITHER IS LEX LUTHOR GIVING A DAMN ABOUT ANYONE BUT HIMSELF.
POINT TAKEN.
AND YOU'RE QUITE CORRECT. SELF-PRESERVATION IS A POWERFUL INCENTIVE.
SO WHAT DO YOU WANT FROM ME?

"I HAVE REASON TO BELIEVE SUPERMAN POSSESSES A *PRECURSOR* OF THIS ALIEN SPECIES.

"ONCE SECURED, IT COULD HELP US UNDERSTAND THE NATURE OF THE *THREAT* THAT'S APPROACHING.

"AND *NOW*, WHILE HE'S OTHERWISE *OCCUPIED*, WOULD BE A GOOD TIME TO *CLAIM IT*."

ALIEN INVADERS. WOW. I THINK I DROPPED A THOUSAND DOLLARS IN *QUARTERS* ON THAT GAME BACK IN THE *LATE '80s*.

AND HEY, LEX WASN'T SUCH A BAD GUY, CONSIDERING HIS REP.

HE'D KILL US IN AN *INSTANT* IF HE THOUGHT IT WOULD GAIN HIM AN ADVANTAGE.

I DON'T TRUST HIM ANY MORE THAN I DO *YOU*.

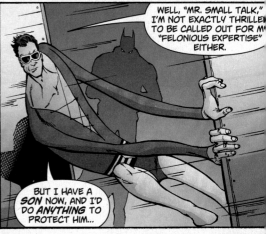

WELL, "MR. SMALL TALK," I'M NOT EXACTLY THRILLE[D] TO BE CALLED OUT FOR M[Y] "FELONIOUS EXPERTISE" EITHER.

BUT I HAVE A *SON* NOW, AND I'D DO *ANYTHING* TO PROTECT HIM...

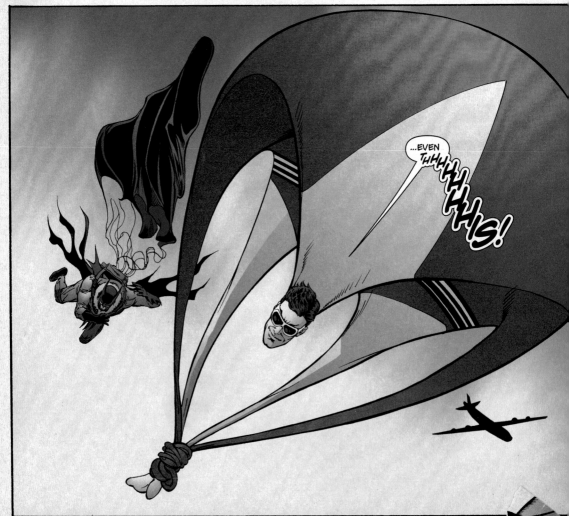

...EVEN *THHHHHHHHHHIS!*

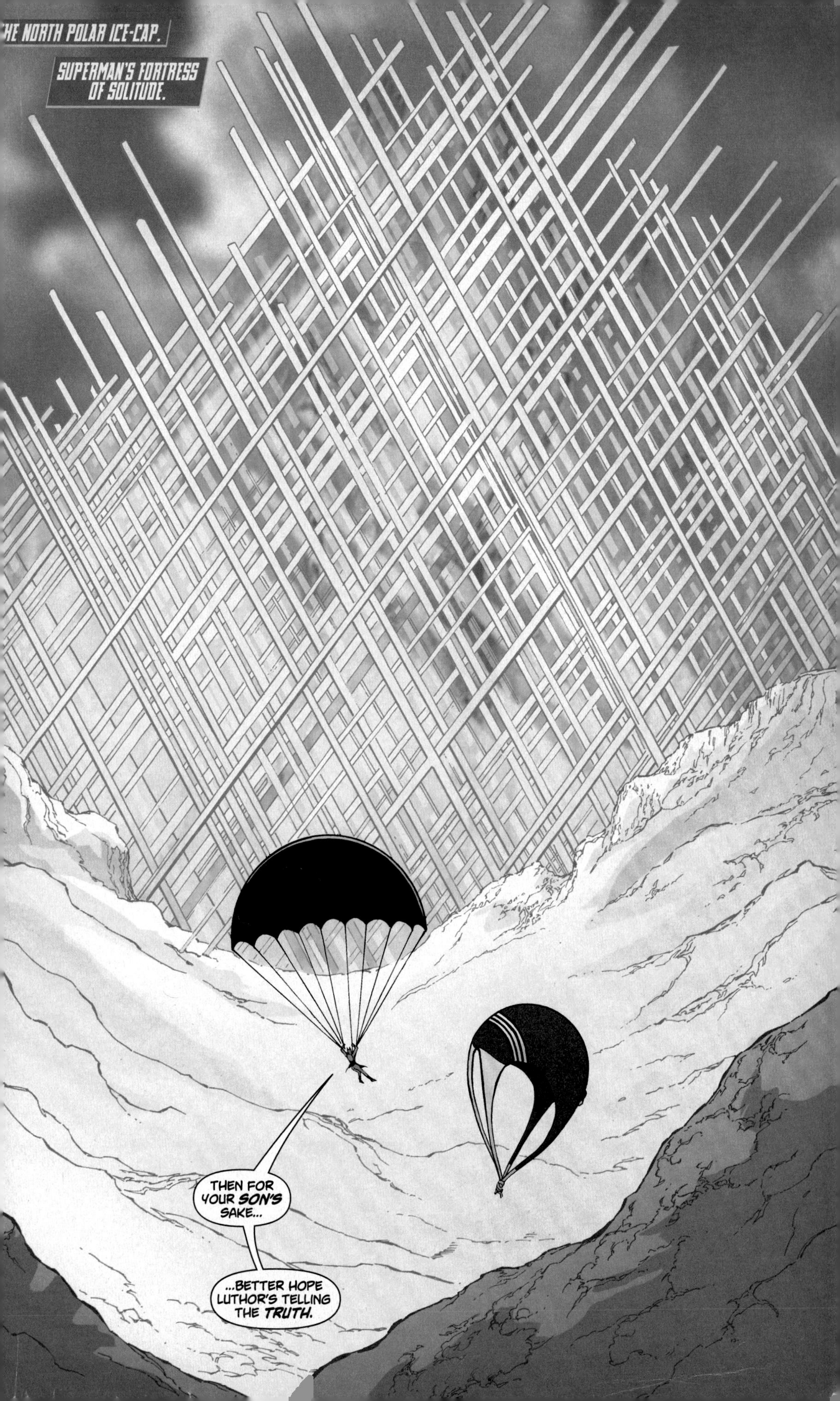
THE NORTH POLAR ICE-CAP.
SUPERMAN'S FORTRESS OF SOLITUDE.
THEN FOR YOUR SON'S SAKE...
...BETTER HOPE LUTHOR'S TELLING THE TRUTH.

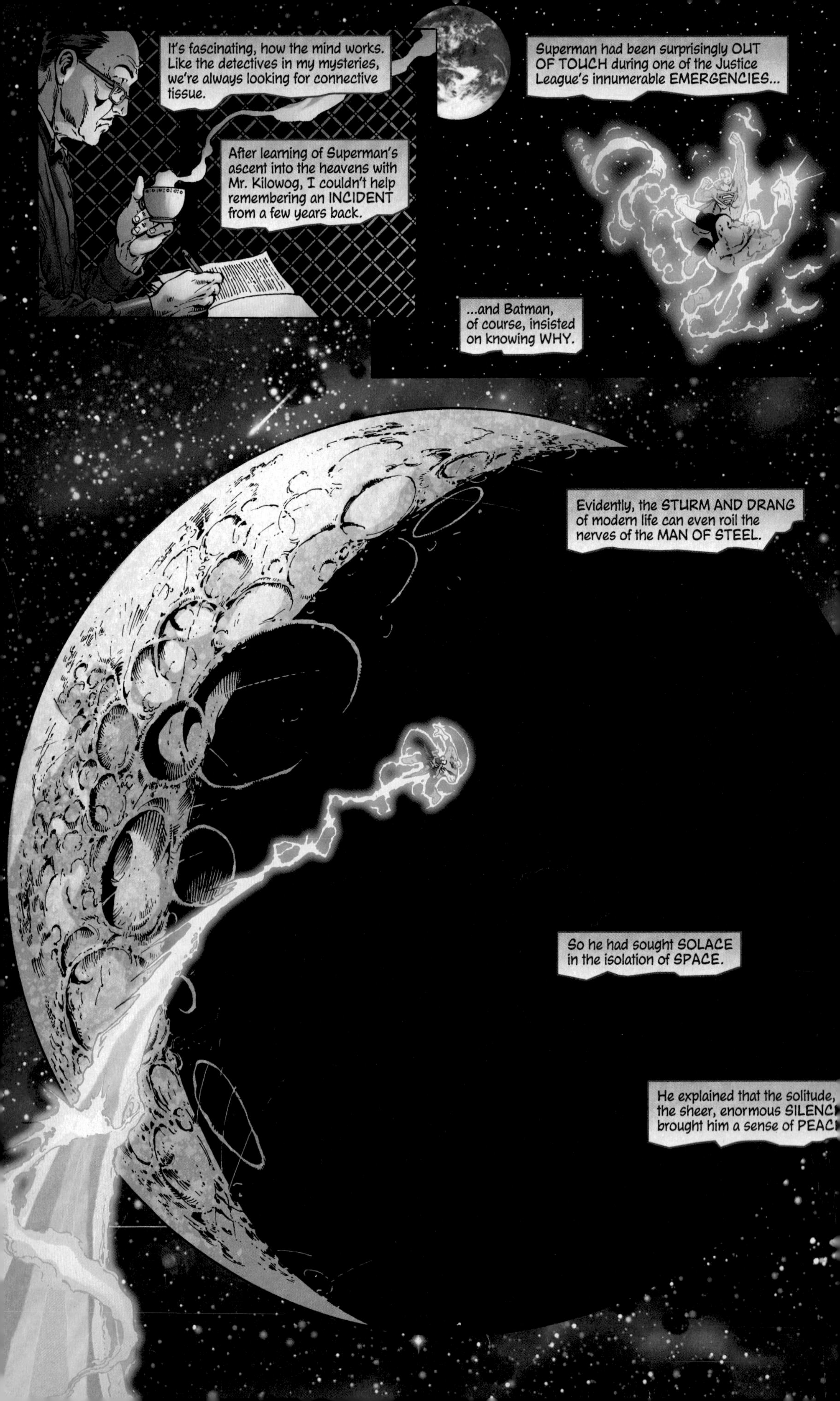

It's fascinating, how the mind works. Like the detectives in my mysteries, we're always looking for connective tissue.
After learning of Superman's ascent into the heavens with Mr. Kilowog, I couldn't help remembering an INCIDENT from a few years back.
Superman had been surprisingly OUT OF TOUCH during one of the Justice League's innumerable EMERGENCIES...
...and Batman, of course, insisted on knowing WHY.
Evidently, the STURM AND DRANG of modern life can even roil the nerves of the MAN OF STEEL.
So he had sought SOLACE in the isolation of SPACE.
He explained that the solitude, the sheer, enormous SILENC brought him a sense of PEAC

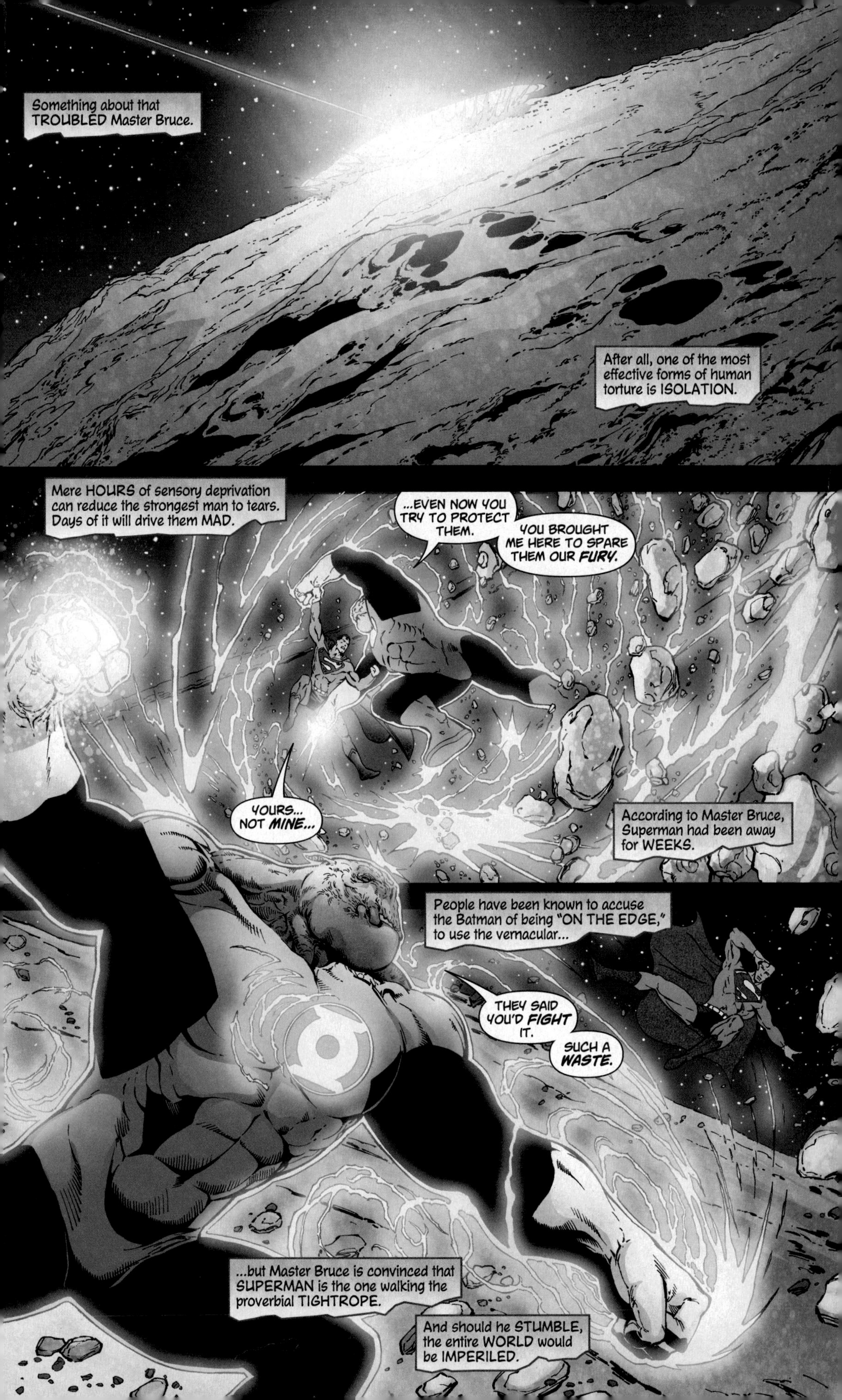

Something about that TROUBLED Master Bruce.
After all, one of the most effective forms of human torture is ISOLATION.
Mere HOURS of sensory deprivation can reduce the strongest man to tears. Days of it will drive them MAD.
...EVEN NOW YOU TRY TO PROTECT THEM.
YOU BROUGHT ME HERE TO SPARE THEM OUR FURY.
YOURS... NOT MINE...
According to Master Bruce, Superman had been away for WEEKS.
People have been known to accuse the Batman of being "ON THE EDGE," to use the vernacular...
THEY SAID YOU'D FIGHT IT.
SUCH A WASTE.
...but Master Bruce is convinced that SUPERMAN is the one walking the proverbial TIGHTROPE.
And should he STUMBLE, the entire WORLD would be IMPERILED.

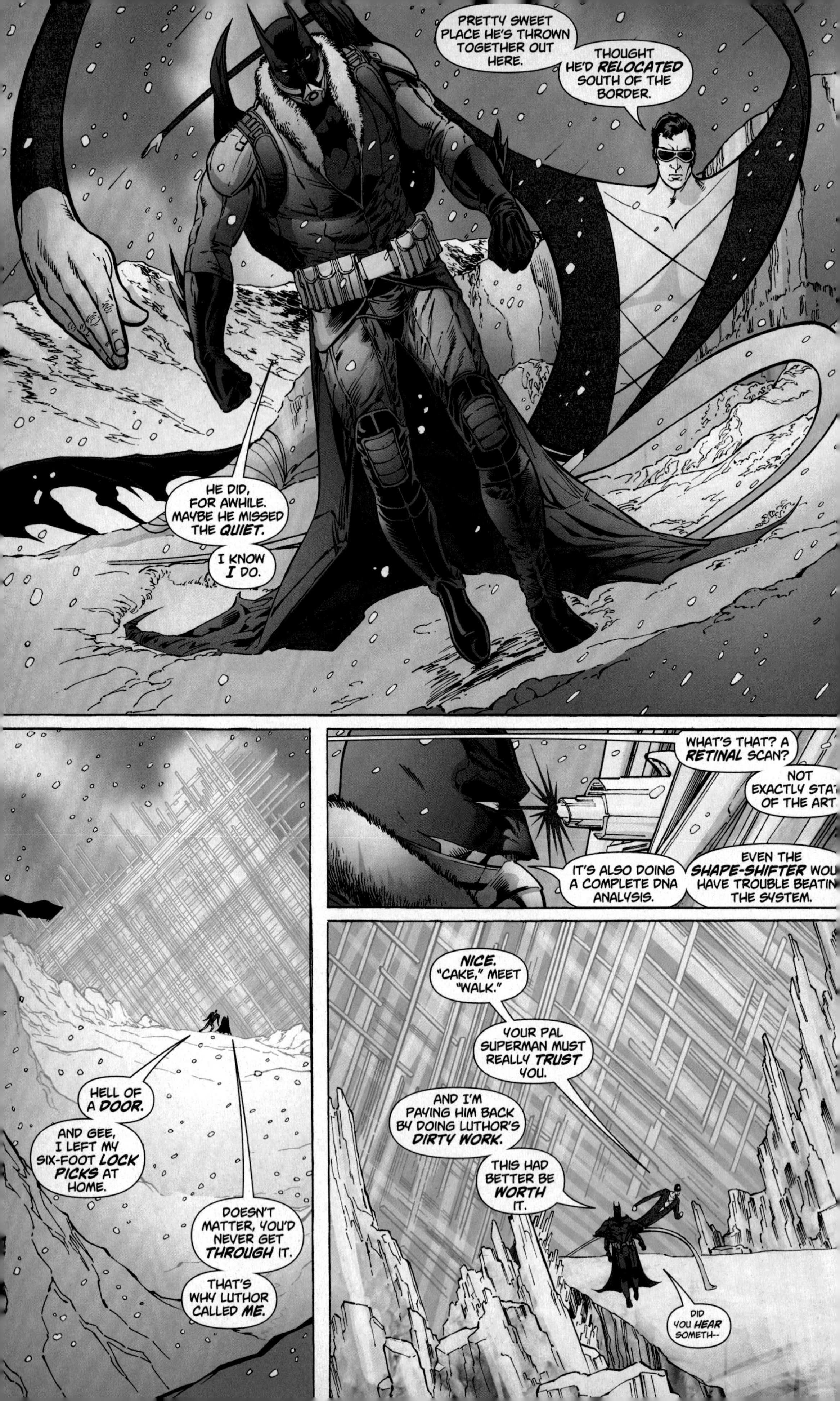

PRETTY SWEET PLACE HE'S THROWN TOGETHER OUT HERE.
THOUGHT HE'D RELOCATED SOUTH OF THE BORDER.
HE DID, FOR AWHILE. MAYBE HE MISSED THE QUIET.
I KNOW I DO.
HELL OF A DOOR.
AND GEE, I LEFT MY SIX-FOOT LOCK PICKS AT HOME.
DOESN'T MATTER, YOU'D NEVER GET THROUGH IT.
THAT'S WHY LUTHOR CALLED ME.
WHAT'S THAT? A RETINAL SCAN?
NOT EXACTLY STA OF THE ART
IT'S ALSO DOING A COMPLETE DNA ANALYSIS.
EVEN THE SHAPE-SHIFTER WOU HAVE TROUBLE BEATIN THE SYSTEM.
NICE. "CAKE," MEET "WALK."
YOUR PAL SUPERMAN MUST REALLY TRUST YOU.
AND I'M PAYING HIM BACK BY DOING LUTHOR'S DIRTY WORK.
THIS HAD BETTER BE WORTH IT.
DID YOU HEAR SOMETH--

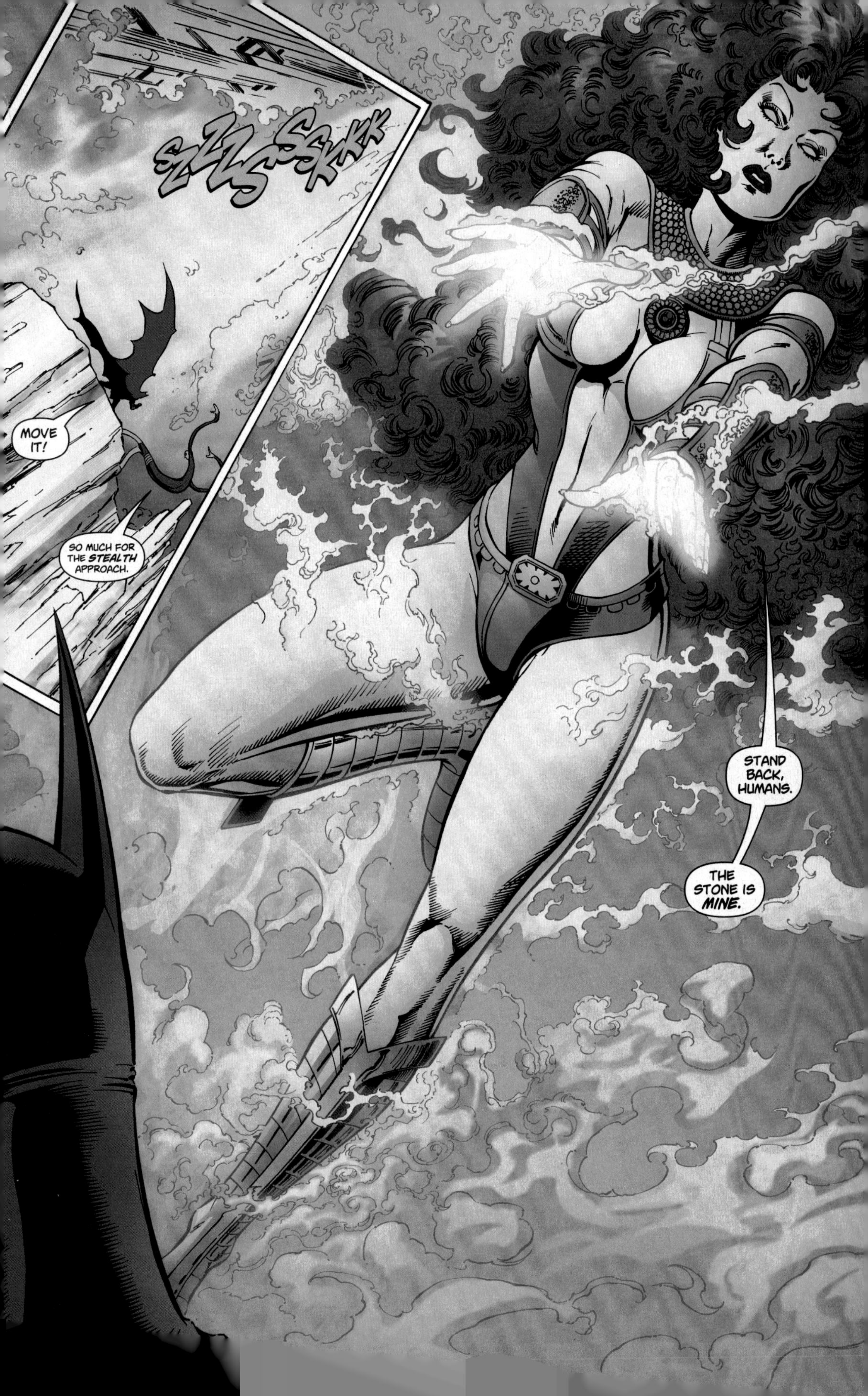
SZZZSSKKKK
MOVE IT!
SO MUCH FOR THE STEALTH APPROACH.
STAND BACK, HUMANS.
THE STONE IS MINE.

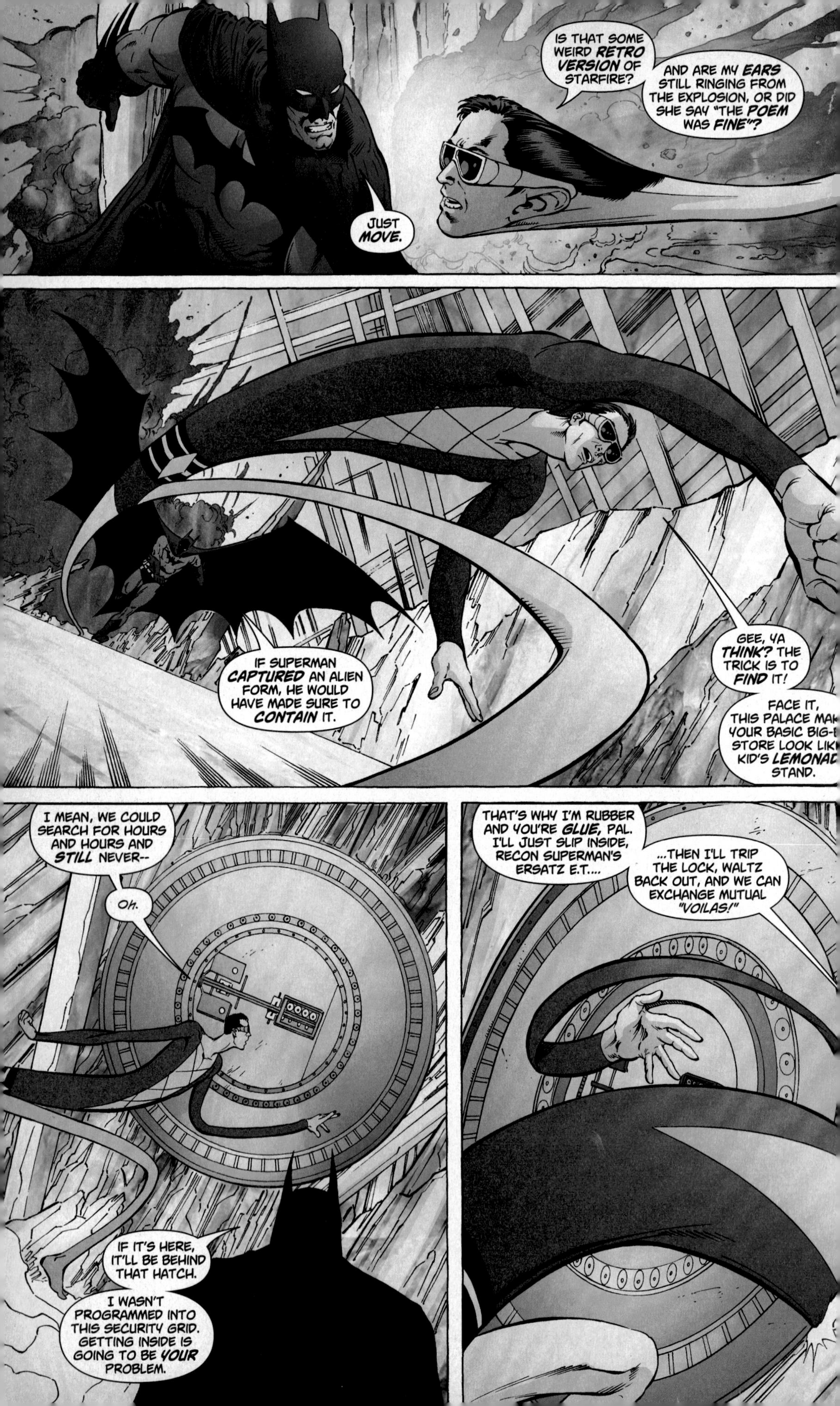

IS THAT SOME WEIRD RETRO VERSION OF STARFIRE?
AND ARE MY EARS STILL RINGING FROM THE EXPLOSION, OR DID SHE SAY "THE POEM WAS FINE"?
JUST MOVE.
IF SUPERMAN CAPTURED AN ALIEN FORM, HE WOULD HAVE MADE SURE TO CONTAIN IT.
GEE, YA THINK? THE TRICK IS TO FIND IT!
FACE IT, THIS PALACE MAK YOUR BASIC BIG- STORE LOOK LIK KID'S LEMONAD STAND.
I MEAN, WE COULD SEARCH FOR HOURS AND HOURS AND STILL NEVER--
Oh.
IF IT'S HERE, IT'LL BE BEHIND THAT HATCH.
I WASN'T PROGRAMMED INTO THIS SECURITY GRID. GETTING INSIDE IS GOING TO BE YOUR PROBLEM.
THAT'S WHY I'M RUBBER AND YOU'RE GLUE, PAL. I'LL JUST SLIP INSIDE, RECON SUPERMAN'S ERSATZ E.T....
...THEN I'LL TRIP THE LOCK, WALTZ BACK OUT, AND WE CAN EXCHANGE MUTUAL "VOILAS!"

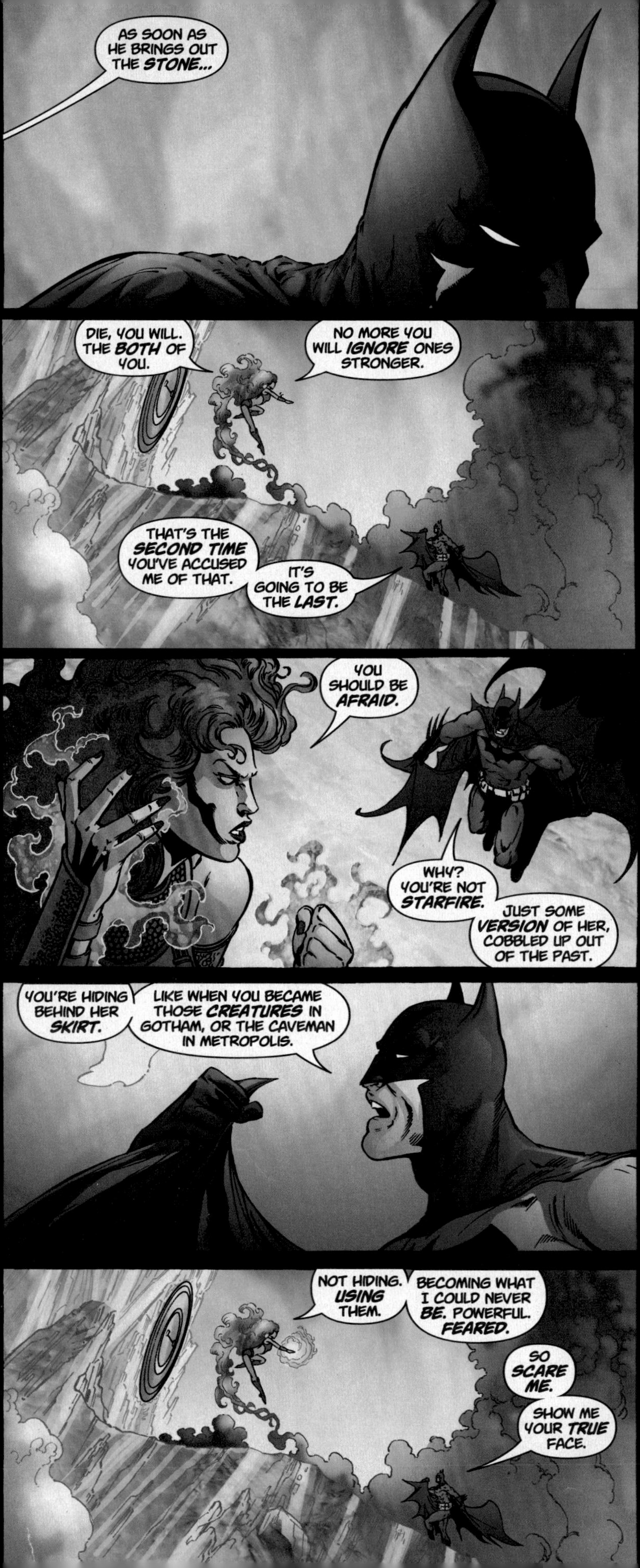
AS SOON AS HE BRINGS OUT THE STONE...
DIE, YOU WILL. THE BOTH OF YOU.
NO MORE YOU WILL IGNORE ONES STRONGER.
THAT'S THE SECOND TIME YOU'VE ACCUSED ME OF THAT.
IT'S GOING TO BE THE LAST.
YOU SHOULD BE AFRAID.
WHY? YOU'RE NOT STARFIRE.
JUST SOME VERSION OF HER, COBBLED UP OUT OF THE PAST.
YOU'RE HIDING BEHIND HER SKIRT.
LIKE WHEN YOU BECAME THOSE CREATURES IN GOTHAM, OR THE CAVEMAN IN METROPOLIS.
NOT HIDING. USING THEM.
BECOMING WHAT I COULD NEVER BE. POWERFUL. FEARED.
SO SCARE ME.
SHOW ME YOUR TRUE FACE.

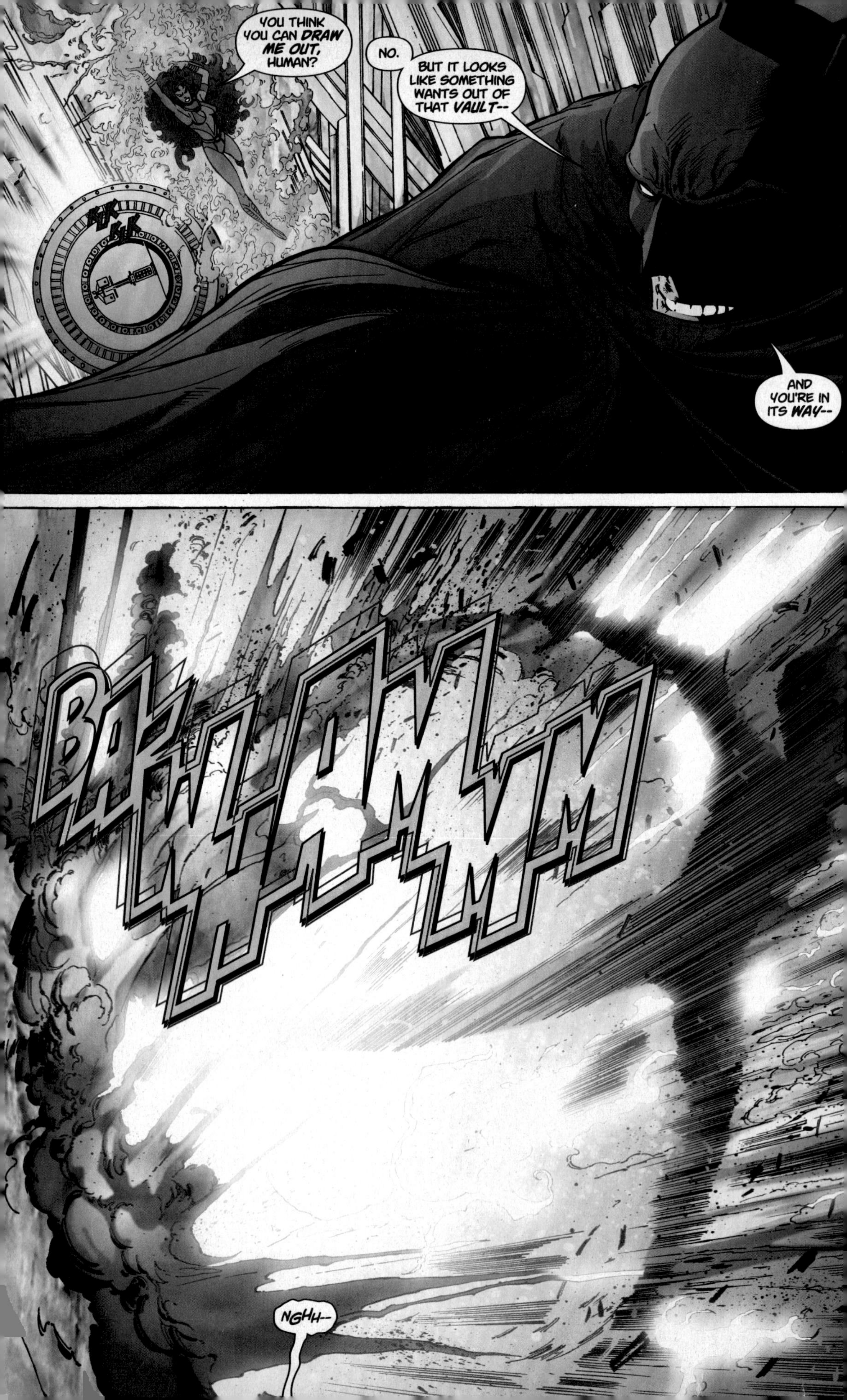
YOU THINK YOU CAN DRAW ME OUT, HUMAN?
NO.
BUT IT LOOKS LIKE SOMETHING WANTS OUT OF THAT VAULT--
AND YOU'RE IN ITS WAY--
NGHH--

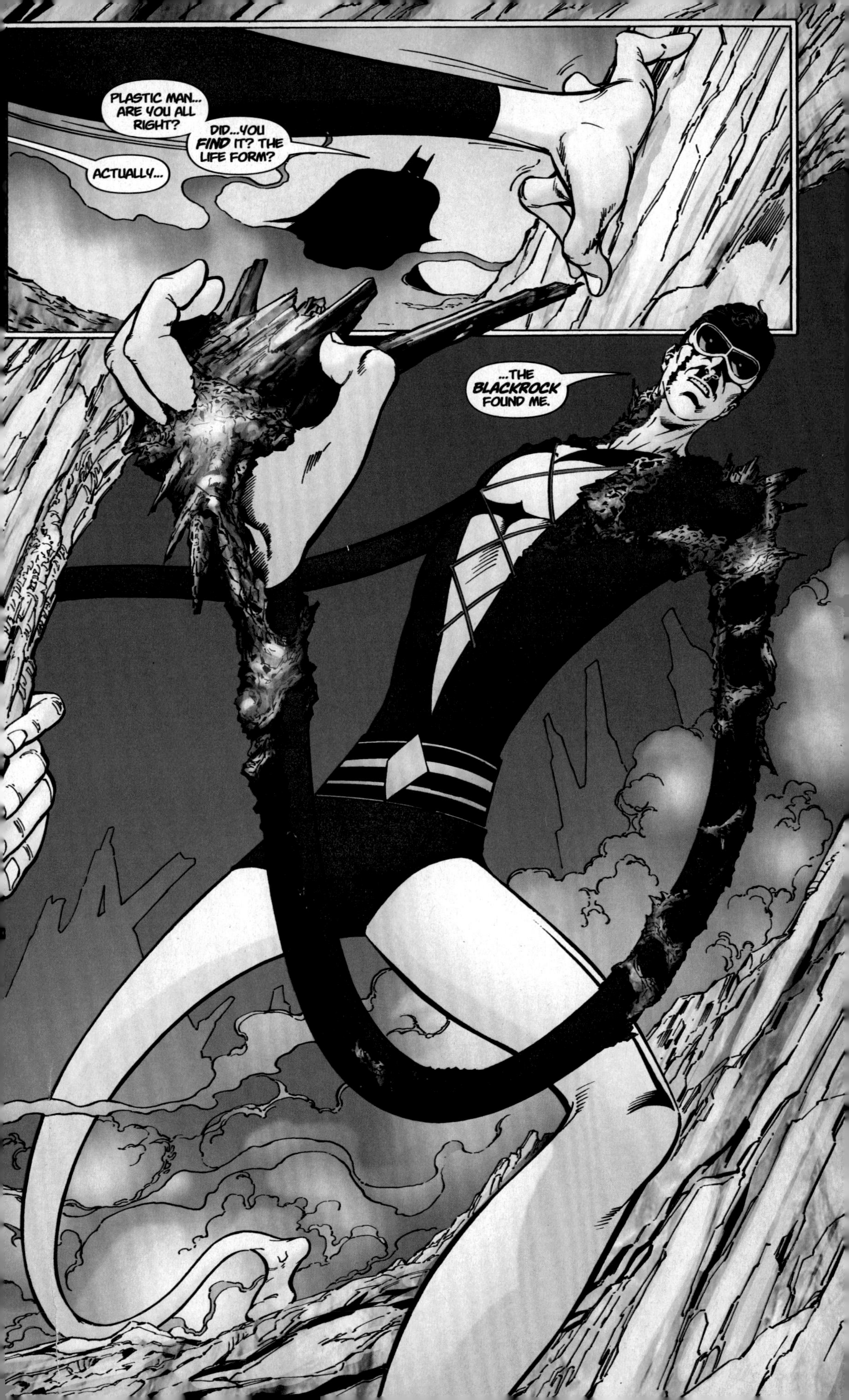
PLASTIC MAN... ARE YOU ALL RIGHT?
DID...YOU FIND IT? THE LIFE FORM?
ACTUALLY...
...THE BLACKROCK FOUND ME.

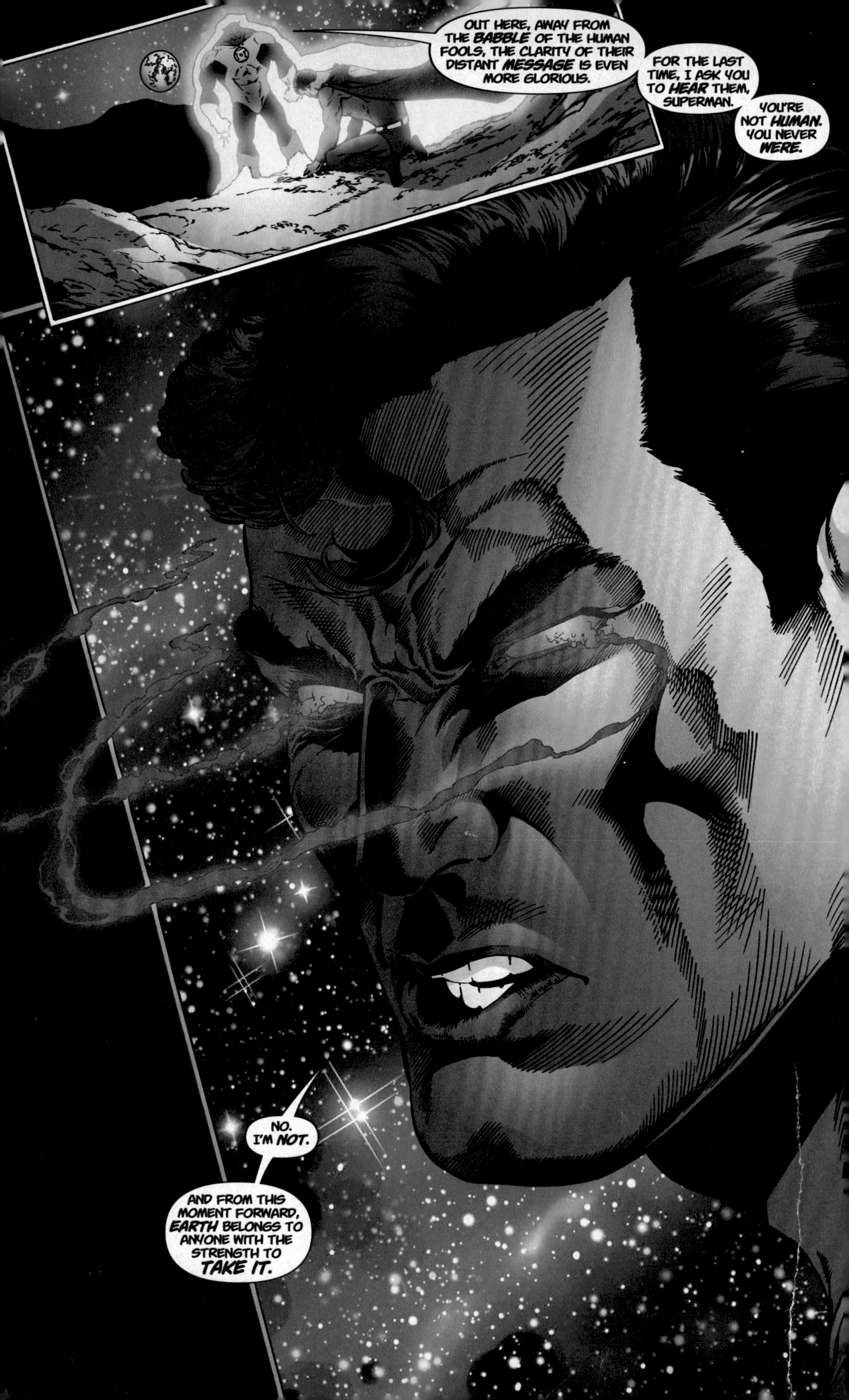
OUT HERE, AWAY FROM THE BABBLE OF THE HUMAN FOOLS, THE CLARITY OF THEIR DISTANT MESSAGE IS EVEN MORE GLORIOUS.
FOR THE LAST TIME, I ASK YOU TO HEAR THEM, SUPERMAN.
YOU'RE NOT HUMAN. YOU NEVER WERE.
NO. I'M NOT.
AND FROM THIS MOMENT FORWARD, EARTH BELONGS TO ANYONE WITH THE STRENGTH TO TAKE IT.

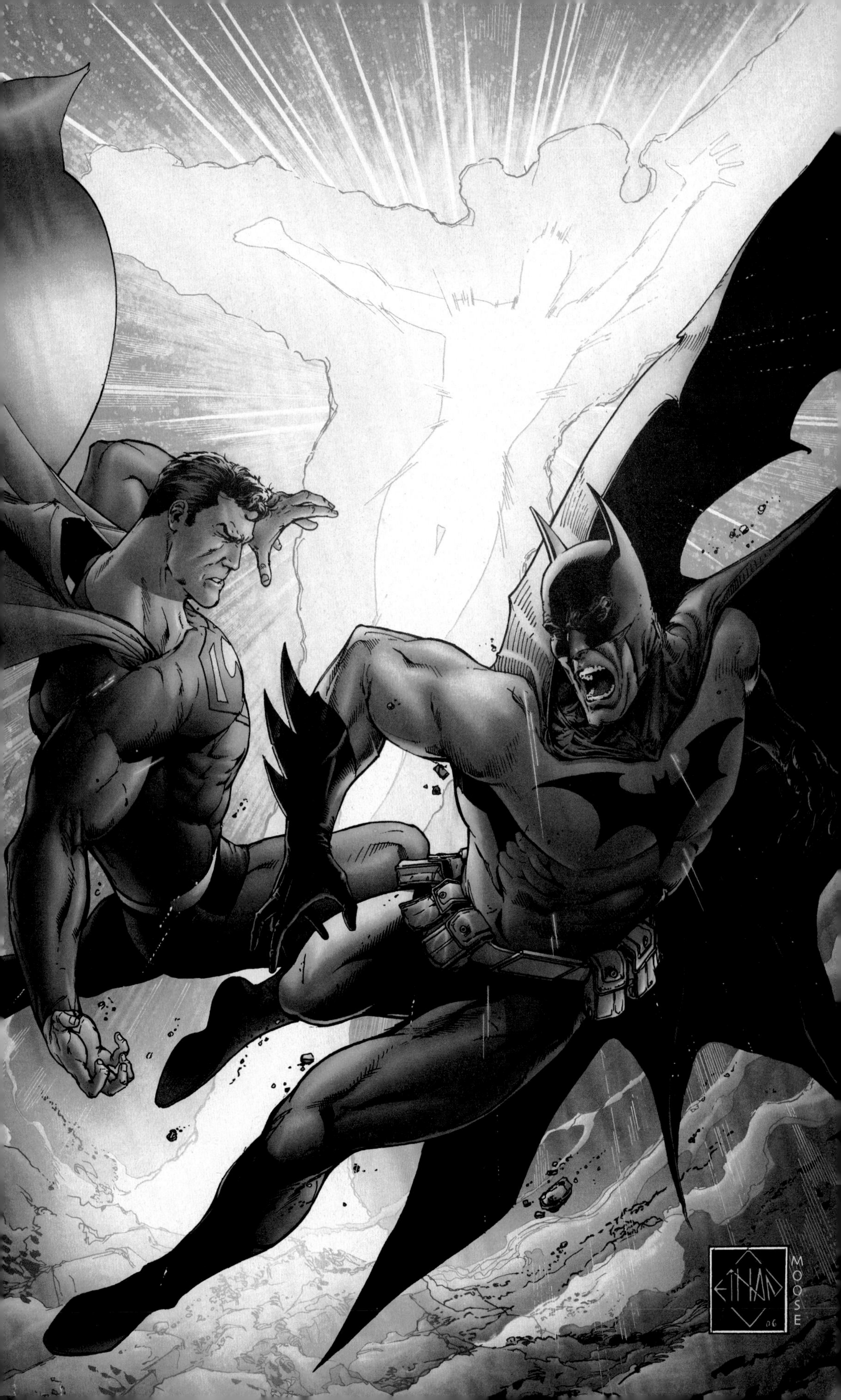
MOOSE

THE ENEMIES AMONG US: PART FOUR
From SUPERMAN/BATMAN 31
Cover by Ethan Van Sciver and Moose Baumann

Mark Verheiden
Writer

Matthew Clark
Pencils

Andy Lanning
Inks

Guy Major
Colors

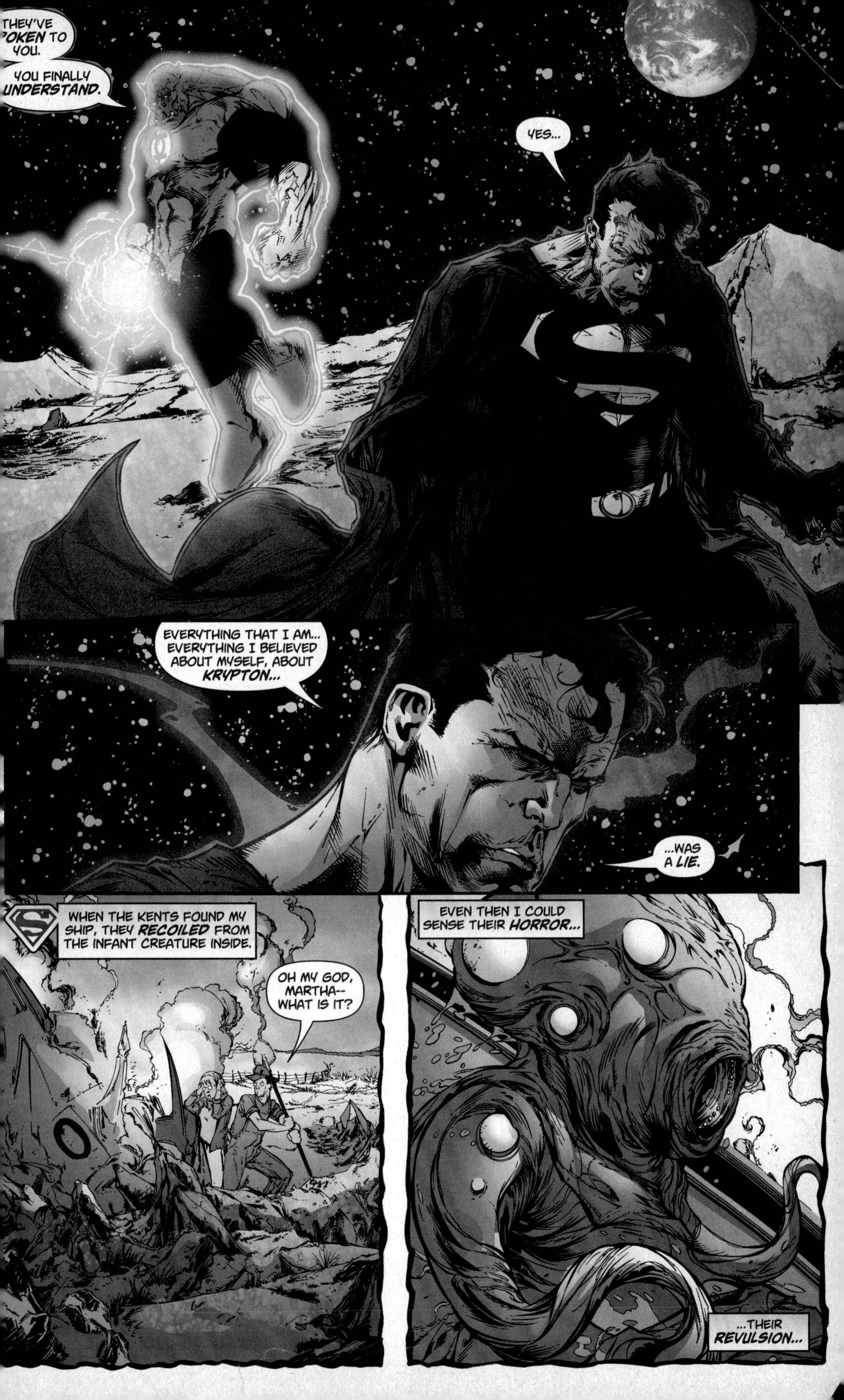
THEY'VE
'OKEN TO
YOU.
YOU FINALLY
UNDERSTAND.
YES...
EVERYTHING THAT I AM... EVERYTHING I BELIEVED ABOUT MYSELF, ABOUT KRYPTON...
...WAS A LIE.
WHEN THE KENTS FOUND MY SHIP, THEY RECOILED FROM THE INFANT CREATURE INSIDE.
OH MY GOD, MARTHA-- WHAT IS IT?
EVEN THEN I COULD SENSE THEIR HORROR...
...THEIR REVULSION...

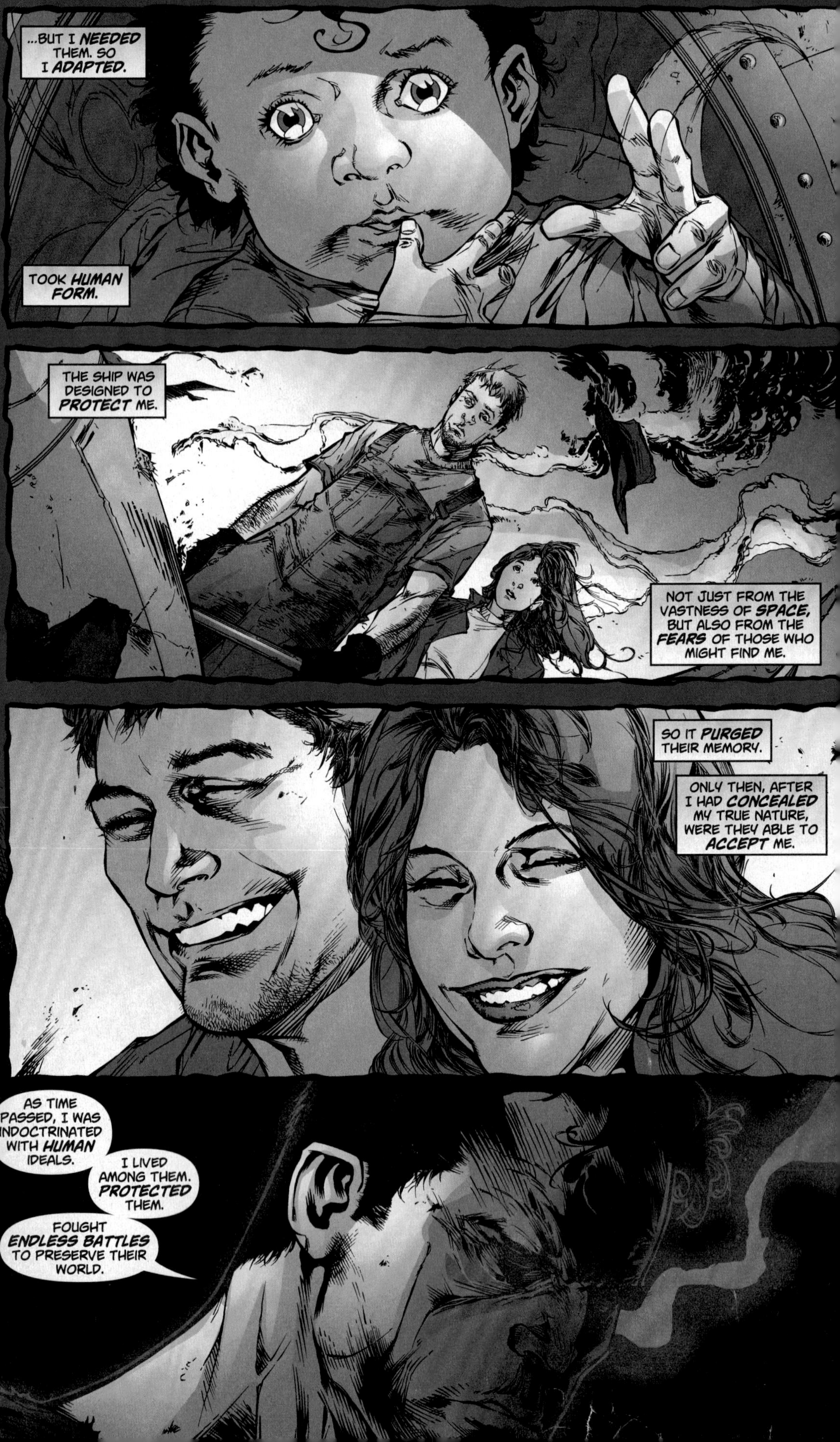

...BUT I NEEDED THEM. SO I ADAPTED.
TOOK HUMAN FORM.
THE SHIP WAS DESIGNED TO PROTECT ME.
NOT JUST FROM THE VASTNESS OF SPACE, BUT ALSO FROM THE FEARS OF THOSE WHO MIGHT FIND ME.
SO IT PURGED THEIR MEMORY.
ONLY THEN, AFTER I HAD CONCEALED MY TRUE NATURE, WERE THEY ABLE TO ACCEPT ME.
AS TIME PASSED, I WAS INDOCTRINATED WITH HUMAN IDEALS.
I LIVED AMONG THEM. PROTECTED THEM.
FOUGHT ENDLESS BATTLES TO PRESERVE THEIR WORLD.

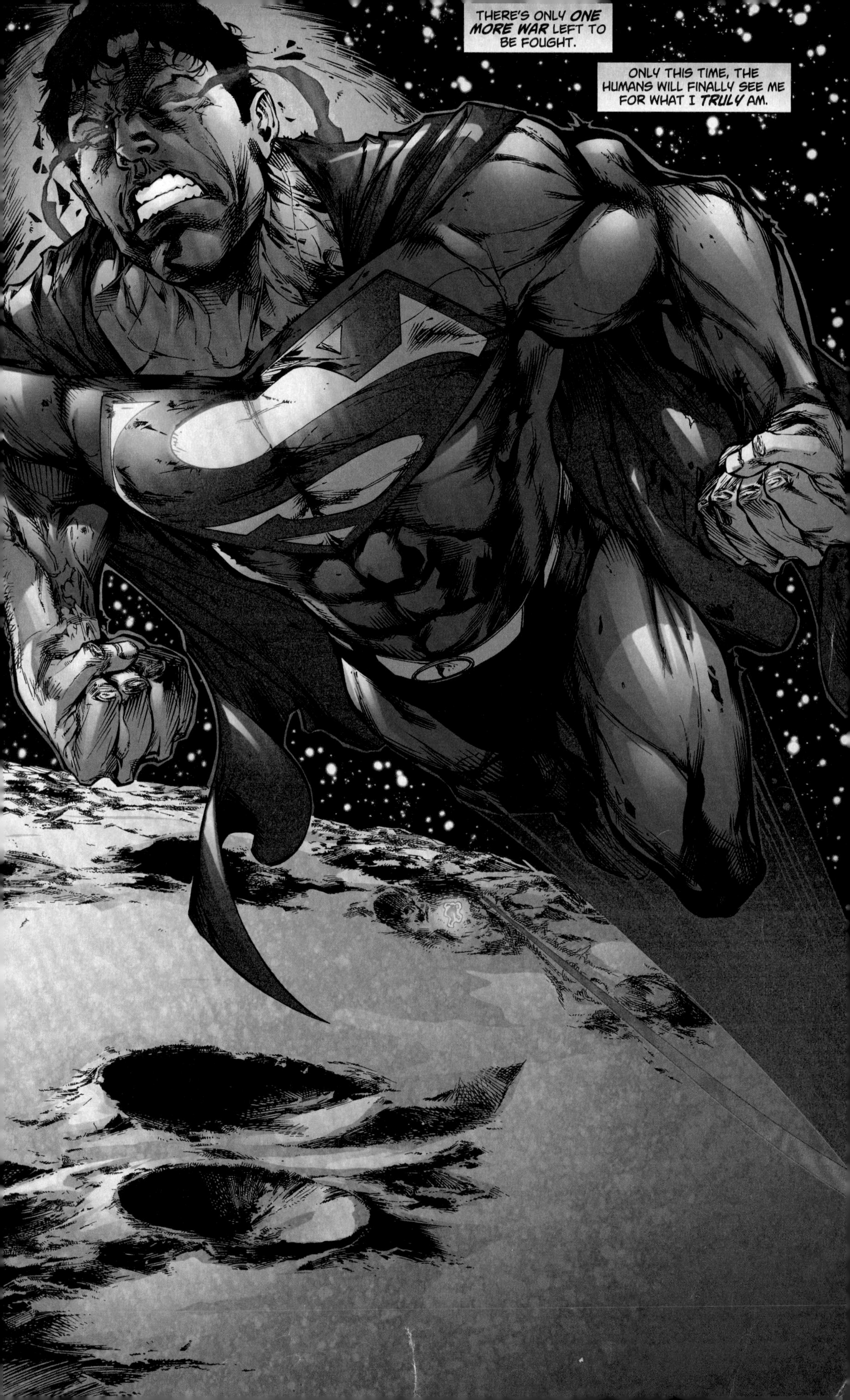
THERE'S ONLY ONE MORE WAR LEFT TO BE FOUGHT.
ONLY THIS TIME, THE HUMANS WILL FINALLY SEE ME FOR WHAT I TRULY AM.

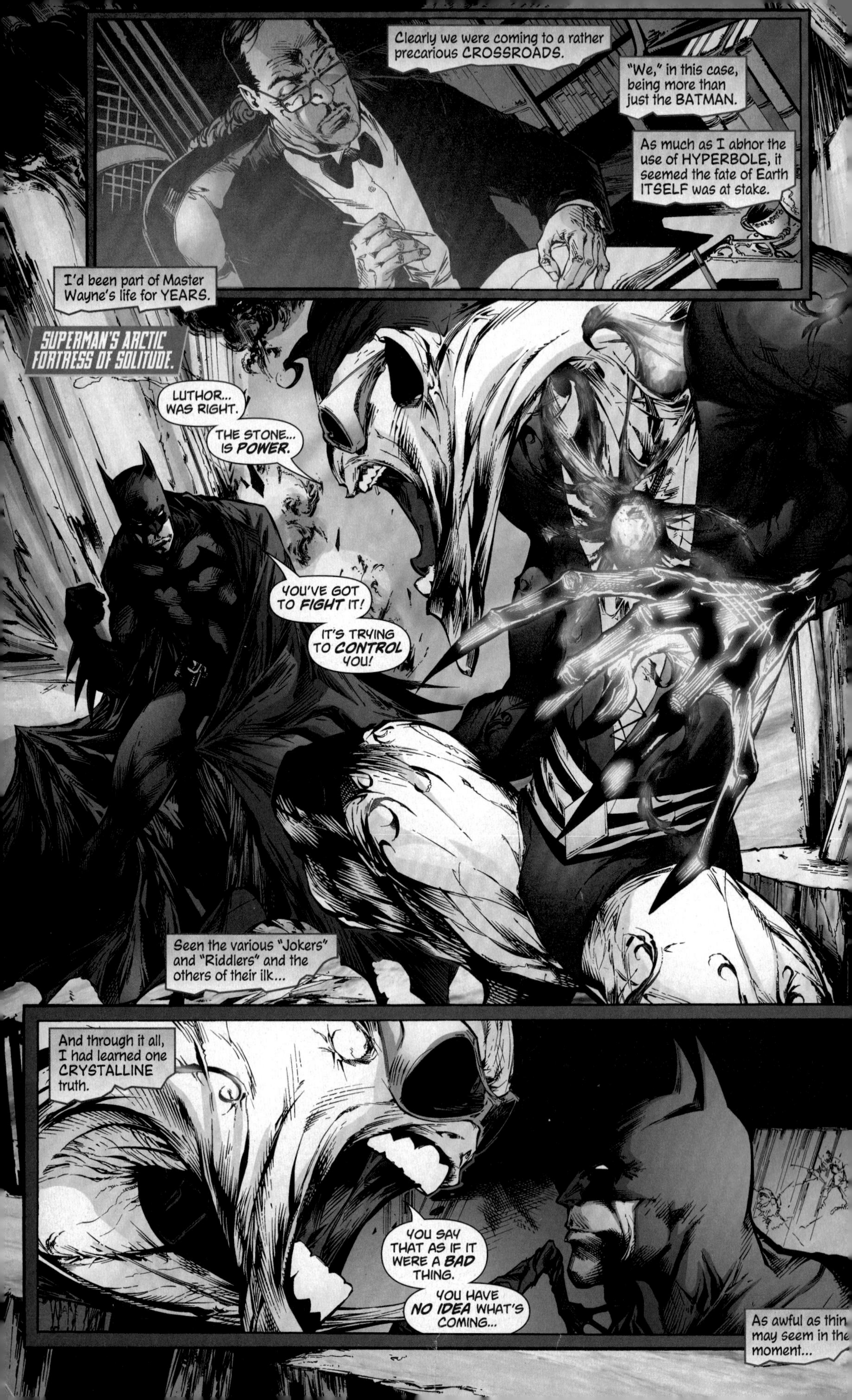
Clearly we were coming to a rather precarious CROSSROADS.
"We," in this case, being more than just the BATMAN.
As much as I abhor the use of HYPERBOLE, it seemed the fate of Earth ITSELF was at stake.
I'd been part of Master Wayne's life for YEARS.
SUPERMAN'S ARCTIC FORTRESS OF SOLITUDE.
LUTHOR... WAS RIGHT.
THE STONE... IS POWER.
YOU'VE GOT TO FIGHT IT!
IT'S TRYING TO CONTROL YOU!
Seen the various "Jokers" and "Riddlers" and the others of their ilk...
And through it all, I had learned one CRYSTALLINE truth.
YOU SAY THAT AS IF IT WERE A BAD THING.
YOU HAVE NO IDEA WHAT'S COMING...
As awful as thin may seem in the moment...

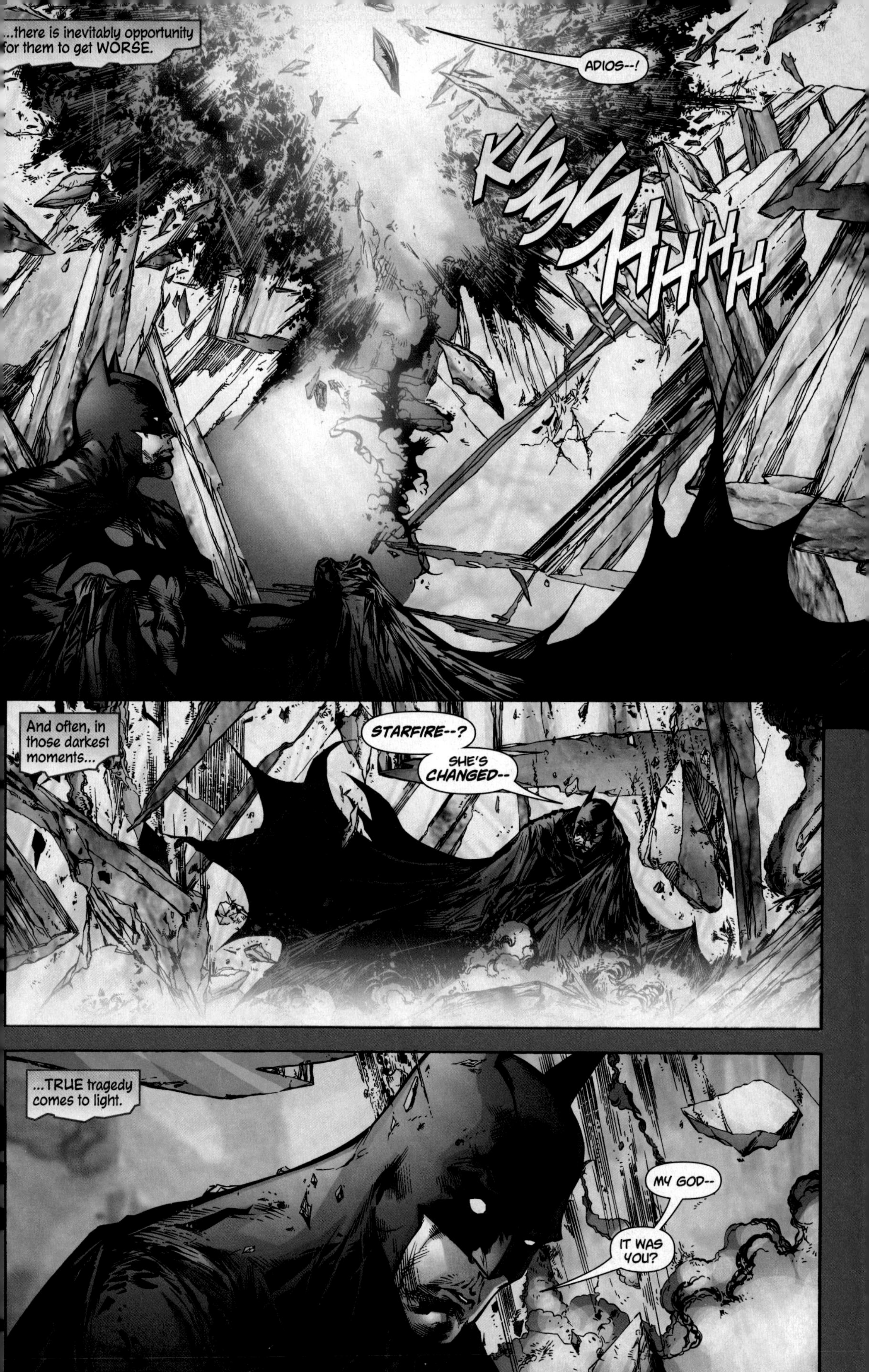

...there is inevitably opportunity for them to get WORSE.
ADIOS--!
KSSSHHHH
And often, in those darkest moments...
STARFIRE--?
SHE'S CHANGED--
...TRUE tragedy comes to light.
MY GOD--
IT WAS YOU?

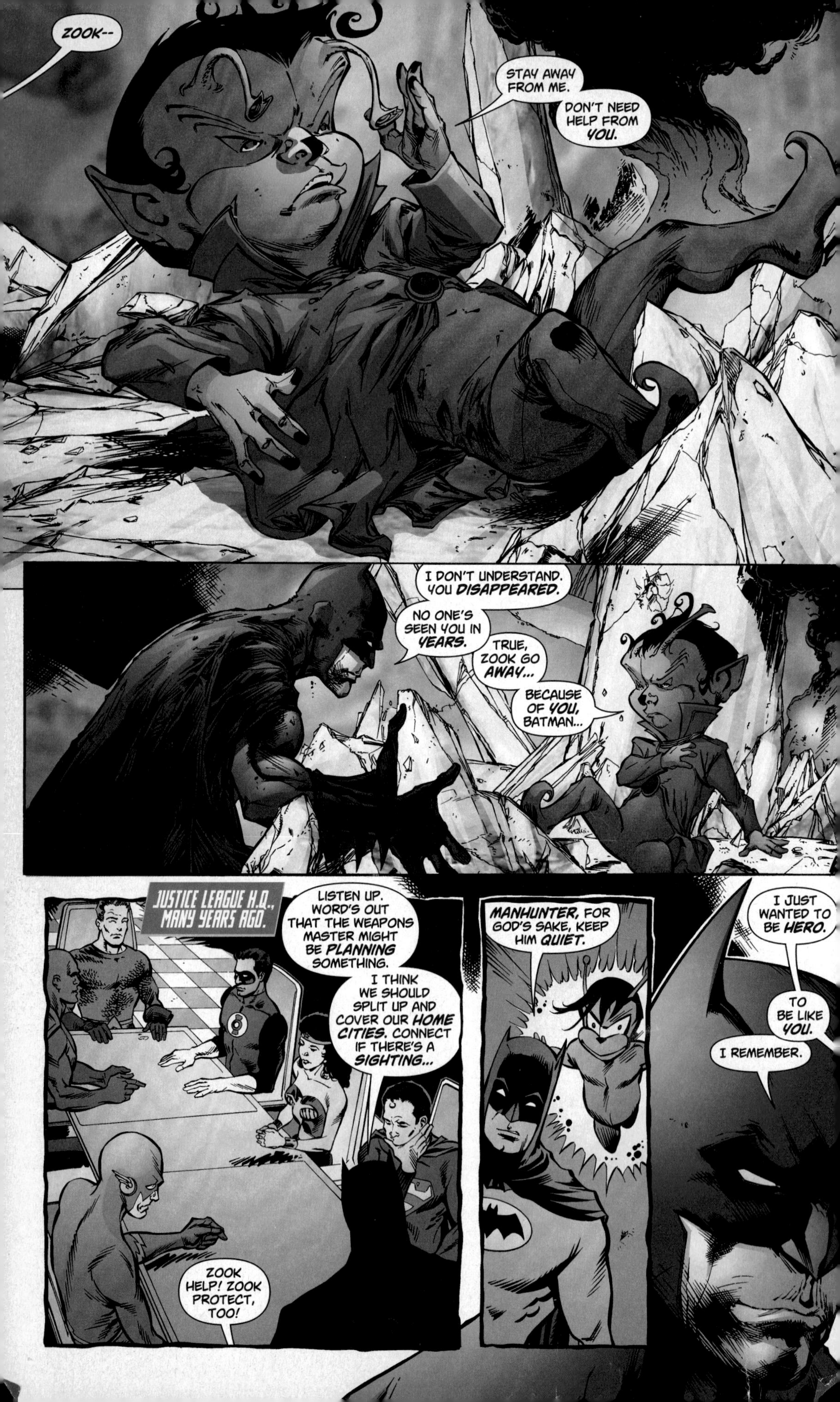

ZOOK--
STAY AWAY FROM ME.
DON'T NEED HELP FROM YOU.
I DON'T UNDERSTAND. YOU DISAPPEARED.
NO ONE'S SEEN YOU IN YEARS.
TRUE, ZOOK GO AWAY...
BECAUSE OF YOU, BATMAN...
JUSTICE LEAGUE H.Q., MANY YEARS AGO.
LISTEN UP. WORD'S OUT THAT THE WEAPONS MASTER MIGHT BE PLANNING SOMETHING.
I THINK WE SHOULD SPLIT UP AND COVER OUR HOME CITIES. CONNECT IF THERE'S A SIGHTING...
ZOOK HELP! ZOOK PROTECT, TOO!
MANHUNTER, FOR GOD'S SAKE, KEEP HIM QUIET.
I JUST WANTED TO BE HERO.
TO BE LIKE YOU.
I REMEMBER.

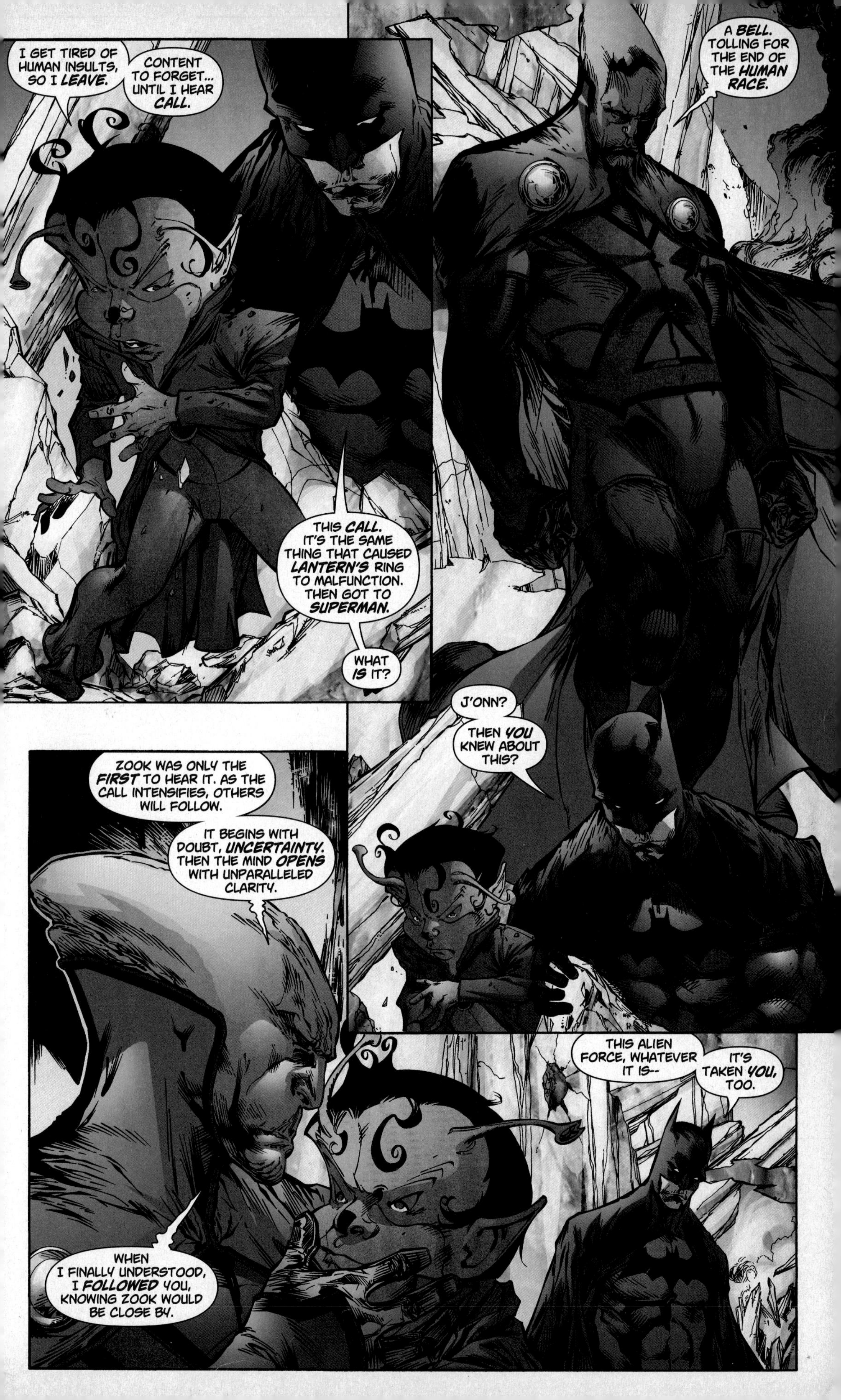

I GET TIRED OF HUMAN INSULTS, SO I LEAVE.
CONTENT TO FORGET... UNTIL I HEAR CALL.
A BELL. TOLLING FOR THE END OF THE HUMAN RACE.
THIS CALL. IT'S THE SAME THING THAT CAUSED LANTERN'S RING TO MALFUNCTION. THEN GOT TO SUPERMAN.
WHAT IS IT?
J'ONN?
THEN YOU KNEW ABOUT THIS?
ZOOK WAS ONLY THE FIRST TO HEAR IT. AS THE CALL INTENSIFIES, OTHERS WILL FOLLOW.
IT BEGINS WITH DOUBT, UNCERTAINTY. THEN THE MIND OPENS WITH UNPARALLELED CLARITY.
THIS ALIEN FORCE, WHATEVER IT IS--
IT'S TAKEN YOU, TOO.
WHEN I FINALLY UNDERSTOOD, I FOLLOWED YOU, KNOWING ZOOK WOULD BE CLOSE BY.

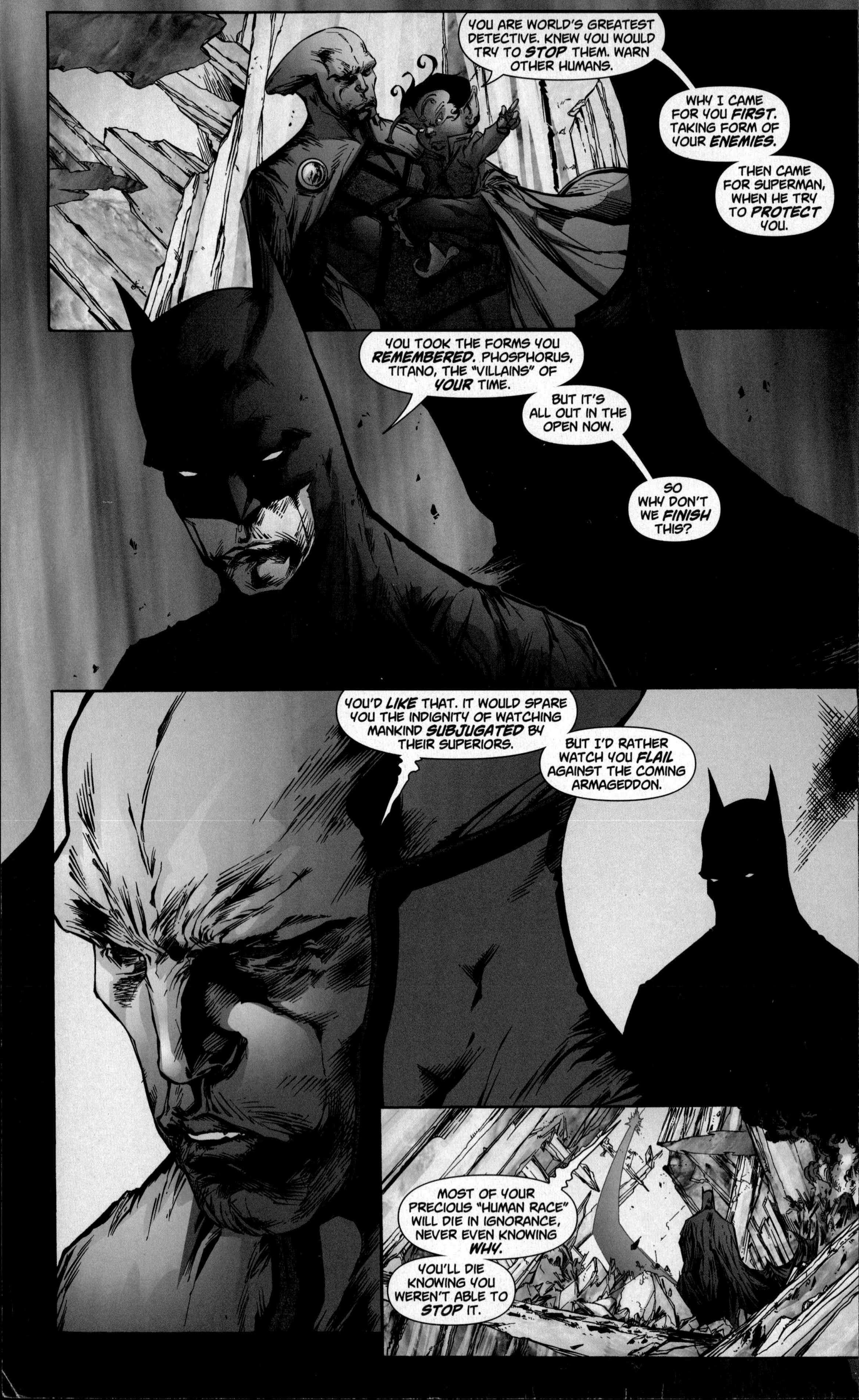

YOU ARE WORLD'S GREATEST DETECTIVE. KNEW YOU WOULD TRY TO STOP THEM. WARN OTHER HUMANS.
WHY I CAME FOR YOU FIRST. TAKING FORM OF YOUR ENEMIES.
THEN CAME FOR SUPERMAN, WHEN HE TRY TO PROTECT YOU.
YOU TOOK THE FORMS YOU REMEMBERED. PHOSPHORUS, TITANO, THE "VILLAINS" OF YOUR TIME.
BUT IT'S ALL OUT IN THE OPEN NOW.
SO WHY DON'T WE FINISH THIS?
YOU'D LIKE THAT. IT WOULD SPARE YOU THE INDIGNITY OF WATCHING MANKIND SUBJUGATED BY THEIR SUPERIORS.
BUT I'D RATHER WATCH YOU FLAIL AGAINST THE COMING ARMAGEDDON.
MOST OF YOUR PRECIOUS "HUMAN RACE" WILL DIE IN IGNORANCE, NEVER EVEN KNOWING WHY.
YOU'LL DIE KNOWING YOU WEREN'T ABLE TO STOP IT.

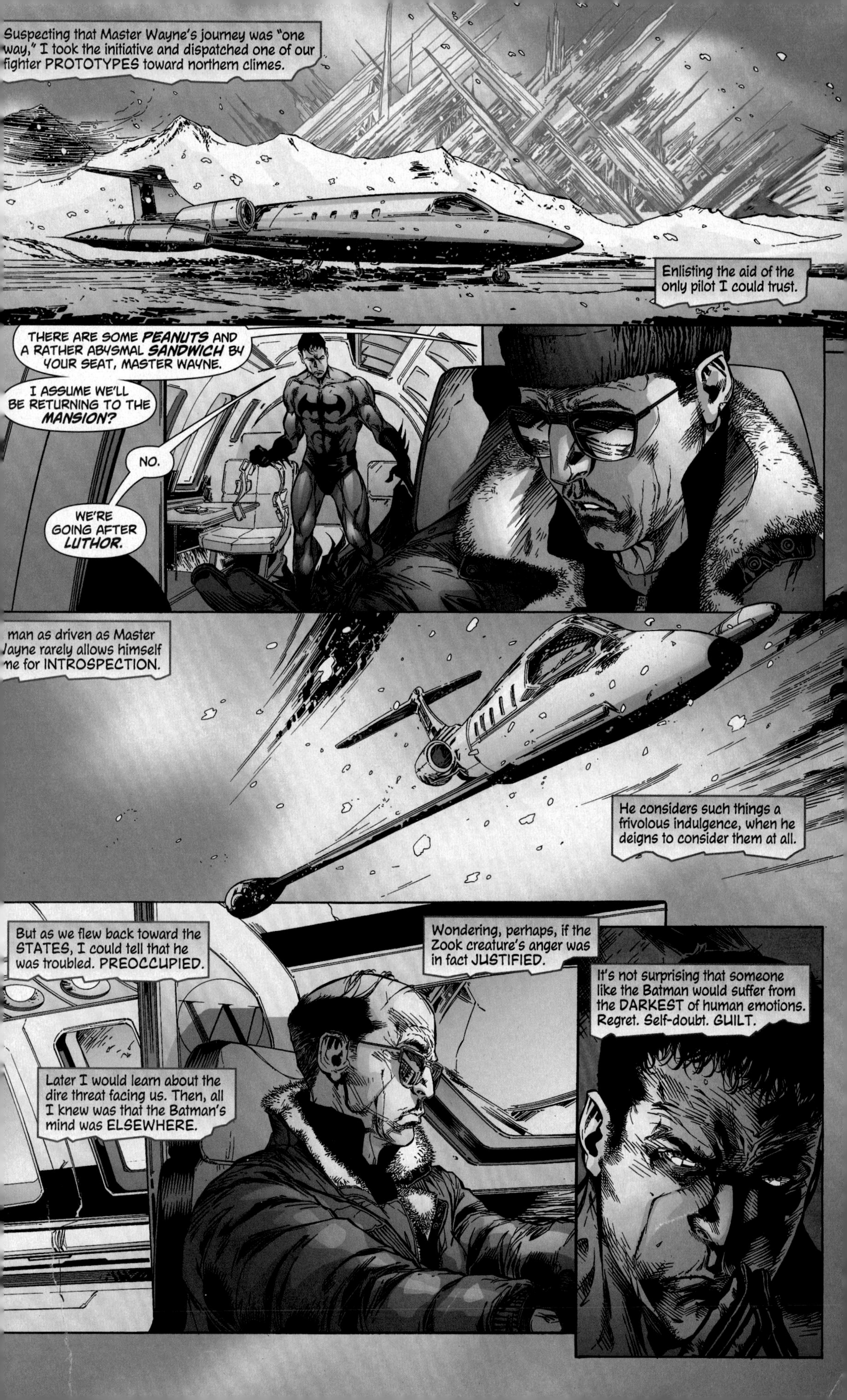
Suspecting that Master Wayne's journey was "one way," I took the initiative and dispatched one of our fighter PROTOTYPES toward northern climes.
Enlisting the aid of the only pilot I could trust.
THERE ARE SOME PEANUTS AND A RATHER ABYSMAL SANDWICH BY YOUR SEAT, MASTER WAYNE.
I ASSUME WE'LL BE RETURNING TO THE MANSION?
NO.
WE'RE GOING AFTER LUTHOR.
man as driven as Master ayne rarely allows himself me for INTROSPECTION.
He considers such things a frivolous indulgence, when he deigns to consider them at all.
But as we flew back toward the STATES, I could tell that he was troubled. PREOCCUPIED.
Wondering, perhaps, if the Zook creature's anger was in fact JUSTIFIED.
It's not surprising that someone like the Batman would suffer from the DARKEST of human emotions. Regret. Self-doubt. GUILT.
Later I would learn about the dire threat facing us. Then, all I knew was that the Batman's mind was ELSEWHERE.

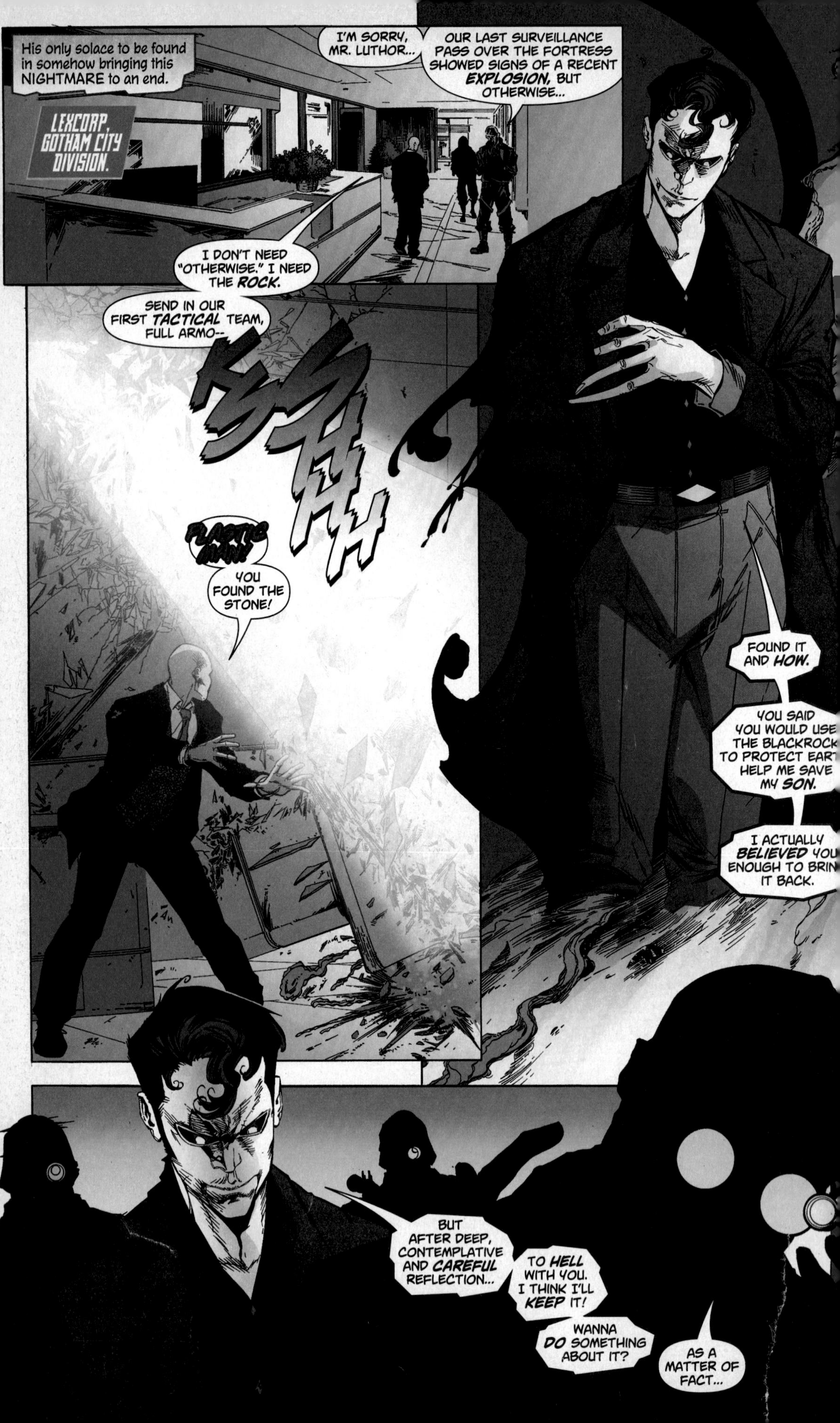
His only solace to be found in somehow bringing this NIGHTMARE to an end.
LEXCORP, GOTHAM CITY DIVISION.
I'M SORRY, MR. LUTHOR...
OUR LAST SURVEILLANCE PASS OVER THE FORTRESS SHOWED SIGNS OF A RECENT EXPLOSION, BUT OTHERWISE...
I DON'T NEED "OTHERWISE." I NEED THE ROCK.
SEND IN OUR FIRST TACTICAL TEAM, FULL ARMO--
KSSHH
PLASTIC MAN!
YOU FOUND THE STONE!
FOUND IT AND HOW.
YOU SAID YOU WOULD USE THE BLACKROCK TO PROTECT EART HELP ME SAVE MY SON.
I ACTUALLY BELIEVED YOU ENOUGH TO BRIN IT BACK.
BUT AFTER DEEP, CONTEMPLATIVE AND CAREFUL REFLECTION...
TO HELL WITH YOU. I THINK I'LL KEEP IT!
WANNA DO SOMETHING ABOUT IT?
AS A MATTER OF FACT...

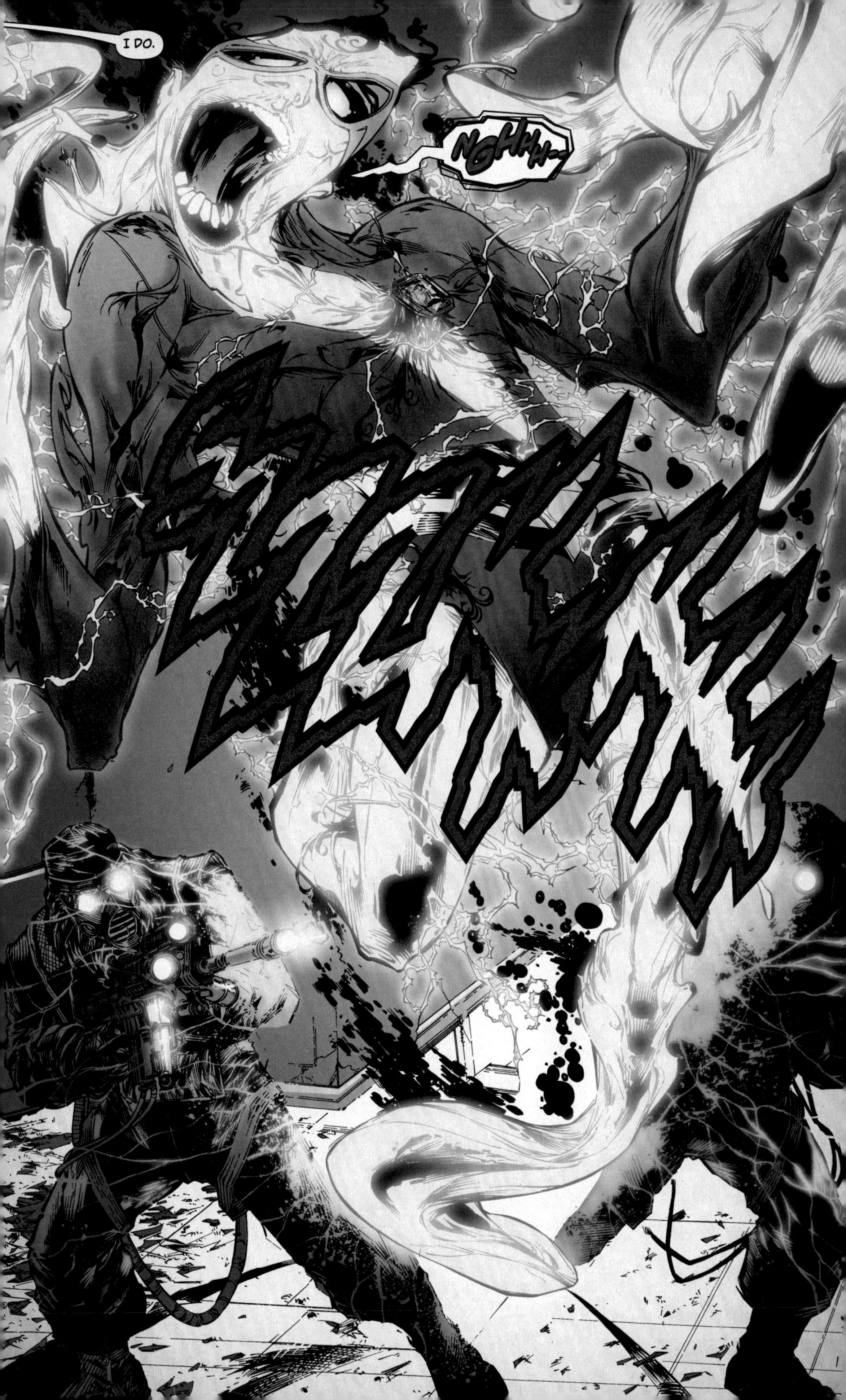
I DO.
NGHHH--

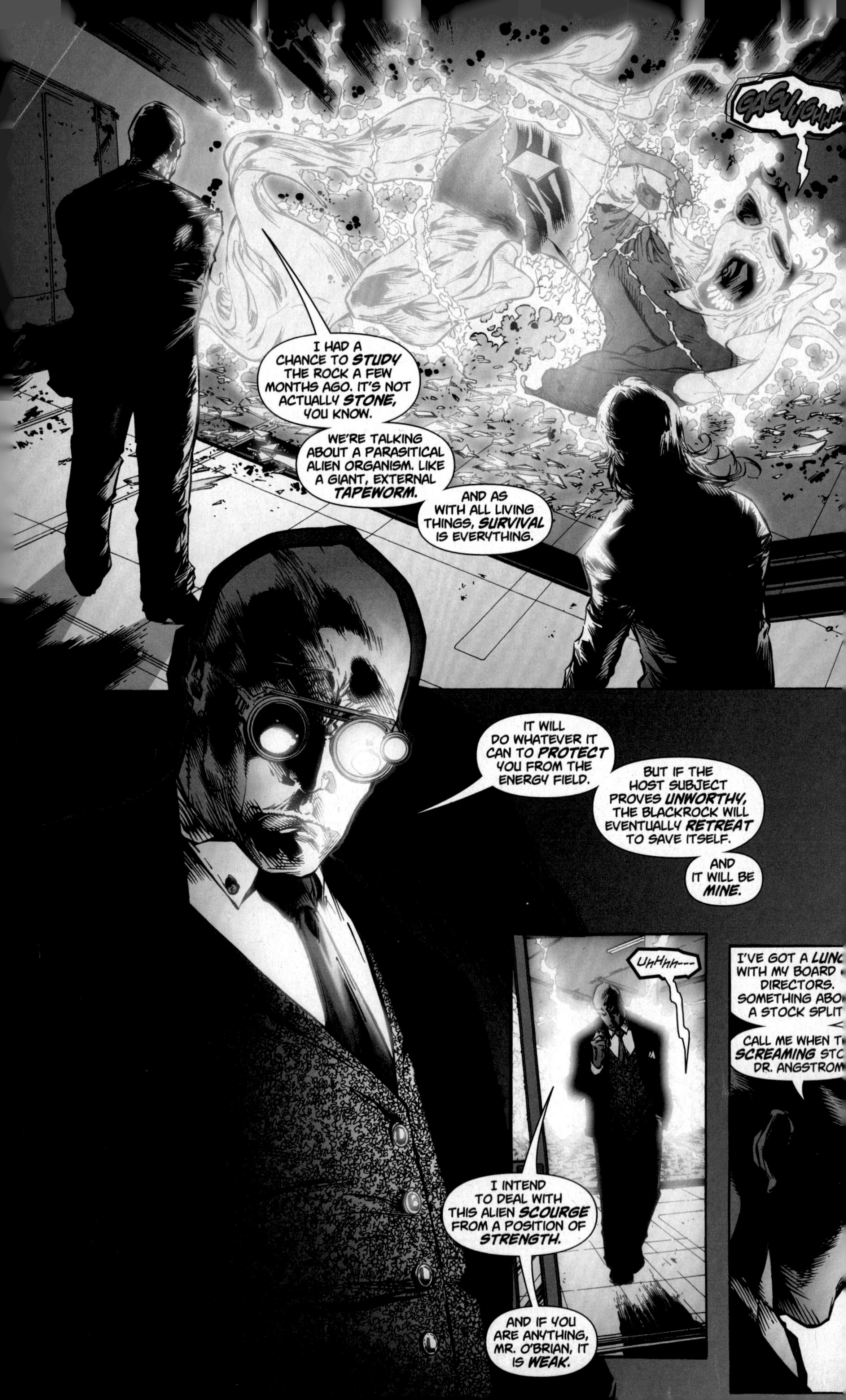
GAGHYCHHHH
I HAD A CHANCE TO STUDY THE ROCK A FEW MONTHS AGO. IT'S NOT ACTUALLY STONE, YOU KNOW.
WE'RE TALKING ABOUT A PARASITICAL ALIEN ORGANISM. LIKE A GIANT, EXTERNAL TAPEWORM.
AND AS WITH ALL LIVING THINGS, SURVIVAL IS EVERYTHING.
IT WILL DO WHATEVER IT CAN TO PROTECT YOU FROM THE ENERGY FIELD.
BUT IF THE HOST SUBJECT PROVES UNWORTHY, THE BLACKROCK WILL EVENTUALLY RETREAT TO SAVE ITSELF.
AND IT WILL BE MINE.
UHHHH---
I INTEND TO DEAL WITH THIS ALIEN SCOURGE FROM A POSITION OF STRENGTH.
AND IF YOU ARE ANYTHING, MR. O'BRIAN, IT IS WEAK.
I'VE GOT A LUNC
WITH MY BOARD
DIRECTORS.
SOMETHING ABO
A STOCK SPLIT
CALL ME WHEN T
SCREAMING STO
DR. ANGSTROM

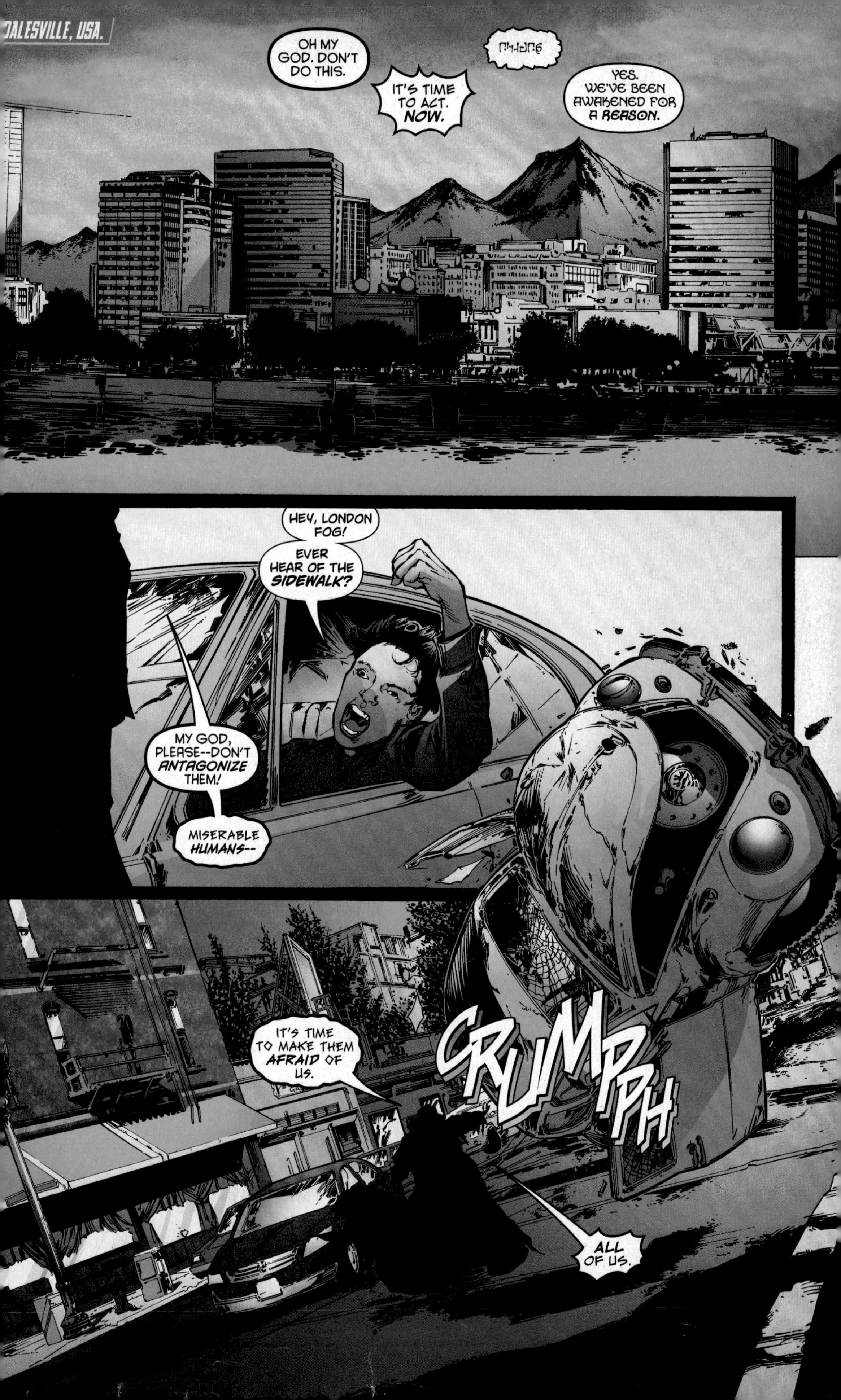
DALESVILLE, USA.
OH MY GOD. DON'T DO THIS.
IT'S TIME TO ACT. NOW.
YES. WE'VE BEEN AWAKENED FOR A REASON.
HEY, LONDON FOG!
EVER HEAR OF THE SIDEWALK?
MY GOD, PLEASE--DON'T ANTAGONIZE THEM!
MISERABLE HUMANS--
IT'S TIME TO MAKE THEM AFRAID OF US.
CRUMPH
ALL OF US.

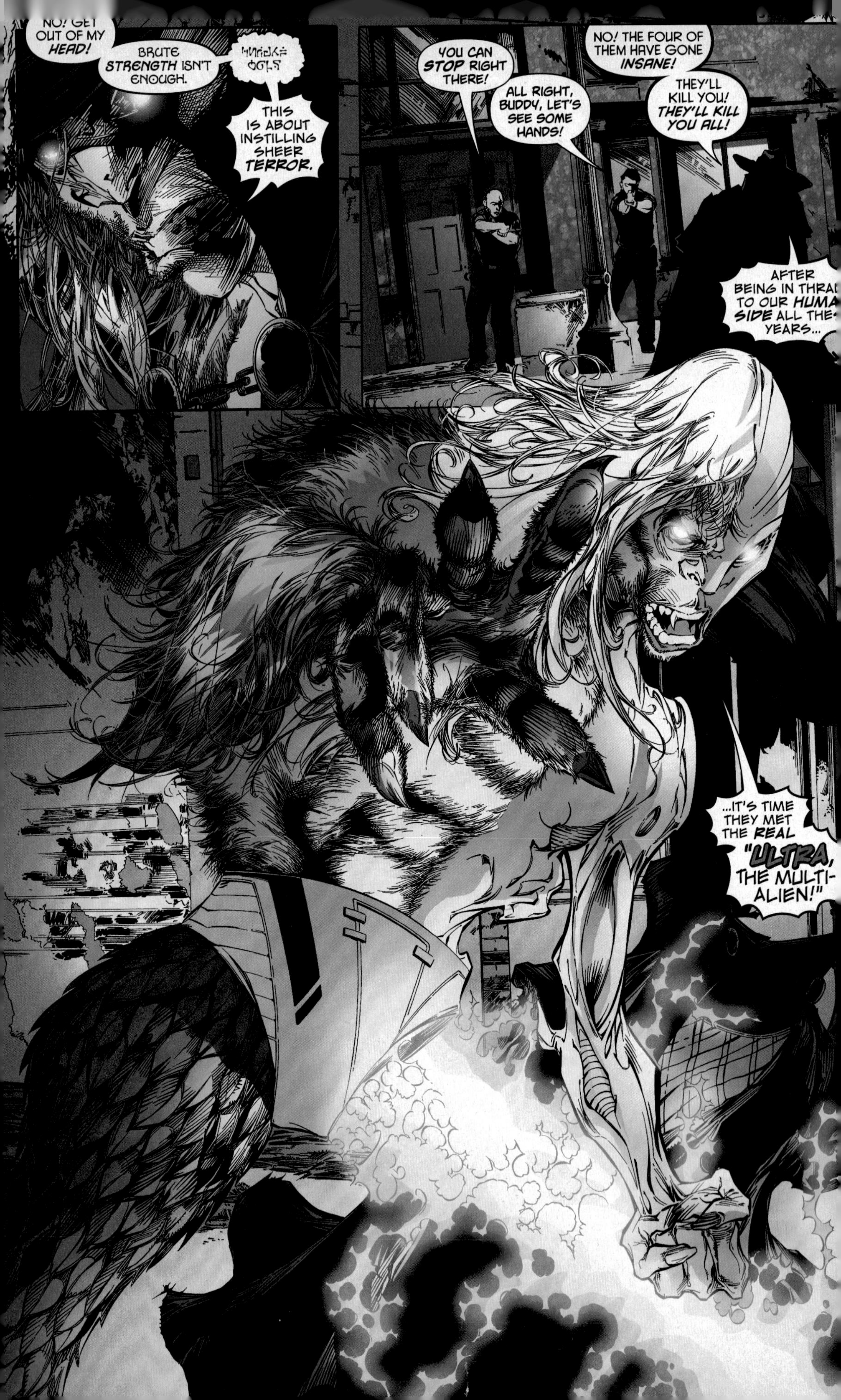

NO! GET OUT OF MY HEAD!
BRUTE STRENGTH ISN'T ENOUGH.
THIS IS ABOUT INSTILLING SHEER TERROR.
YOU CAN STOP RIGHT THERE!
ALL RIGHT, BUDDY, LET'S SEE SOME HANDS!
NO! THE FOUR OF THEM HAVE GONE INSANE!
THEY'LL KILL YOU! THEY'LL KILL YOU ALL!
AFTER BEING IN THRAL TO OUR HUMA SIDE ALL THE YEARS...
...IT'S TIME THEY MET THE REAL "ULTRA, THE MULTI-ALIEN!"

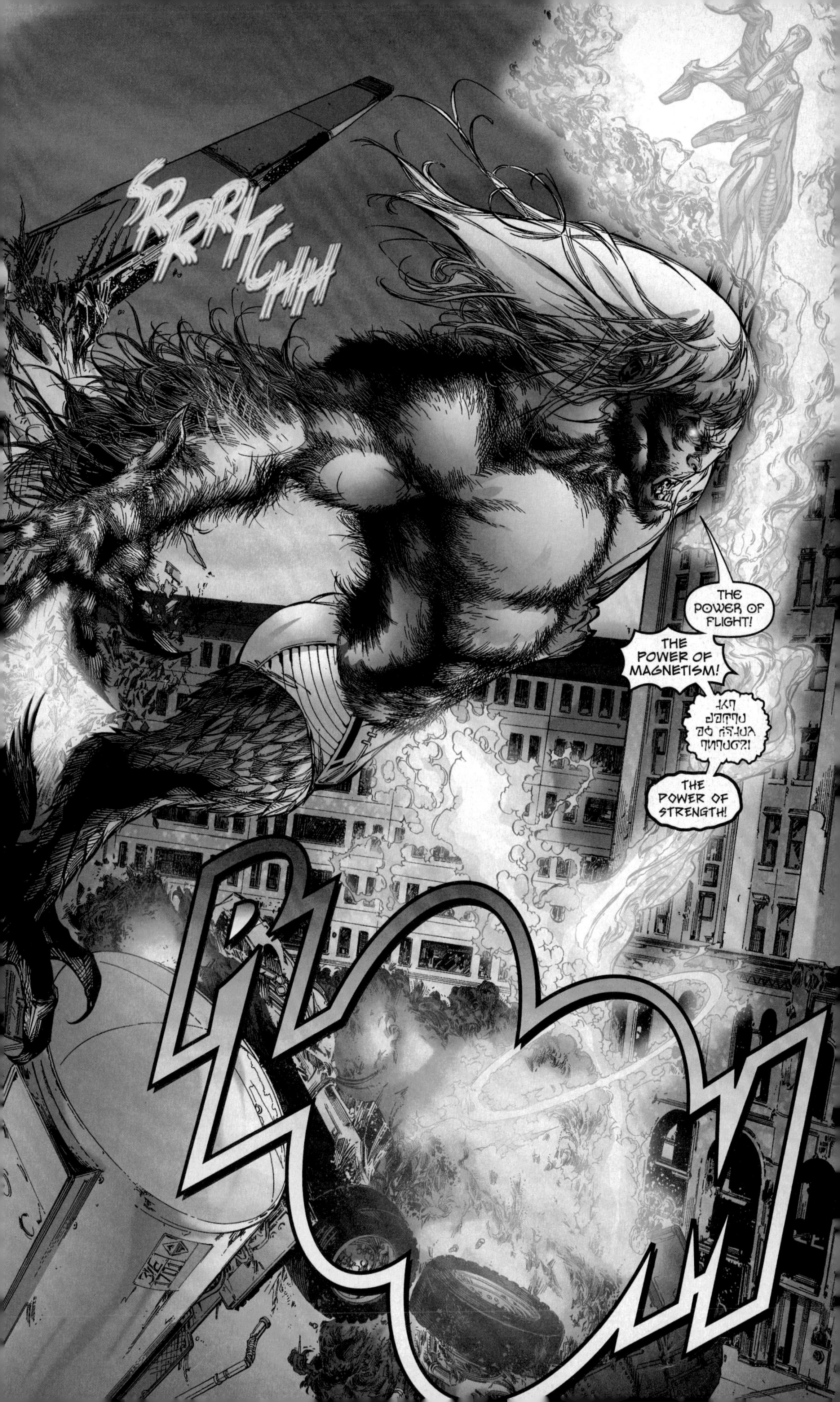
THE POWER OF FLIGHT!
THE POWER OF MAGNETISM!
THE POWER OF STRENGTH!

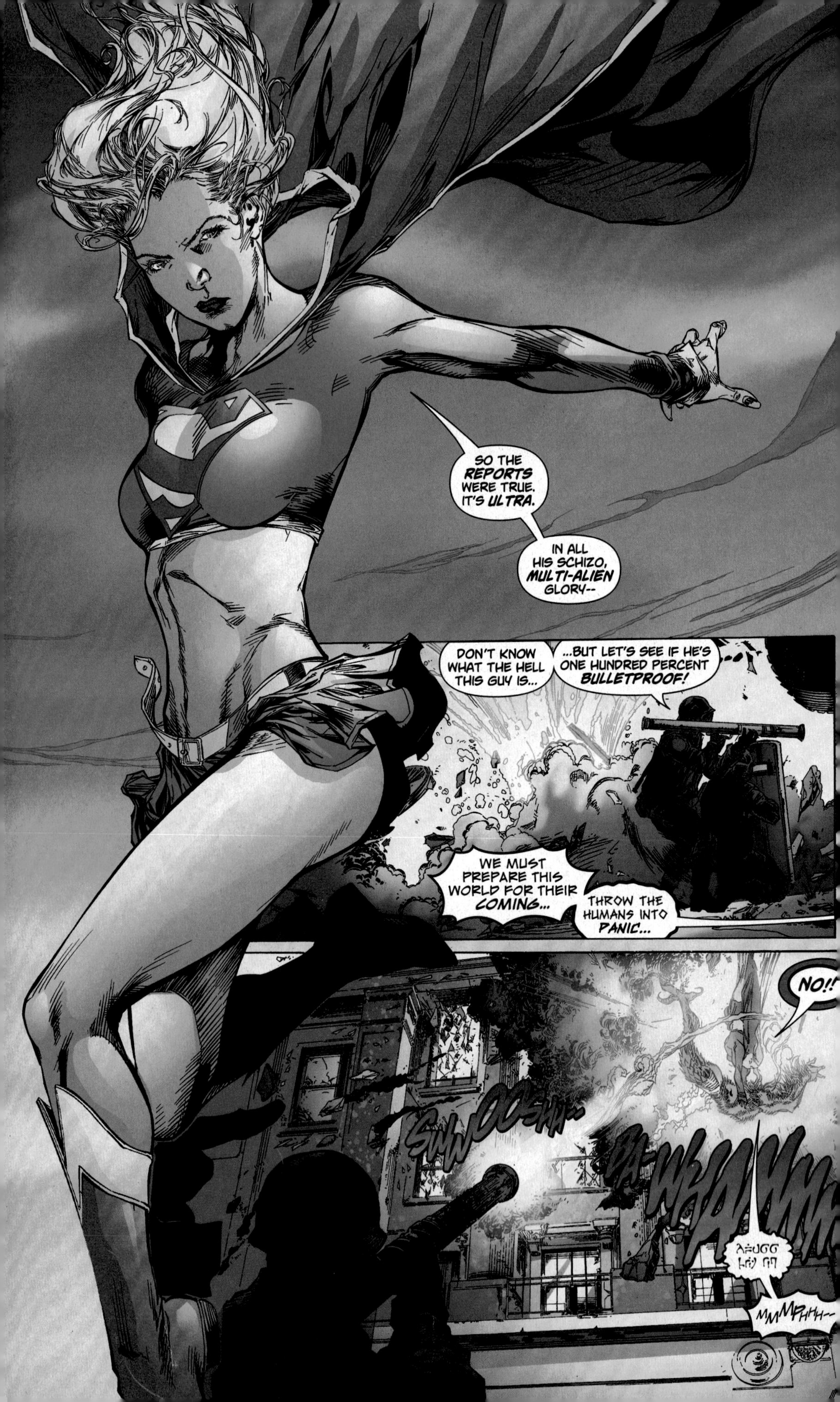
SO THE REPORTS WERE TRUE. IT'S ULTRA.
IN ALL HIS SCHIZO, MULTI-ALIEN GLORY--
DON'T KNOW WHAT THE HELL THIS GUY IS...
...BUT LET'S SEE IF HE'S ONE HUNDRED PERCENT BULLETPROOF!
WE MUST PREPARE THIS WORLD FOR THEIR COMING...
THROW THE HUMANS INTO PANIC...
NO!!
SHWOOSHH--
BA-WHAMMM
MMMPHHH--

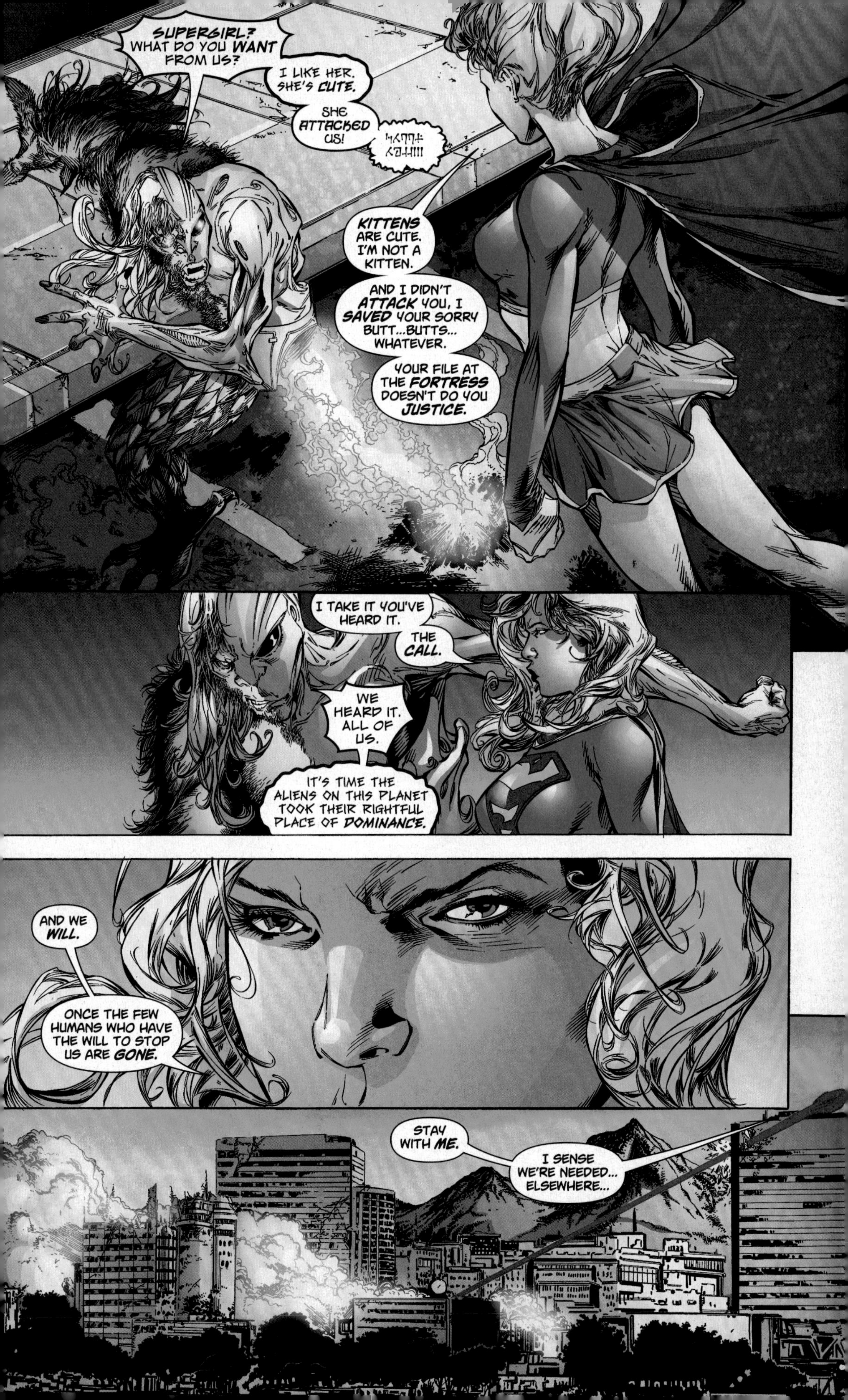
SUPERGIRL? WHAT DO YOU WANT FROM US?
I LIKE HER. SHE'S CUTE.
SHE ATTACKED US!
KITTENS ARE CUTE. I'M NOT A KITTEN.
AND I DIDN'T ATTACK YOU, I SAVED YOUR SORRY BUTT...BUTTS... WHATEVER.
YOUR FILE AT THE FORTRESS DOESN'T DO YOU JUSTICE.
I TAKE IT YOU'VE HEARD IT.
THE CALL.
WE HEARD IT. ALL OF US.
IT'S TIME THE ALIENS ON THIS PLANET TOOK THEIR RIGHTFUL PLACE OF DOMINANCE.
AND WE WILL.
ONCE THE FEW HUMANS WHO HAVE THE WILL TO STOP US ARE GONE.
STAY WITH ME.
I SENSE WE'RE NEEDED... ELSEWHERE...

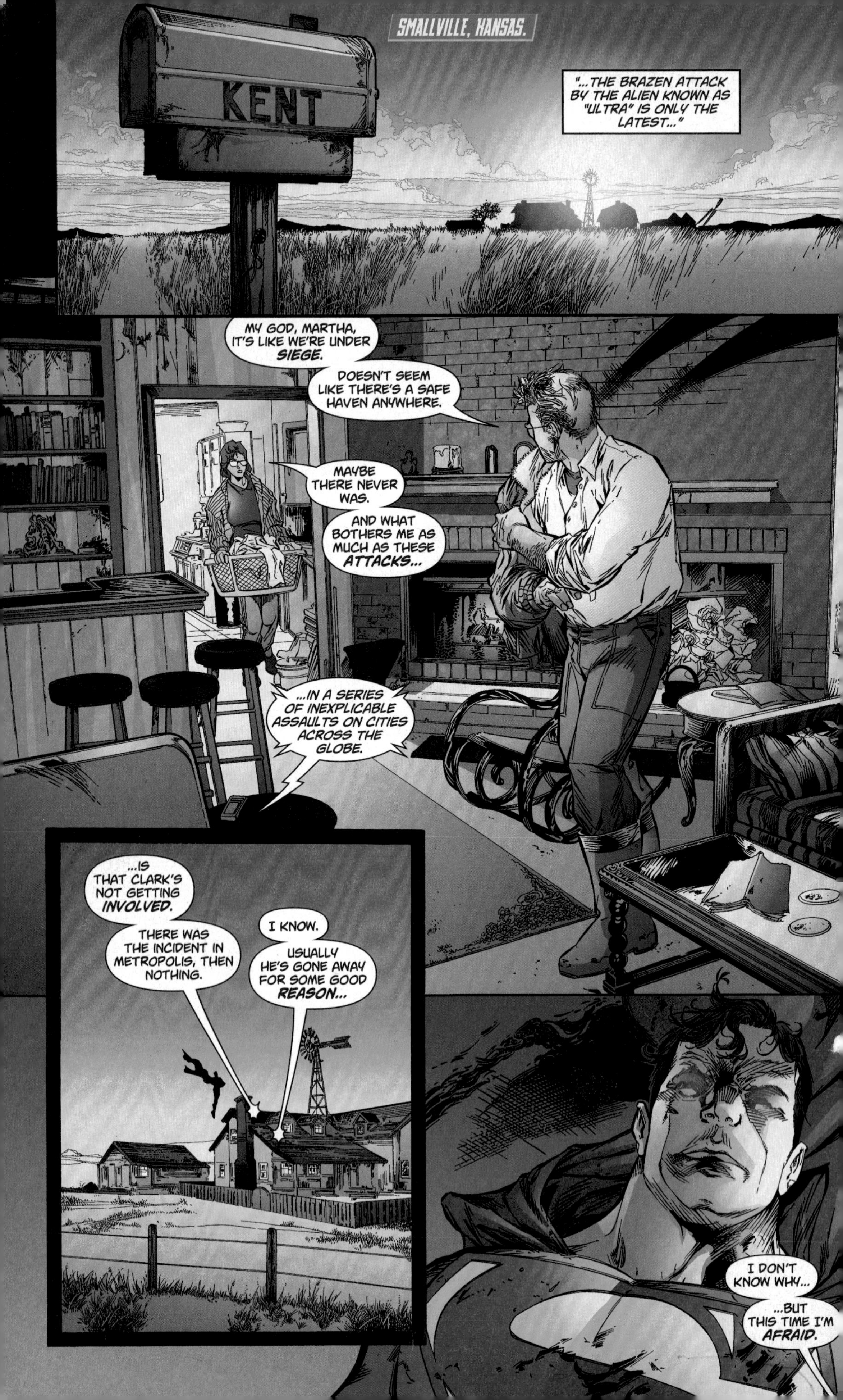
SMALLVILLE, KANSAS.
KENT
"...THE BRAZEN ATTACK BY THE ALIEN KNOWN AS "ULTRA" IS ONLY THE LATEST..."
MY GOD, MARTHA, IT'S LIKE WE'RE UNDER SIEGE.
DOESN'T SEEM LIKE THERE'S A SAFE HAVEN ANYWHERE.
MAYBE THERE NEVER WAS.
AND WHAT BOTHERS ME AS MUCH AS THESE ATTACKS...
...IN A SERIES OF INEXPLICABLE ASSAULTS ON CITIES ACROSS THE GLOBE.
...IS THAT CLARK'S NOT GETTING INVOLVED.
THERE WAS THE INCIDENT IN METROPOLIS, THEN NOTHING.
I KNOW.
USUALLY HE'S GONE AWAY FOR SOME GOOD REASON...
I DON'T KNOW WHY...
...BUT THIS TIME I'M AFRAID.

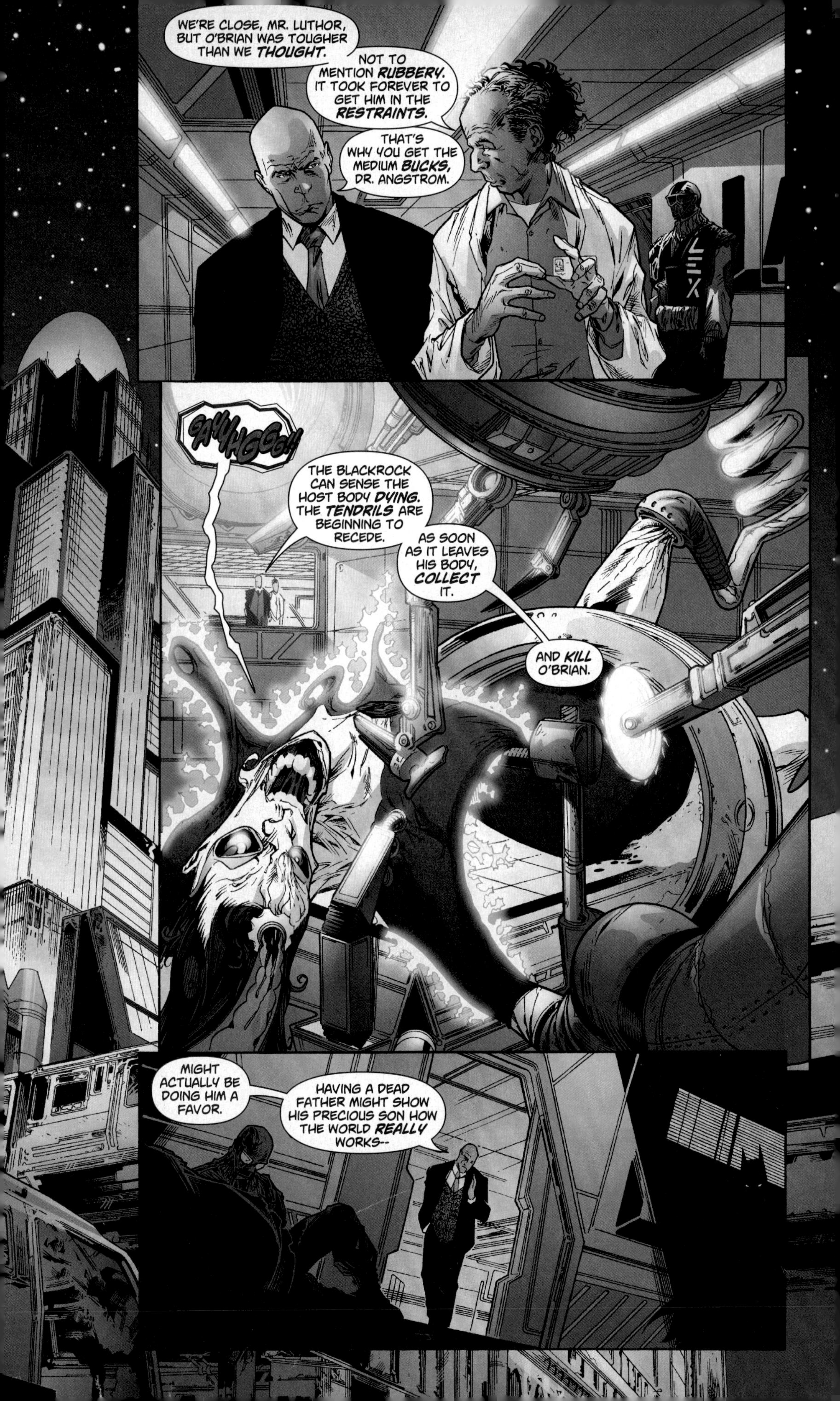

WE'RE CLOSE, MR. LUTHOR, BUT O'BRIAN WAS TOUGHER THAN WE THOUGHT.
NOT TO MENTION RUBBERY. IT TOOK FOREVER TO GET HIM IN THE RESTRAINTS.
THAT'S WHY YOU GET THE MEDIUM BUCKS, DR. ANGSTROM.
THE BLACKROCK CAN SENSE THE HOST BODY DYING. THE TENDRILS ARE BEGINNING TO RECEDE.
AS SOON AS IT LEAVES HIS BODY, COLLECT IT.
AND KILL O'BRIAN.
MIGHT ACTUALLY BE DOING HIM A FAVOR.
HAVING A DEAD FATHER MIGHT SHOW HIS PRECIOUS SON HOW THE WORLD REALLY WORKS--

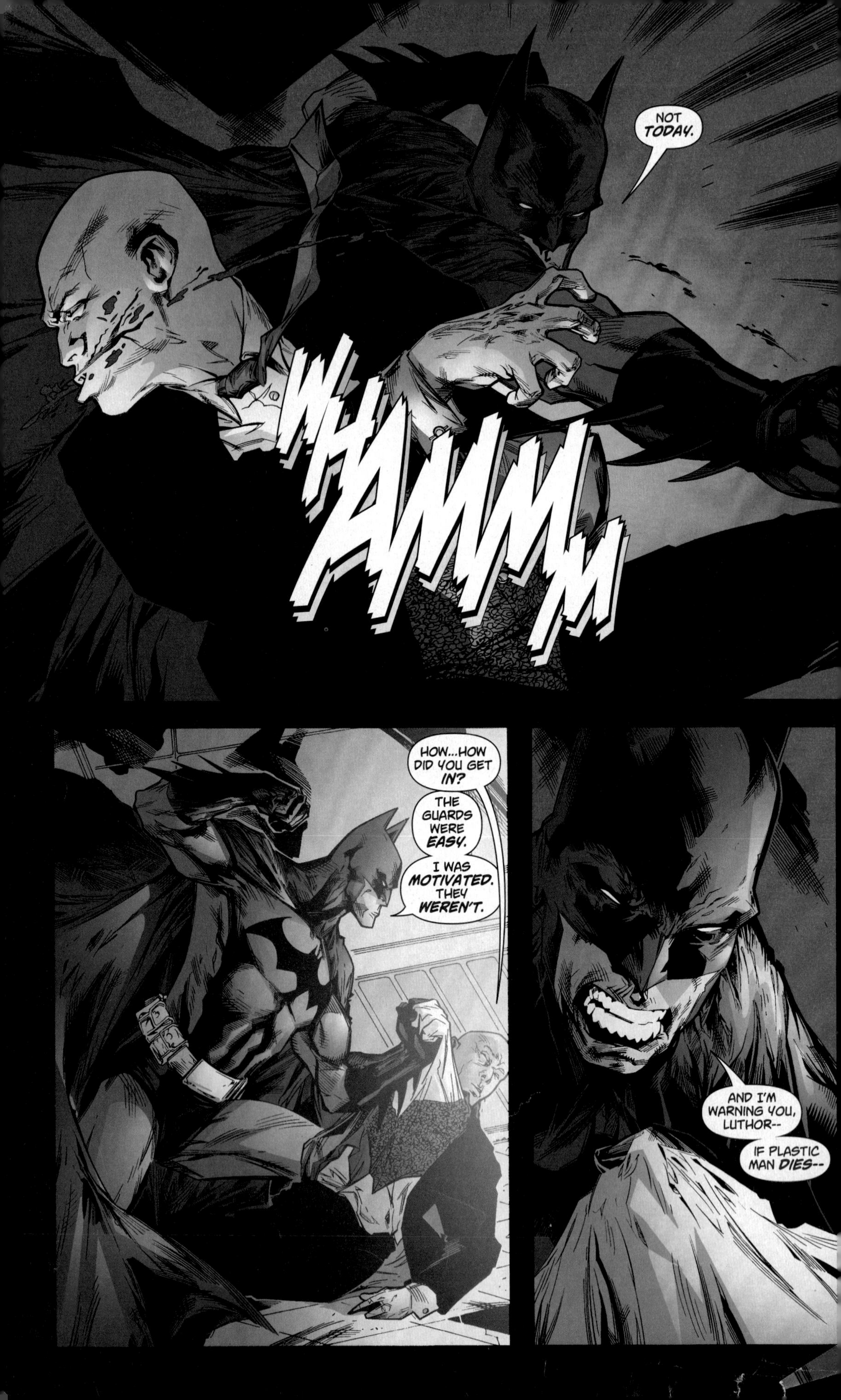
NOT TODAY.
WHAMMM
HOW...HOW DID YOU GET IN?
THE GUARDS WERE EASY.
I WAS MOTIVATED. THEY WEREN'T.
AND I'M WARNING YOU, LUTHOR--
IF PLASTIC MAN DIES--

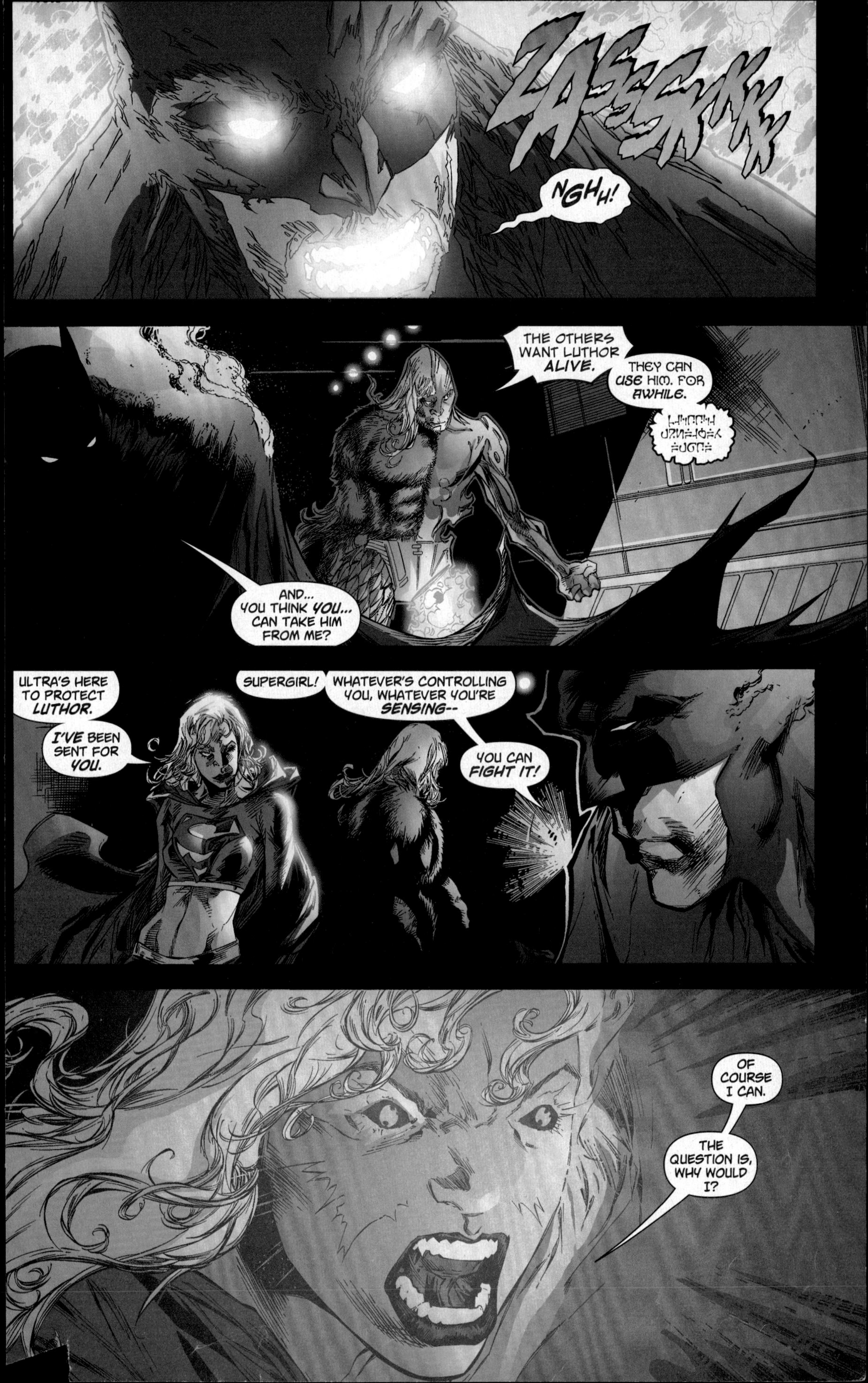
ZASSSKRKK
NGHH!
THE OTHERS WANT LUTHOR ALIVE.
THEY CAN USE HIM. FOR AWHILE.
AND... YOU THINK YOU... CAN TAKE HIM FROM ME?
ULTRA'S HERE TO PROTECT LUTHOR.
I'VE BEEN SENT FOR YOU.
SUPERGIRL!
WHATEVER'S CONTROLLING YOU, WHATEVER YOU'RE SENSING--
YOU CAN FIGHT IT!
OF COURSE I CAN.
THE QUESTION IS, WHY WOULD I?

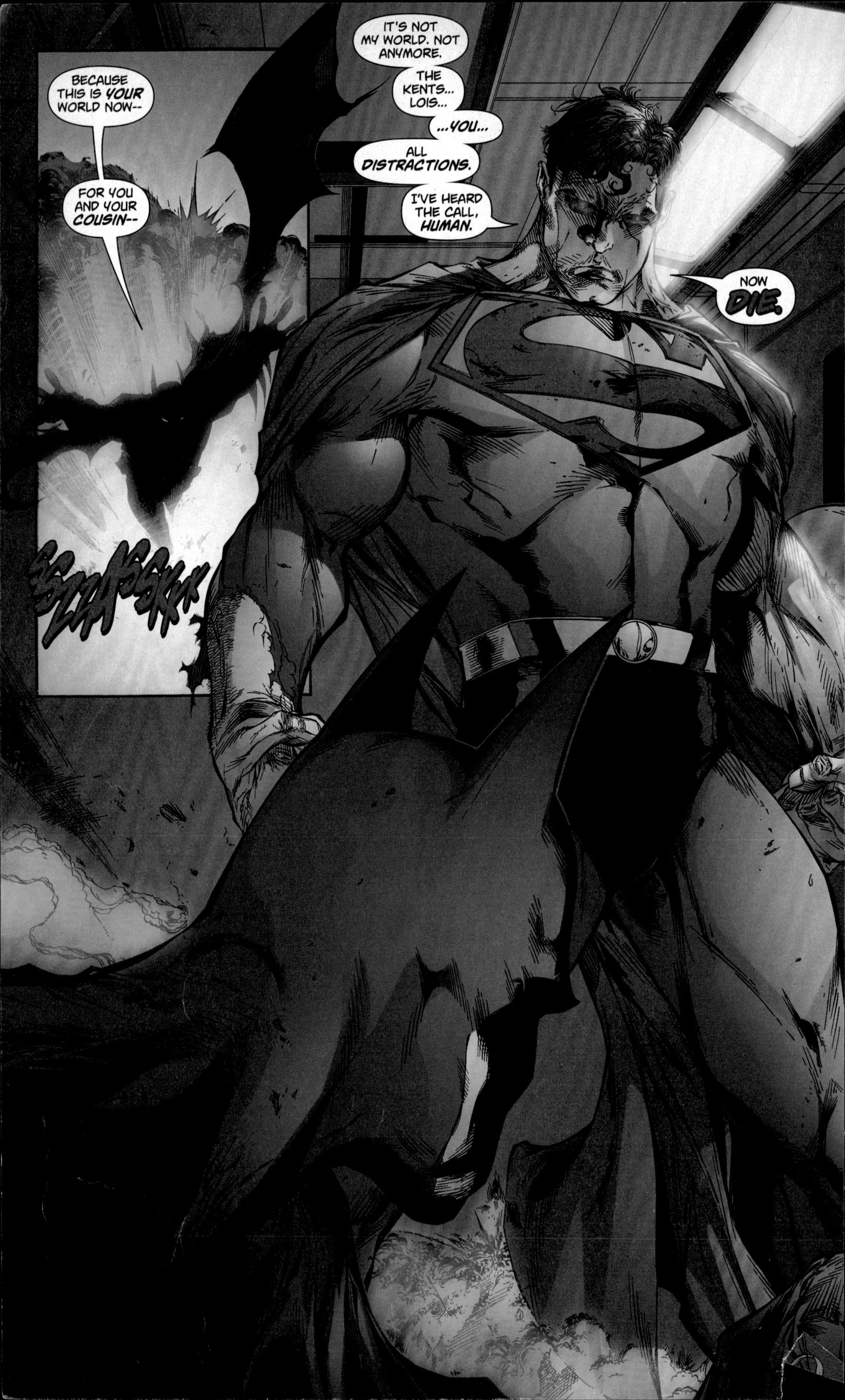
BECAUSE THIS IS *YOUR* WORLD NOW--
FOR YOU AND YOUR *COUSIN*--
IT'S NOT MY WORLD. NOT ANYMORE.
THE KENTS... LOIS...
...YOU...
ALL *DISTRACTIONS.*
I'VE HEARD THE CALL, *HUMAN.*
NOW *DIE.*
SSZZASSKKK

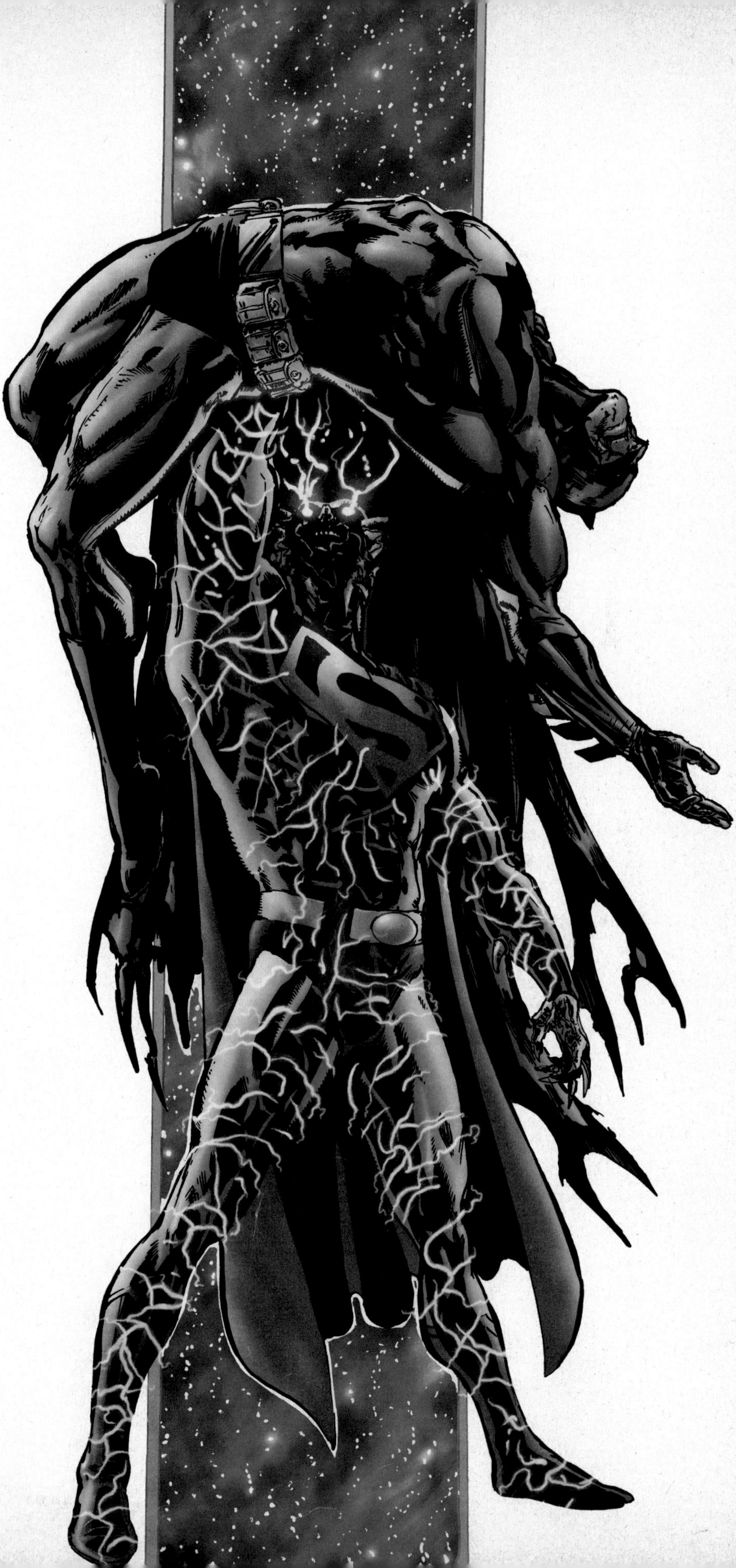

THE ENEMIES AMONG US: PART FIVE
From SUPERMAN/BATMAN 32
Cover by Phil Jimenez, Andy Lanning and Moose Baumann

Mark Verheiden
Writer

Matthew Clark & Ron Randall
Pencils

Andy Lanning & Don Hillsman
Inks

Guy Major
Colors

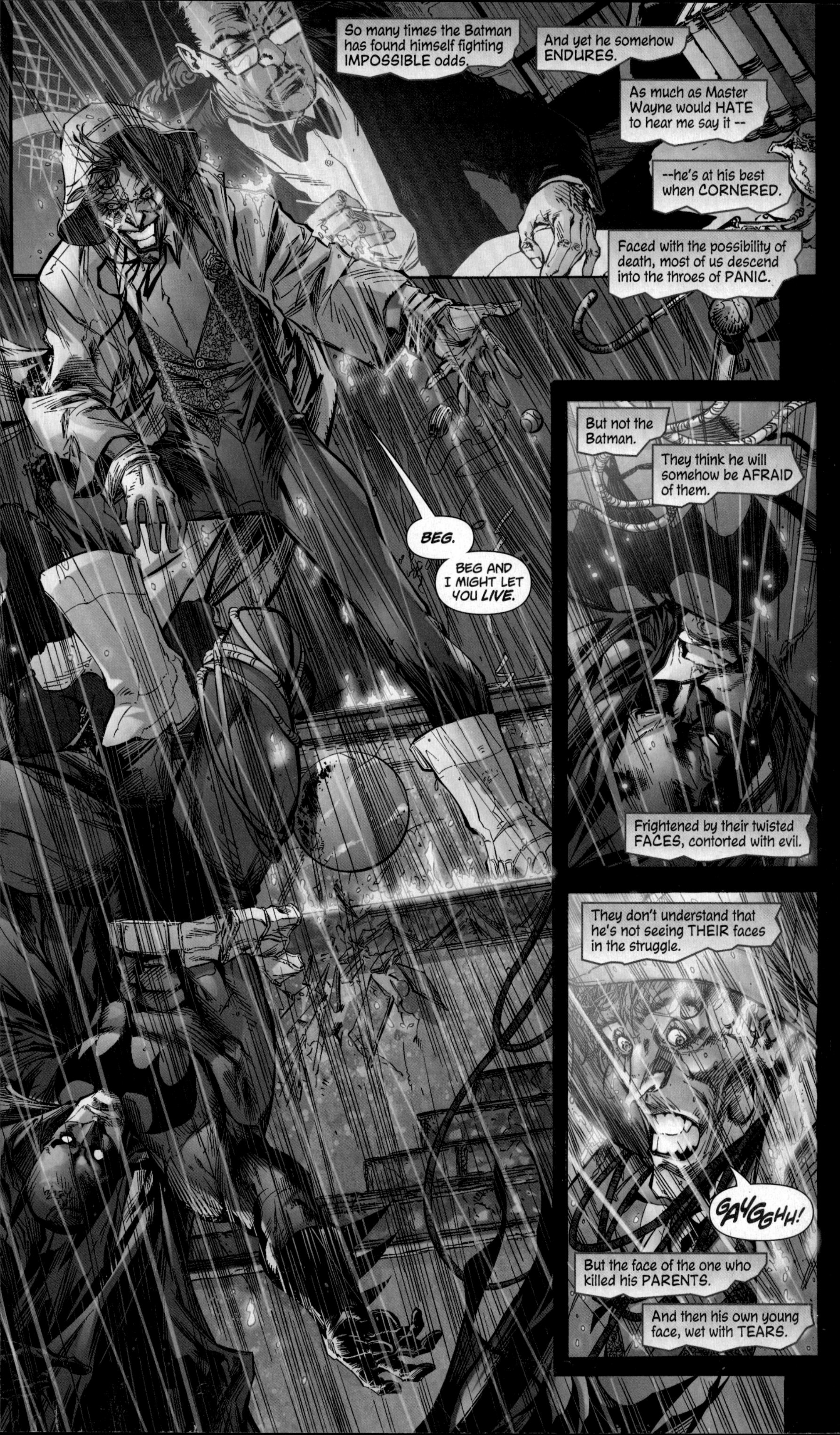
So many times the Batman has found himself fighting IMPOSSIBLE odds.
And yet he somehow ENDURES.
As much as Master Wayne would HATE to hear me say it --
--he's at his best when CORNERED.
Faced with the possibility of death, most of us descend into the throes of PANIC.
BEG.
BEG AND I MIGHT LET YOU LIVE.
But not the Batman.
They think he will somehow be AFRAID of them.
Frightened by their twisted FACES, contorted with evil.
They don't understand that he's not seeing THEIR faces in the struggle.
GAYGGHH!
But the face of the one who killed his PARENTS.
And then his own young face, wet with TEARS.

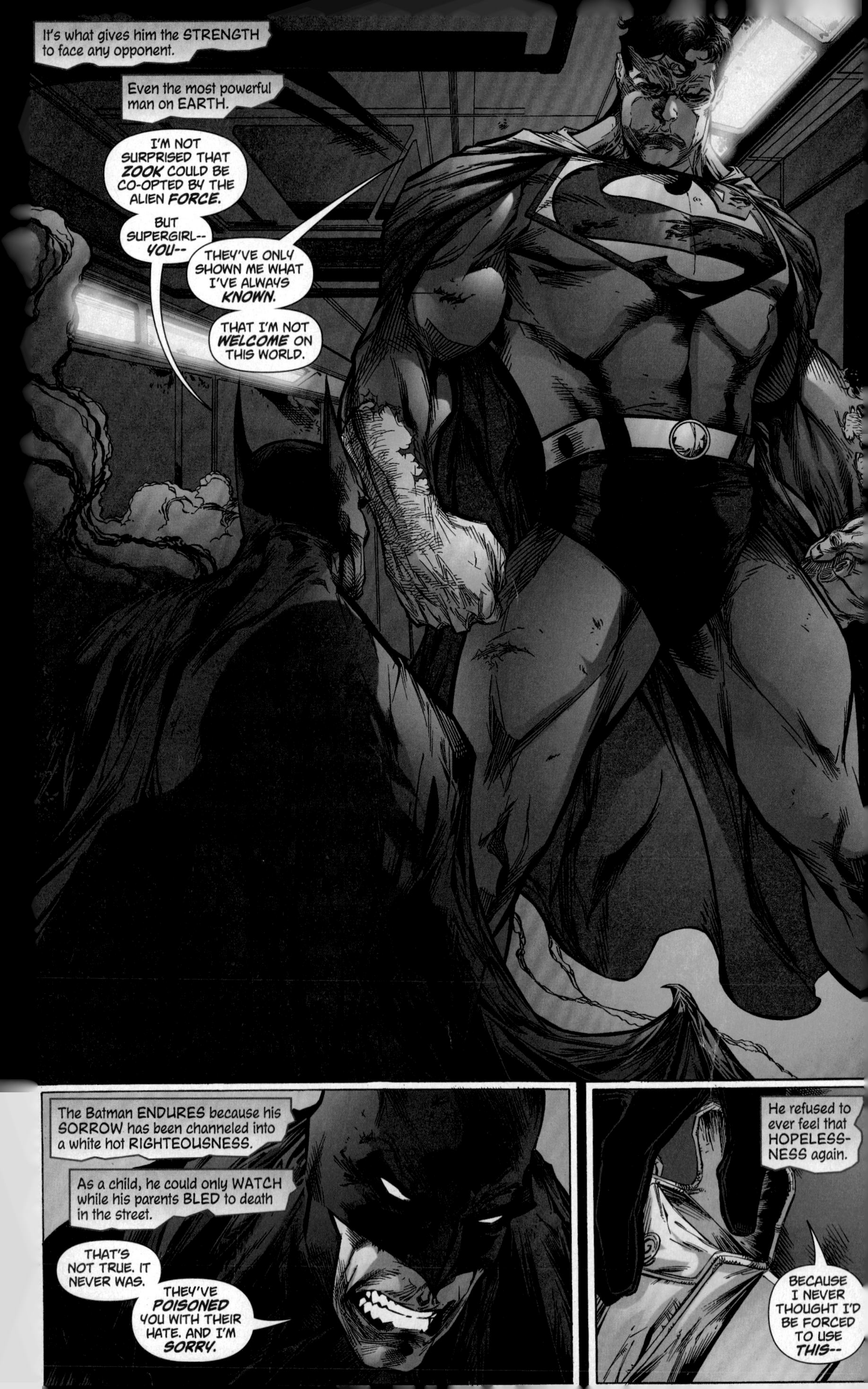

It's what gives him the STRENGTH to face any opponent.
Even the most powerful man on EARTH.
I'M NOT SURPRISED THAT ZOOK COULD BE CO-OPTED BY THE ALIEN FORCE.
BUT SUPERGIRL-- YOU--
THEY'VE ONLY SHOWN ME WHAT I'VE ALWAYS KNOWN.
THAT I'M NOT WELCOME ON THIS WORLD.
The Batman ENDURES because his SORROW has been channeled into a white hot RIGHTEOUSNESS.
As a child, he could only WATCH while his parents BLED to death in the street.
THAT'S NOT TRUE. IT NEVER WAS.
THEY'VE POISONED YOU WITH THEIR HATE. AND I'M SORRY.
He refused to ever feel that HOPELESS-NESS again.
BECAUSE I NEVER THOUGHT I'D BE FORCED TO USE THIS--

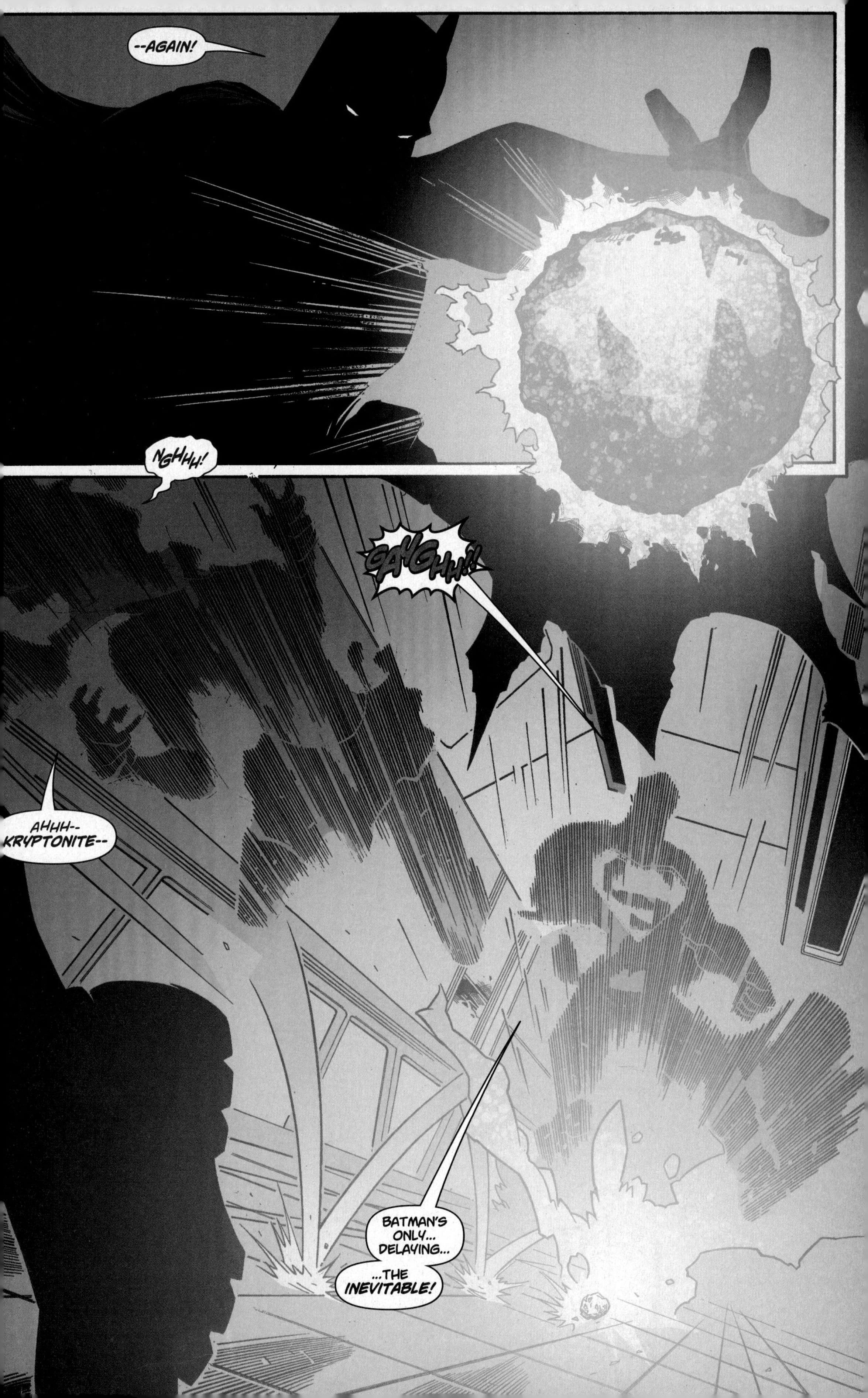
--AGAIN!
NGHHH!
GAHGHH!!
AHHH--
KRYPTONITE--
BATMAN'S ONLY... DELAYING...
...THE INEVITABLE!

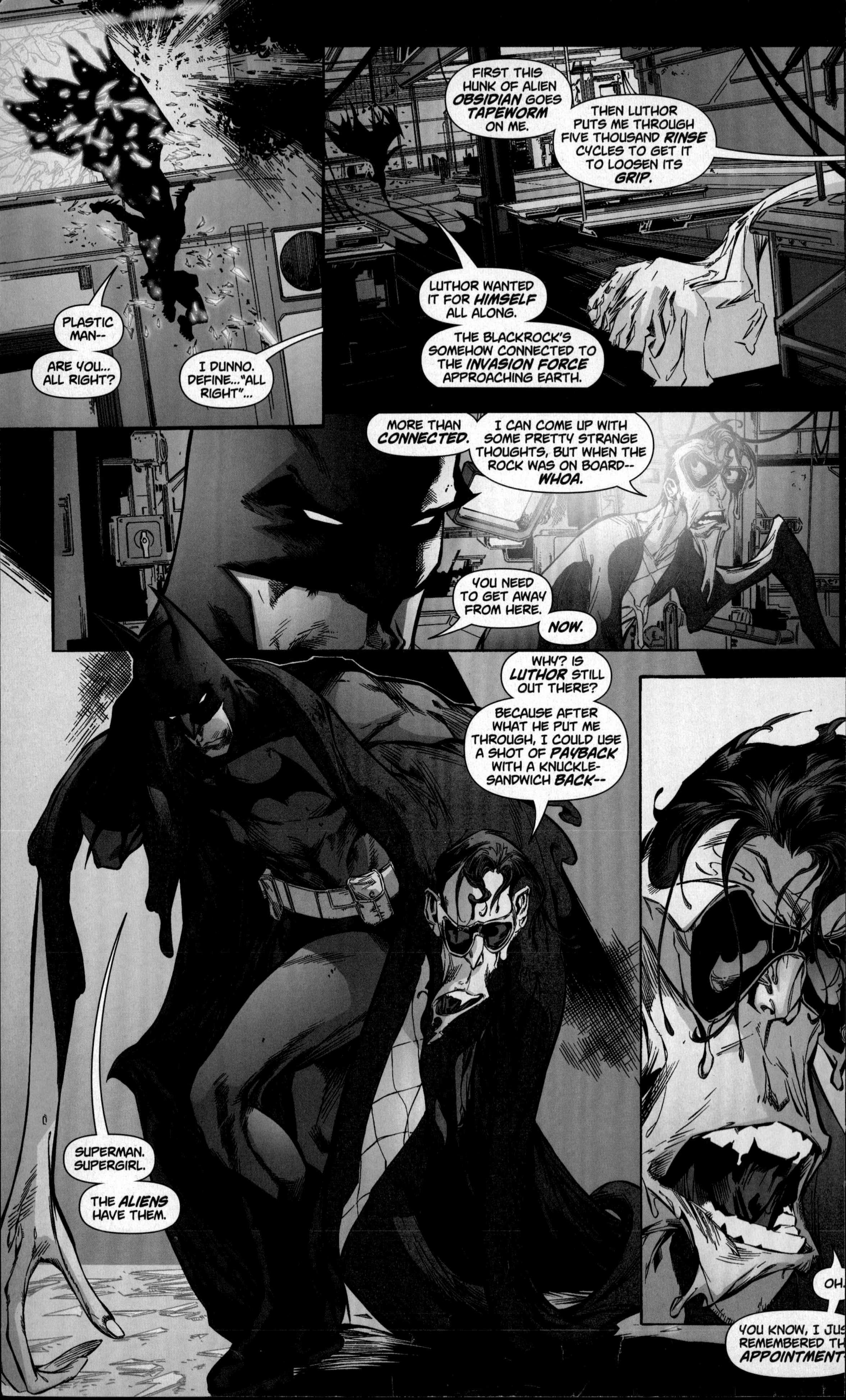
PLASTIC MAN--
ARE YOU... ALL RIGHT?
I DUNNO. DEFINE..."ALL RIGHT"...
FIRST THIS HUNK OF ALIEN OBSIDIAN GOES TAPEWORM ON ME.
THEN LUTHOR PUTS ME THROUGH FIVE THOUSAND RINSE CYCLES TO GET IT TO LOOSEN ITS GRIP.
LUTHOR WANTED IT FOR HIMSELF ALL ALONG.
THE BLACKROCK'S SOMEHOW CONNECTED TO THE INVASION FORCE APPROACHING EARTH.
MORE THAN CONNECTED.
I CAN COME UP WITH SOME PRETTY STRANGE THOUGHTS, BUT WHEN THE ROCK WAS ON BOARD-- WHOA.
YOU NEED TO GET AWAY FROM HERE.
NOW.
WHY? IS LUTHOR STILL OUT THERE?
BECAUSE AFTER WHAT HE PUT ME THROUGH, I COULD USE A SHOT OF PAYBACK WITH A KNUCKLE-SANDWICH BACK--
SUPERMAN. SUPERGIRL.
THE ALIENS HAVE THEM.
OH.
YOU KNOW, I JUS REMEMBERED TH APPOINTMENT

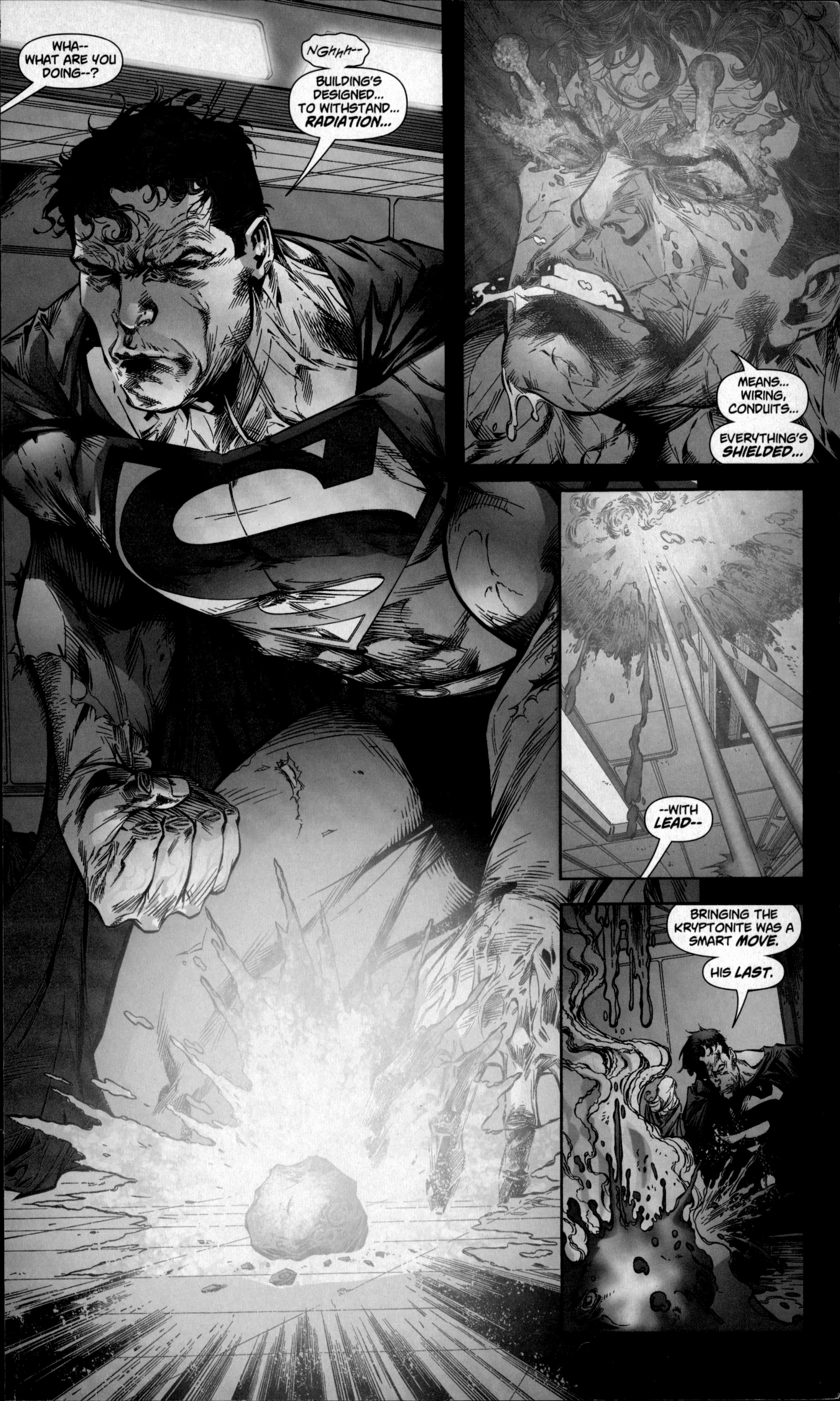
WHA-- WHAT ARE YOU DOING--?
NGhhh--
BUILDING'S DESIGNED... TO WITHSTAND... RADIATION...
MEANS... WIRING, CONDUITS...
EVERYTHING'S SHIELDED...
--WITH LEAD--
BRINGING THE KRYPTONITE WAS A SMART MOVE.
HIS LAST.

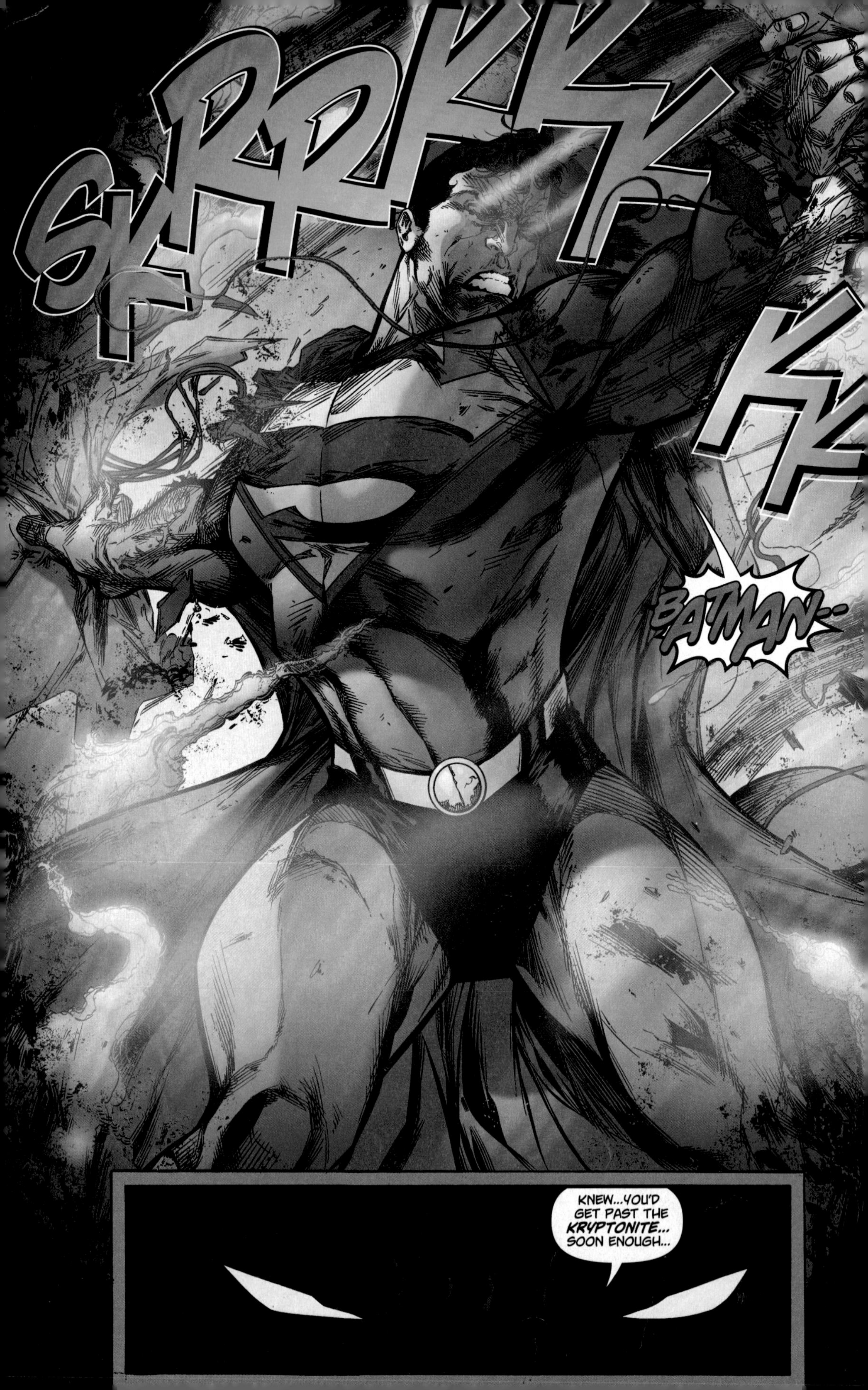

SKRAKK
KK
BATMAN--
KNEW...YOU'D GET PAST THE KRYPTONITE... SOON ENOUGH...

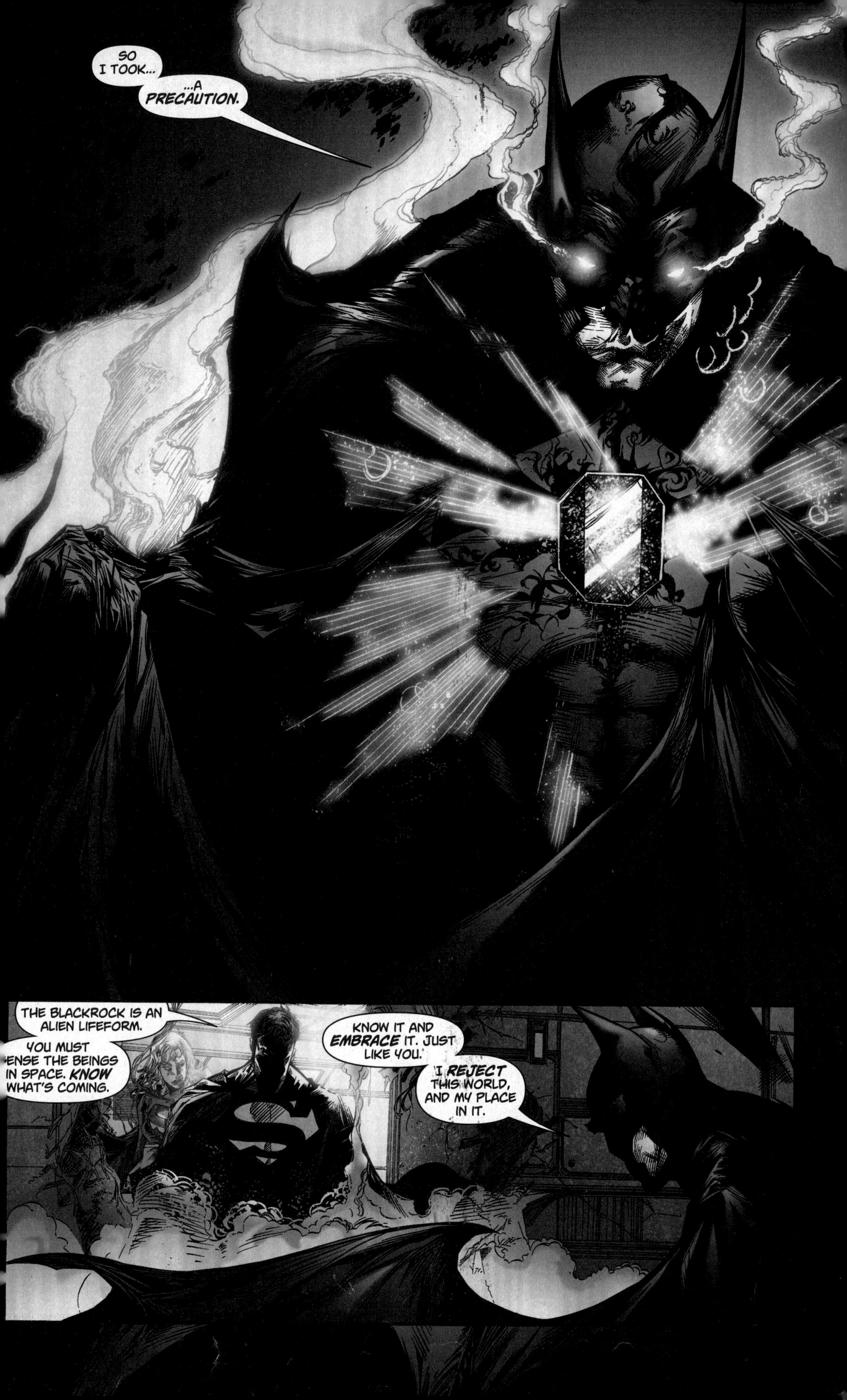
SO I TOOK...
...A PRECAUTION.
THE BLACKROCK IS AN ALIEN LIFEFORM.
YOU MUST ENSE THE BEINGS IN SPACE. KNOW WHAT'S COMING.
KNOW IT AND EMBRACE IT. JUST LIKE YOU.
I REJECT THIS WORLD, AND MY PLACE IN IT.

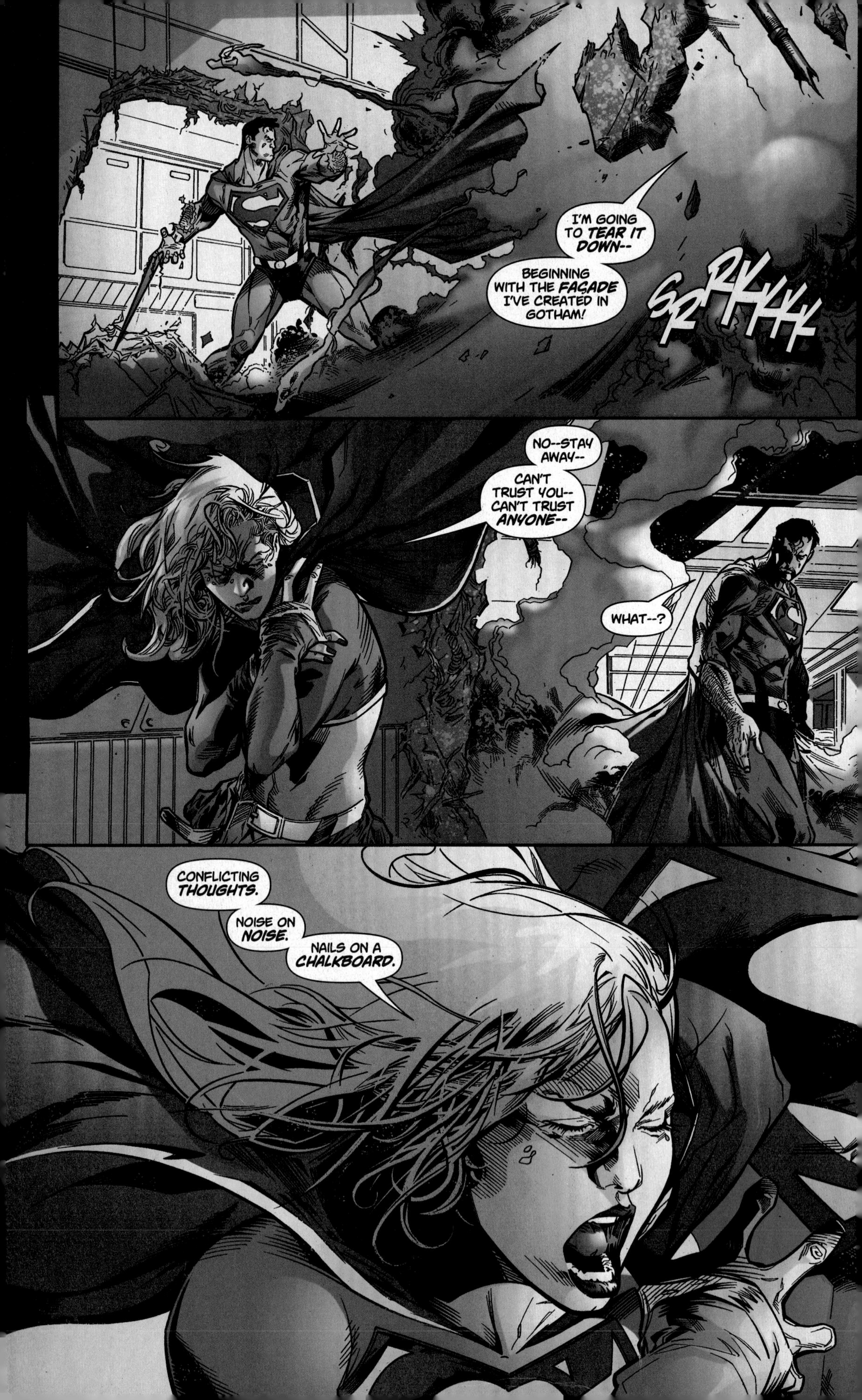
I'M GOING TO TEAR IT DOWN--
BEGINNING WITH THE FAÇADE I'VE CREATED IN GOTHAM!
SRRKKKK
NO--STAY AWAY--
CAN'T TRUST YOU-- CAN'T TRUST ANYONE--
WHAT--?
CONFLICTING THOUGHTS.
NOISE ON NOISE.
NAILS ON A CHALKBOARD.

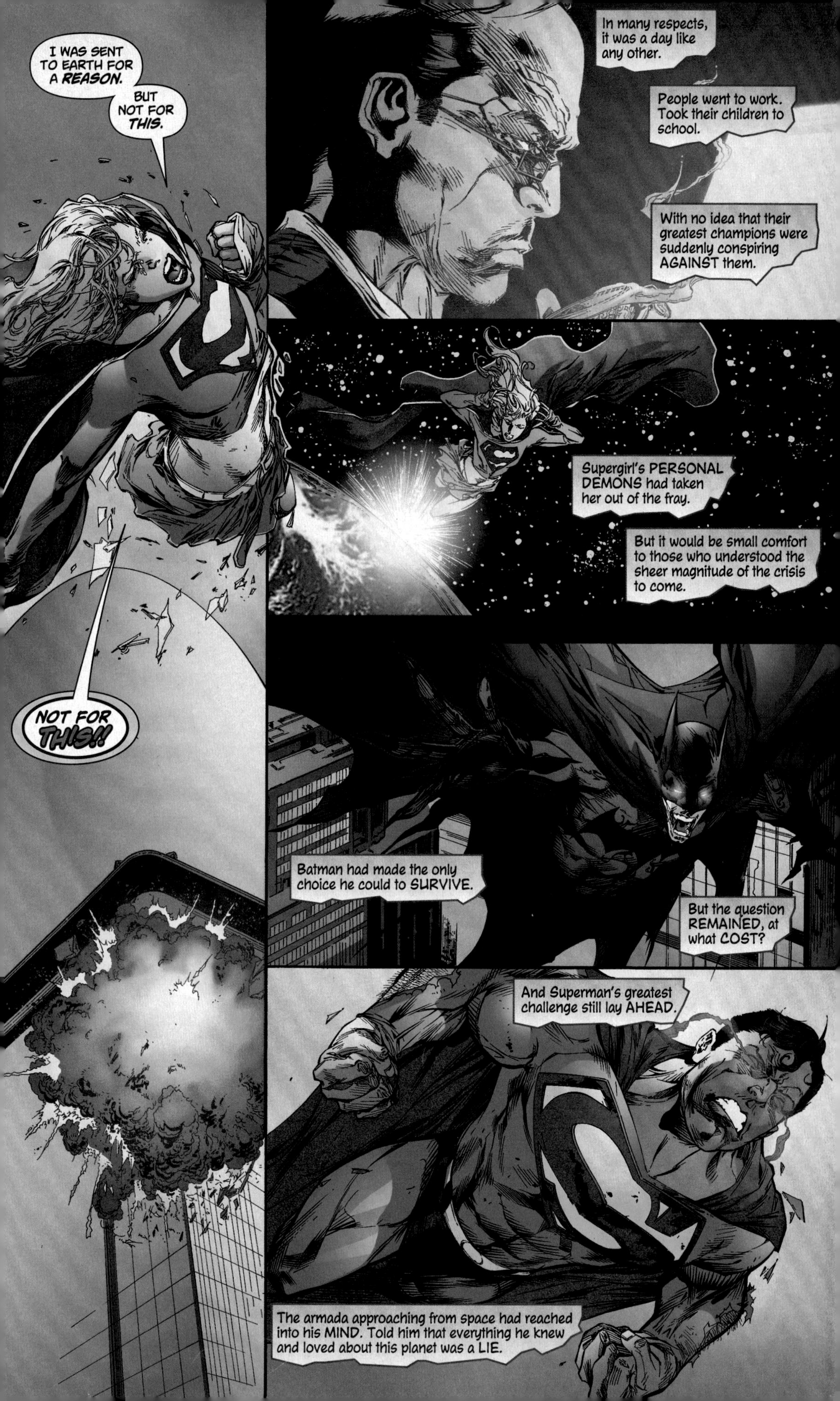

I WAS SENT TO EARTH FOR A *REASON.*
BUT NOT FOR *THIS.*
NOT FOR *THIS!!*
In many respects, it was a day like any other.
People went to work. Took their children to school.
With no idea that their greatest champions were suddenly conspiring AGAINST them.
Supergirl's PERSONAL DEMONS had taken her out of the fray.
But it would be small comfort to those who understood the sheer magnitude of the crisis to come.
Batman had made the only choice he could to SURVIVE.
But the question REMAINED, at what COST?
And Superman's greatest challenge still lay AHEAD.
The armada approaching from space had reached into his MIND. Told him that everything he knew and loved about this planet was a LIE.

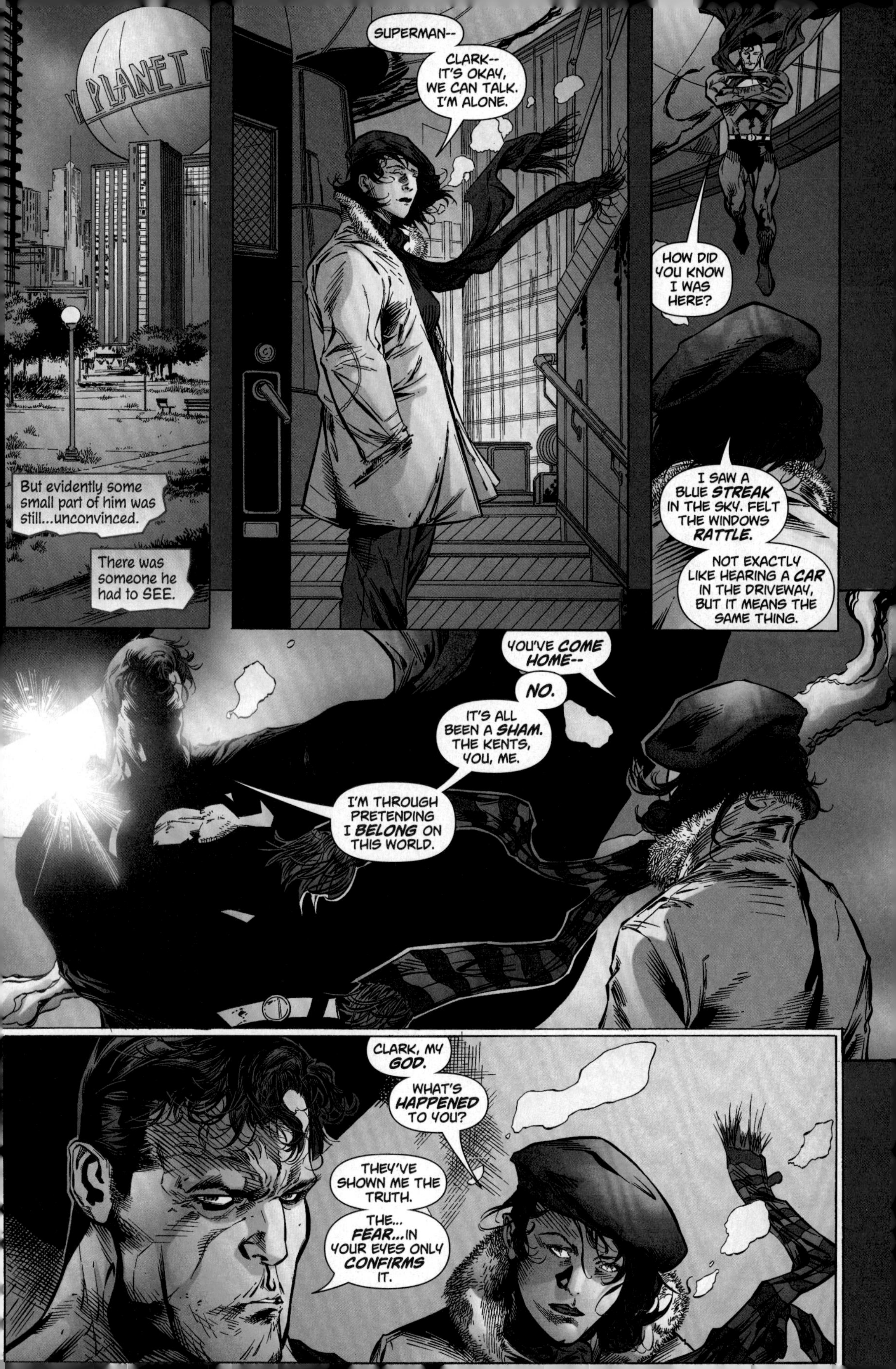

PLANET
But evidently some small part of him was still...unconvinced.
There was someone he had to SEE.
SUPERMAN--
CLARK-- IT'S OKAY, WE CAN TALK. I'M ALONE.
HOW DID YOU KNOW I WAS HERE?
I SAW A BLUE STREAK IN THE SKY. FELT THE WINDOWS RATTLE.
NOT EXACTLY LIKE HEARING A CAR IN THE DRIVEWAY, BUT IT MEANS THE SAME THING.
YOU'VE COME HOME--
NO.
IT'S ALL BEEN A SHAM. THE KENTS, YOU, ME.
I'M THROUGH PRETENDING I BELONG ON THIS WORLD.
CLARK, MY GOD.
WHAT'S HAPPENED TO YOU?
THEY'VE SHOWN ME THE TRUTH.
THE... FEAR...IN YOUR EYES ONLY CONFIRMS IT.

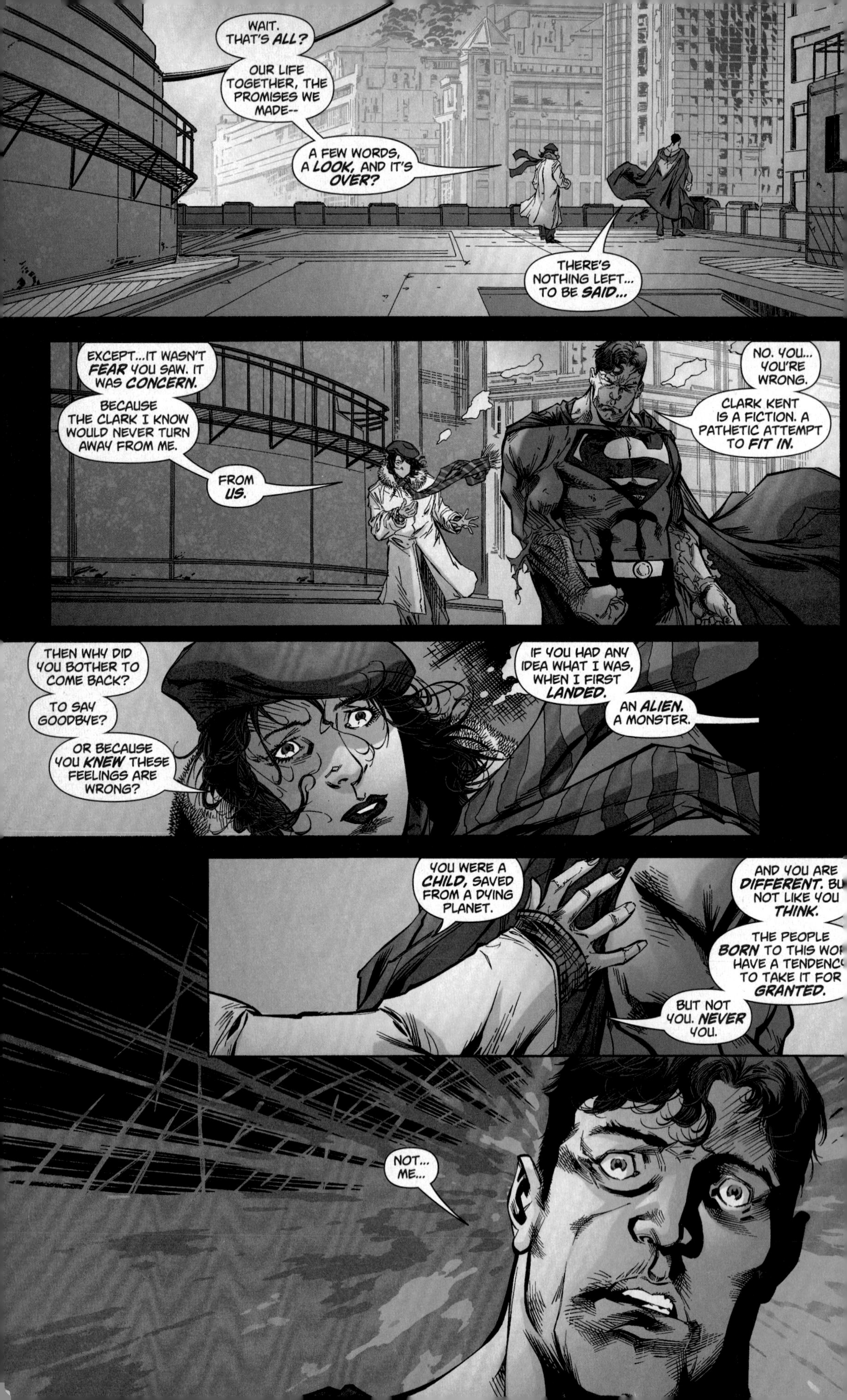
WAIT. THAT'S ALL?
OUR LIFE TOGETHER, THE PROMISES WE MADE--
A FEW WORDS, A LOOK, AND IT'S OVER?
THERE'S NOTHING LEFT... TO BE SAID...
EXCEPT...IT WASN'T FEAR YOU SAW. IT WAS CONCERN.
BECAUSE THE CLARK I KNOW WOULD NEVER TURN AWAY FROM ME.
FROM US.
NO. YOU... YOU'RE WRONG.
CLARK KENT IS A FICTION. A PATHETIC ATTEMPT TO FIT IN.
THEN WHY DID YOU BOTHER TO COME BACK?
TO SAY GOODBYE?
OR BECAUSE YOU KNEW THESE FEELINGS ARE WRONG?
IF YOU HAD ANY IDEA WHAT I WAS, WHEN I FIRST LANDED.
AN ALIEN. A MONSTER.
YOU WERE A CHILD, SAVED FROM A DYING PLANET.
AND YOU ARE DIFFERENT. BU NOT LIKE YOU THINK.
THE PEOPLE BORN TO THIS WO HAVE A TENDENC TO TAKE IT FOR GRANTED.
BUT NOT YOU. NEVER YOU.
NOT... ME...

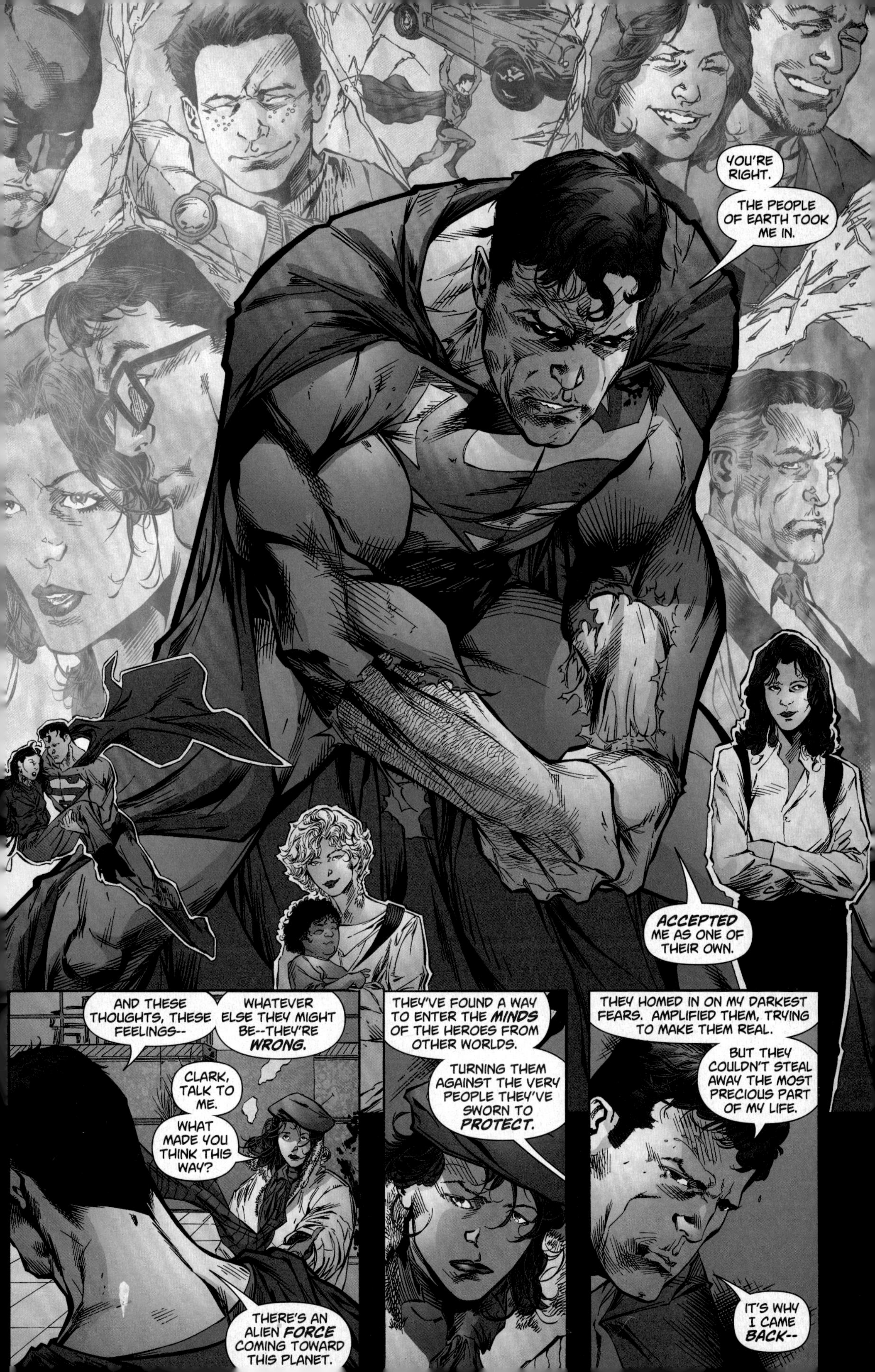
YOU'RE RIGHT.
THE PEOPLE OF EARTH TOOK ME IN.
ACCEPTED ME AS ONE OF THEIR OWN.
AND THESE THOUGHTS, THESE FEELINGS--
WHATEVER ELSE THEY MIGHT BE--THEY'RE WRONG.
CLARK, TALK TO ME.
WHAT MADE YOU THINK THIS WAY?
THERE'S AN ALIEN FORCE COMING TOWARD THIS PLANET.
THEY'VE FOUND A WAY TO ENTER THE MINDS OF THE HEROES FROM OTHER WORLDS.
TURNING THEM AGAINST THE VERY PEOPLE THEY'VE SWORN TO PROTECT.
THEY HOMED IN ON MY DARKEST FEARS. AMPLIFIED THEM, TRYING TO MAKE THEM REAL.
BUT THEY COULDN'T STEAL AWAY THE MOST PRECIOUS PART OF MY LIFE.
IT'S WHY I CAME BACK--

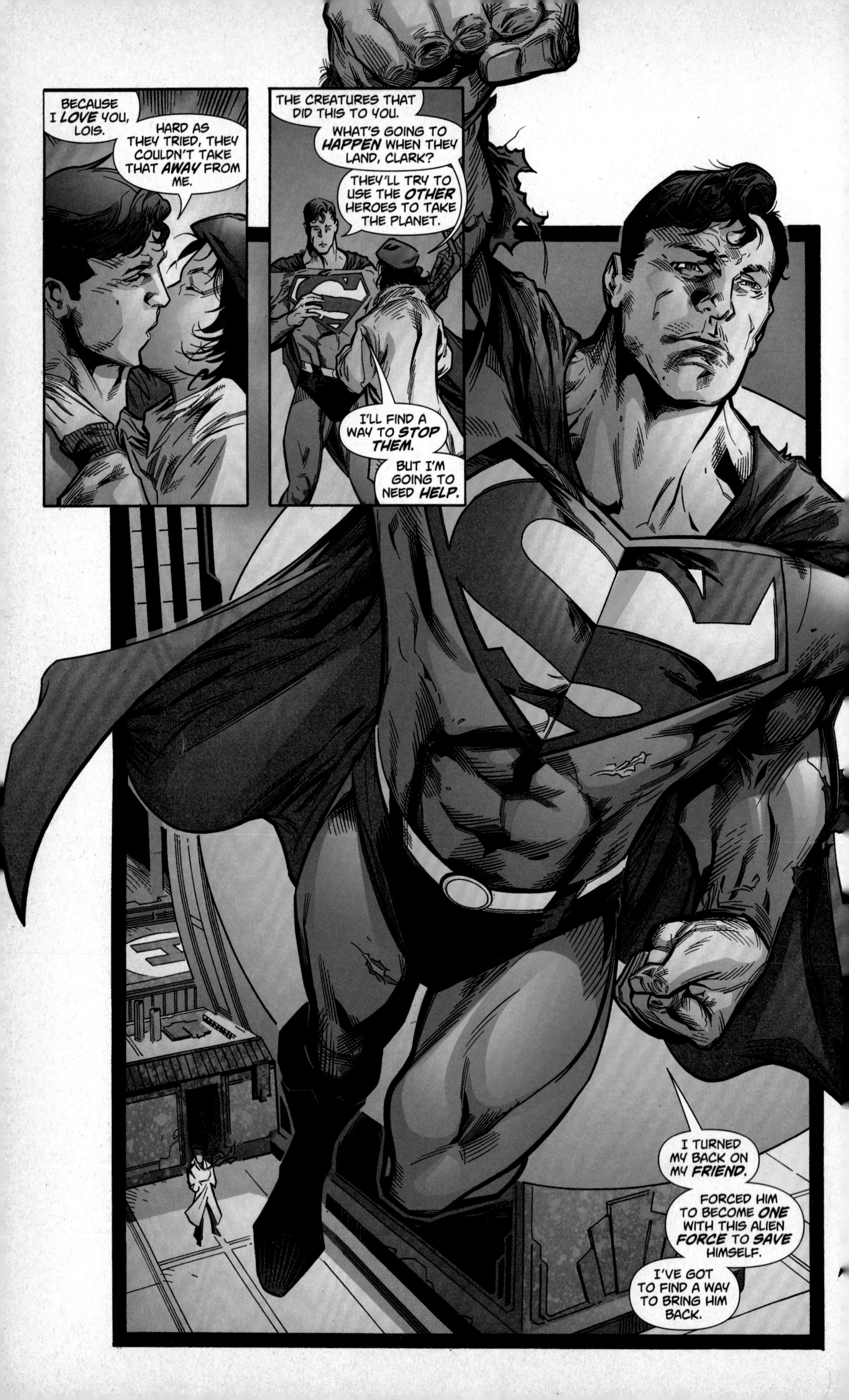
BECAUSE I LOVE YOU, LOIS.
HARD AS THEY TRIED, THEY COULDN'T TAKE THAT AWAY FROM ME.
THE CREATURES THAT DID THIS TO YOU.
WHAT'S GOING TO HAPPEN WHEN THEY LAND, CLARK?
THEY'LL TRY TO USE THE OTHER HEROES TO TAKE THE PLANET.
I'LL FIND A WAY TO STOP THEM.
BUT I'M GOING TO NEED HELP.
I TURNED MY BACK ON MY FRIEND.
FORCED HIM TO BECOME ONE WITH THIS ALIEN FORCE TO SAVE HIMSELF.
I'VE GOT TO FIND A WAY TO BRING HIM BACK.

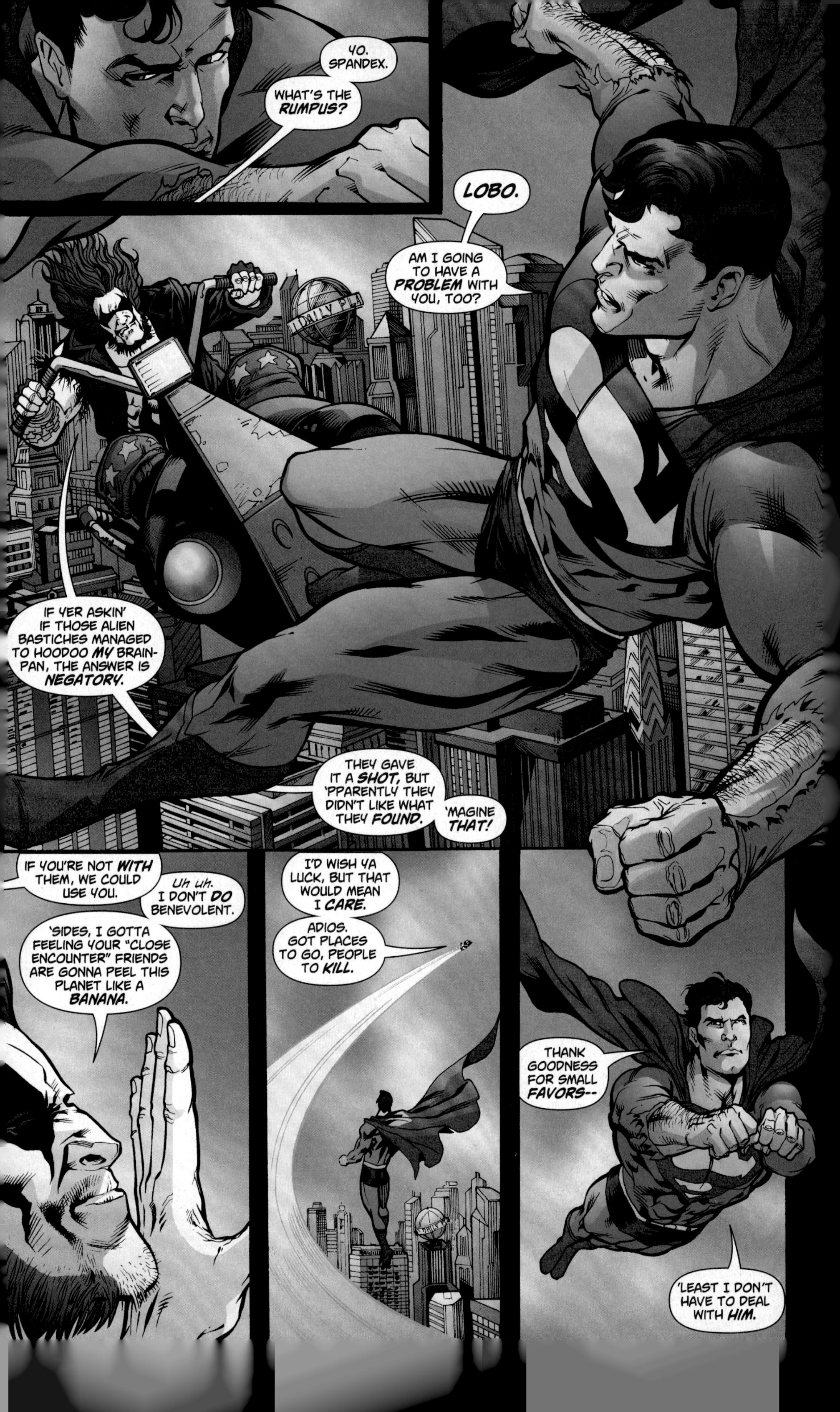
YO. SPANDEX.
WHAT'S THE RUMPUS?
LOBO.
AM I GOING TO HAVE A PROBLEM WITH YOU, TOO?
IF YER ASKIN' IF THOSE ALIEN BASTICHES MANAGED TO HOODOO MY BRAIN-PAN, THE ANSWER IS NEGATORY.
THEY GAVE IT A SHOT, BUT 'PPARENTLY THEY DIDN'T LIKE WHAT THEY FOUND.
'MAGINE THAT!
IF YOU'RE NOT WITH THEM, WE COULD USE YOU.
Uh uh. I DON'T DO BENEVOLENT.
'SIDES, I GOTTA FEELING YOUR "CLOSE ENCOUNTER" FRIENDS ARE GONNA PEEL THIS PLANET LIKE A BANANA.
I'D WISH YA LUCK, BUT THAT WOULD MEAN I CARE.
ADIOS. GOT PLACES TO GO, PEOPLE TO KILL.
THANK GOODNESS FOR SMALL FAVORS--
'LEAST I DON'T HAVE TO DEAL WITH HIM.

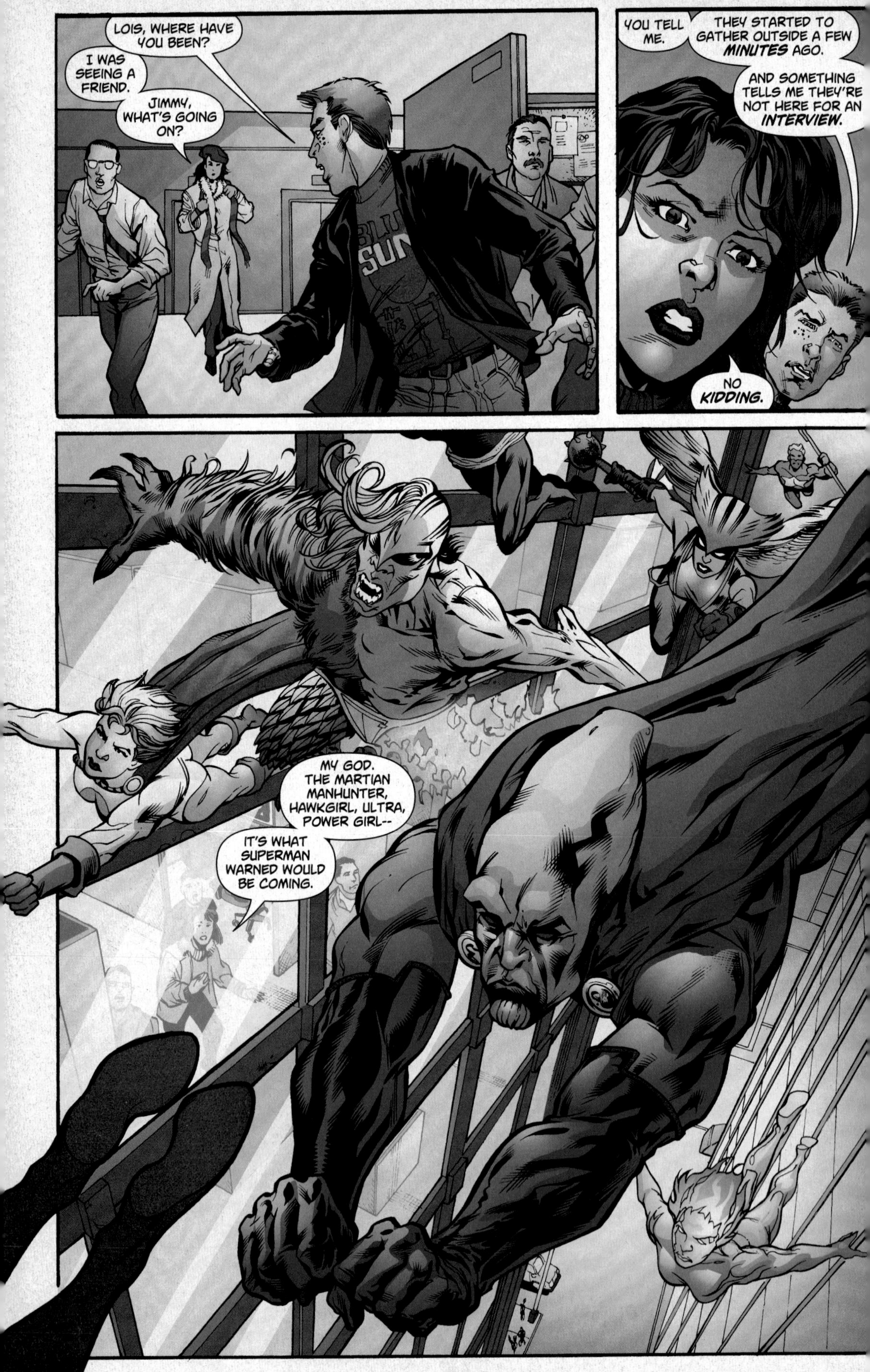
LOIS, WHERE HAVE YOU BEEN?
I WAS SEEING A FRIEND.
JIMMY, WHAT'S GOING ON?
YOU TELL ME.
THEY STARTED TO GATHER OUTSIDE A FEW MINUTES AGO.
AND SOMETHING TELLS ME THEY'RE NOT HERE FOR AN INTERVIEW.
NO KIDDING.
MY GOD. THE MARTIAN MANHUNTER, HAWKGIRL, ULTRA, POWER GIRL--
IT'S WHAT SUPERMAN WARNED WOULD BE COMING.

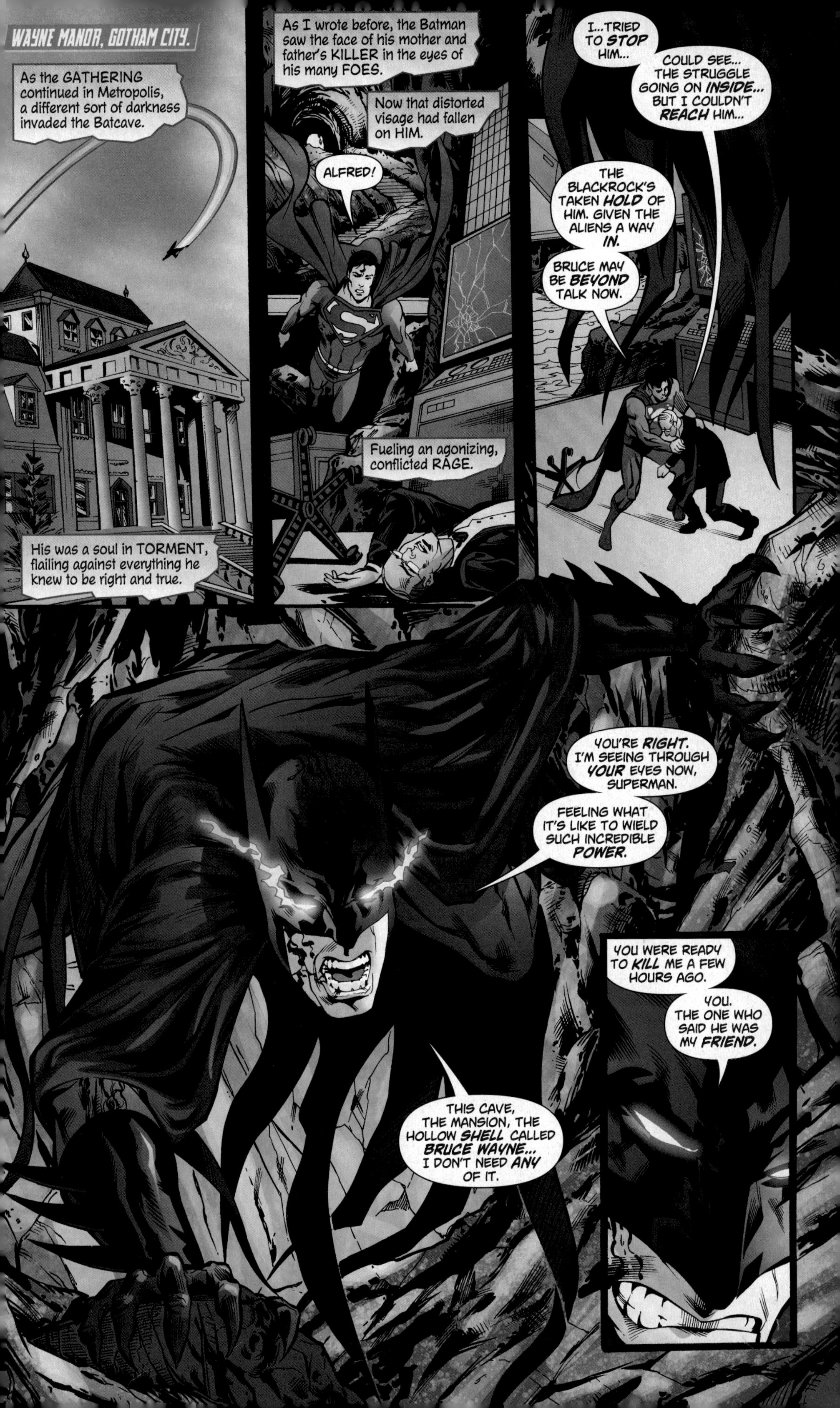
WAYNE MANOR, GOTHAM CITY.
As the GATHERING continued in Metropolis, a different sort of darkness invaded the Batcave.
His was a soul in TORMENT, flailing against everything he knew to be right and true.
As I wrote before, the Batman saw the face of his mother and father's KILLER in the eyes of his many FOES.
Now that distorted visage had fallen on HIM.
ALFRED!
Fueling an agonizing, conflicted RAGE.
I...TRIED TO STOP HIM...
COULD SEE... THE STRUGGLE GOING ON INSIDE... BUT I COULDN'T REACH HIM...
THE BLACKROCK'S TAKEN HOLD OF HIM. GIVEN THE ALIENS A WAY IN.
BRUCE MAY BE BEYOND TALK NOW.
YOU'RE RIGHT. I'M SEEING THROUGH YOUR EYES NOW, SUPERMAN.
FEELING WHAT IT'S LIKE TO WIELD SUCH INCREDIBLE POWER.
THIS CAVE, THE MANSION, THE HOLLOW SHELL CALLED BRUCE WAYNE... I DON'T NEED ANY OF IT.
YOU WERE READY TO KILL ME A FEW HOURS AGO.
YOU. THE ONE WHO SAID HE WAS MY FRIEND.

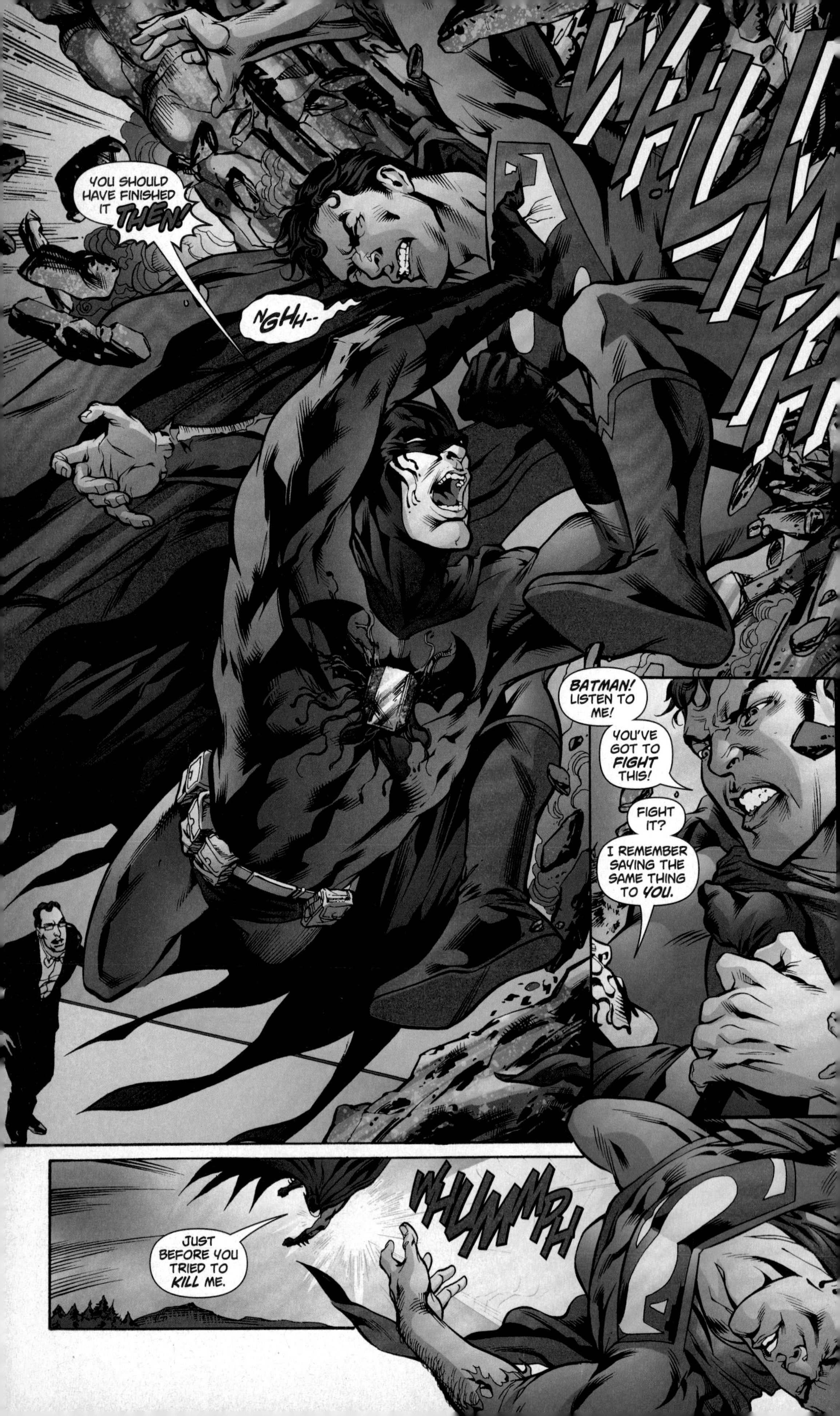
WHUMMPH
YOU SHOULD HAVE FINISHED IT THEN!
NGHH--
BATMAN! LISTEN TO ME!
YOU'VE GOT TO FIGHT THIS!
FIGHT IT?
I REMEMBER SAYING THE SAME THING TO YOU.
JUST BEFORE YOU TRIED TO KILL ME.
WHUMMPH

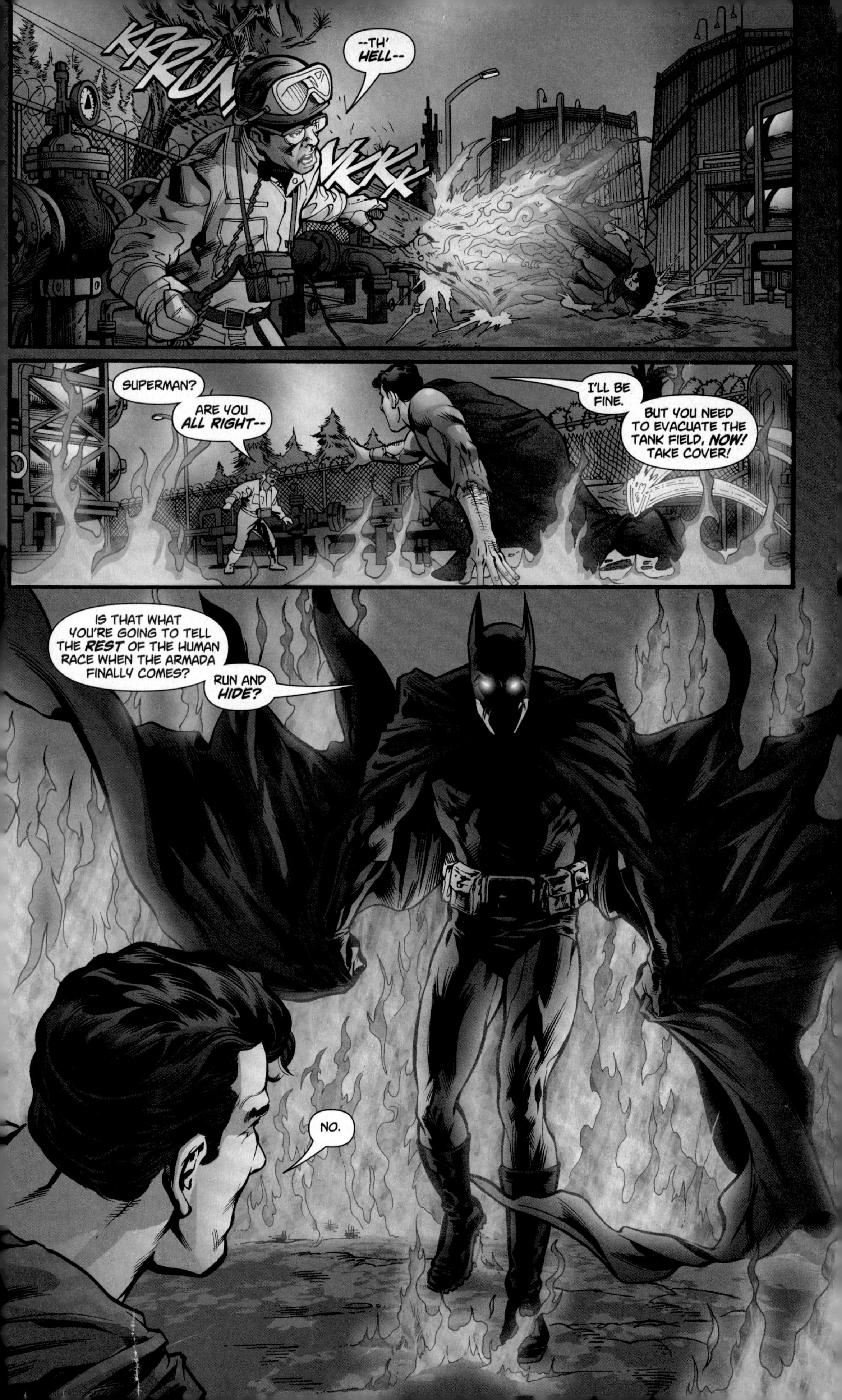
KRRUNNKKK
--TH' HELL--
SUPERMAN?
ARE YOU ALL RIGHT--
I'LL BE FINE.
BUT YOU NEED TO EVACUATE THE TANK FIELD, NOW! TAKE COVER!
IS THAT WHAT YOU'RE GOING TO TELL THE REST OF THE HUMAN RACE WHEN THE ARMADA FINALLY COMES?
RUN AND HIDE?
NO.

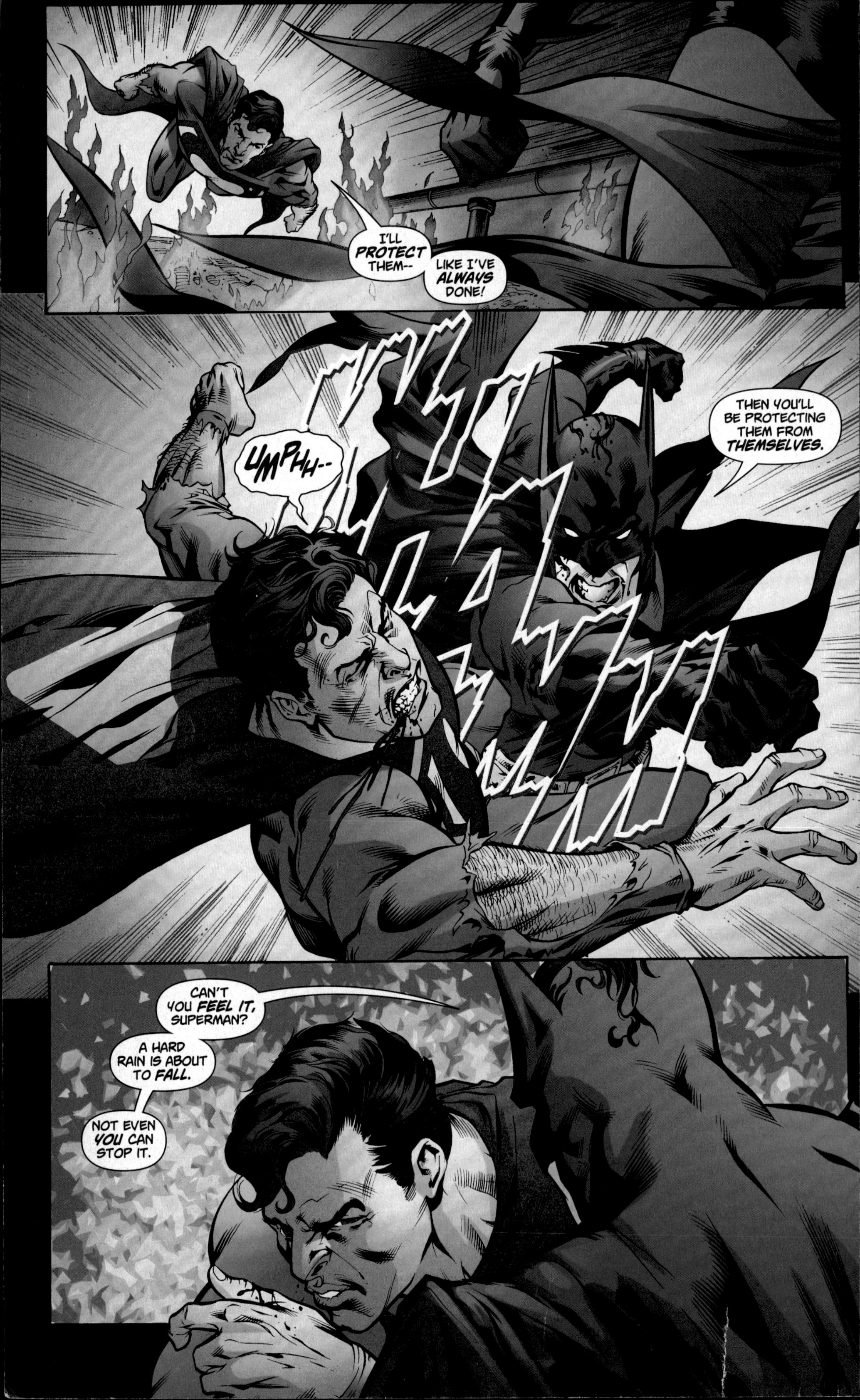
I'LL PROTECT THEM--
LIKE I'VE ALWAYS DONE!
UMPHH--
THEN YOU'LL BE PROTECTING THEM FROM THEMSELVES.
CAN'T YOU FEEL IT, SUPERMAN?
A HARD RAIN IS ABOUT TO FALL.
NOT EVEN YOU CAN STOP IT.

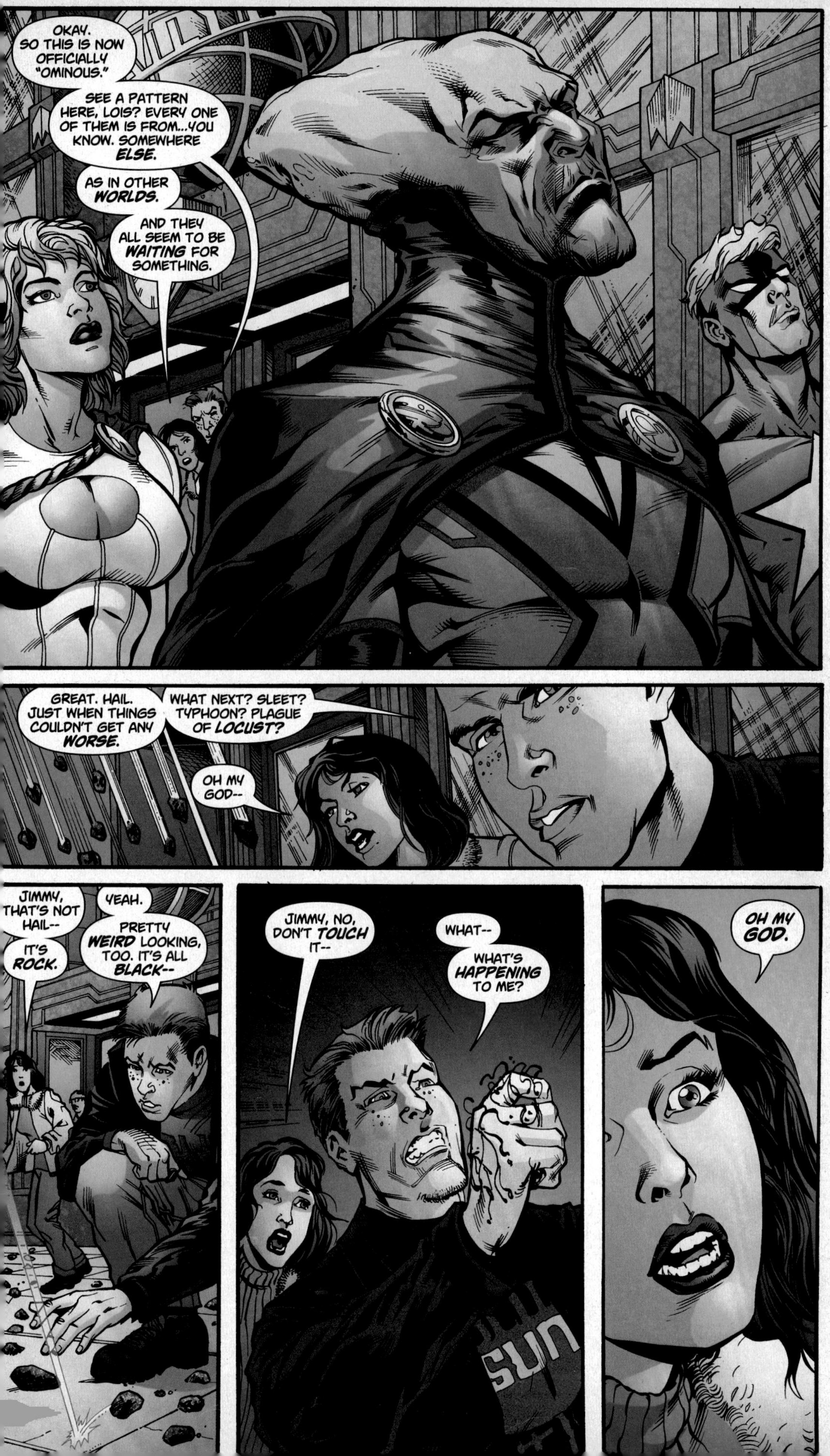
OKAY. SO THIS IS NOW OFFICIALLY "OMINOUS."
SEE A PATTERN HERE, LOIS? EVERY ONE OF THEM IS FROM...YOU KNOW. SOMEWHERE ELSE.
AS IN OTHER WORLDS.
AND THEY ALL SEEM TO BE WAITING FOR SOMETHING.
GREAT. HAIL. JUST WHEN THINGS COULDN'T GET ANY WORSE.
WHAT NEXT? SLEET? TYPHOON? PLAGUE OF LOCUST?
OH MY GOD--
JIMMY, THAT'S NOT HAIL--
IT'S ROCK.
YEAH.
PRETTY WEIRD LOOKING, TOO. IT'S ALL BLACK--
JIMMY, NO, DON'T TOUCH IT--
WHAT--
WHAT'S HAPPENING TO ME?
OH MY GOD.

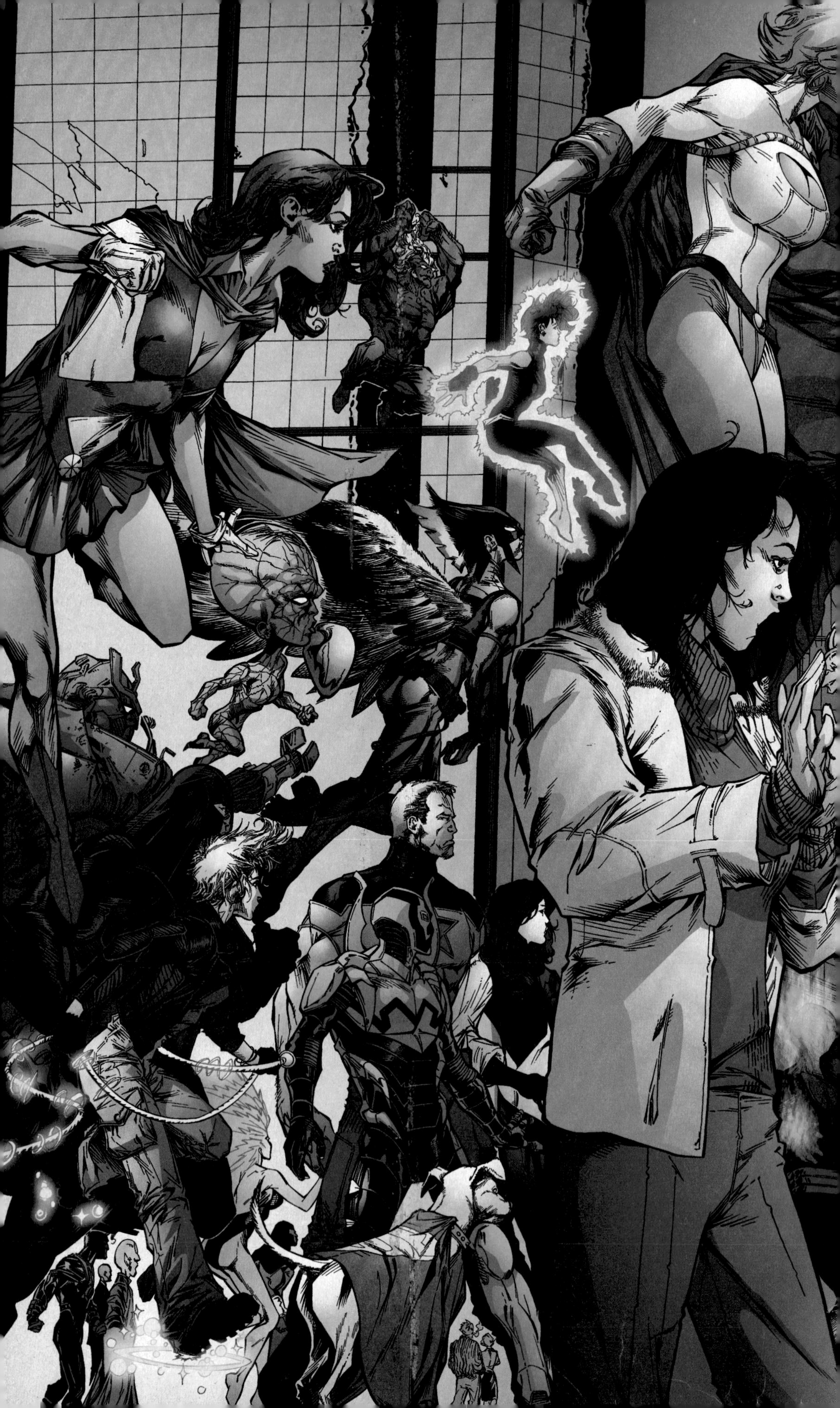

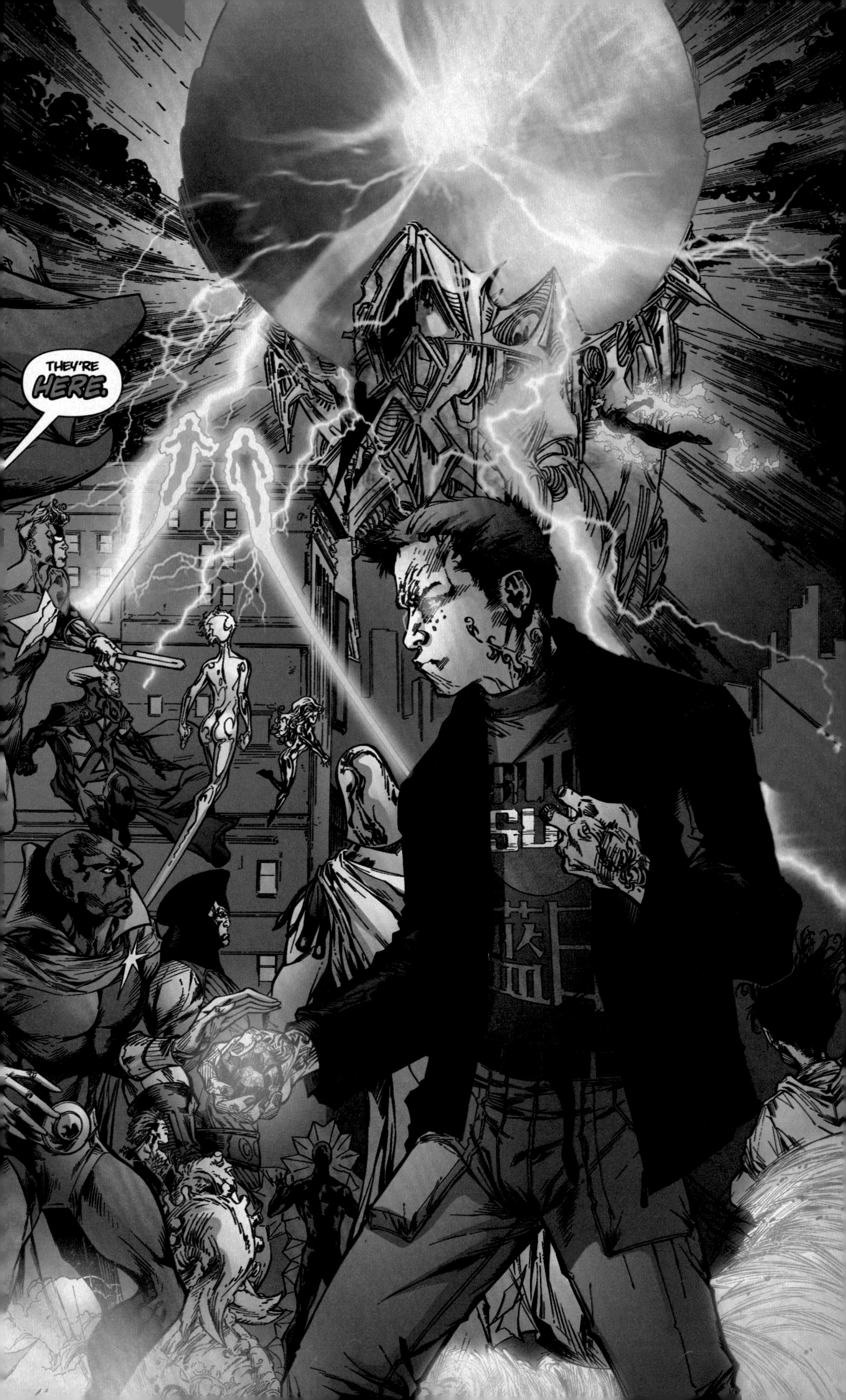
THEY'RE HERE.

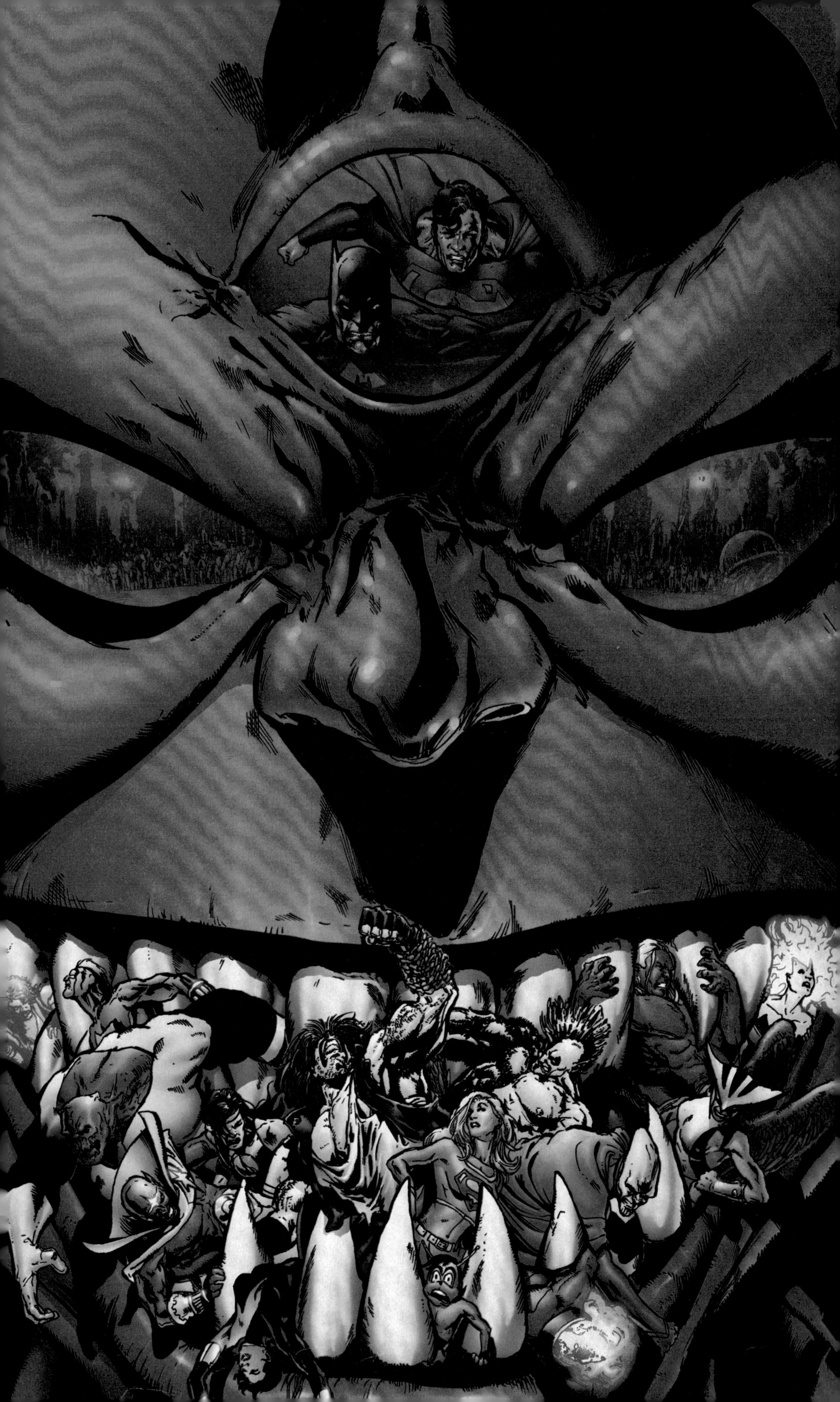

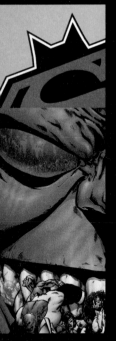

THE ENEMIES AMONG US: PART SIX
From SUPERMAN/BATMAN 33
Cover by Phil Jimenez, Andy Lanning and Moose Baumann

Mark Verheiden
Writer

Joe Benitez
Pencils

Victor Llamas
Inks

Guy Major
Colors

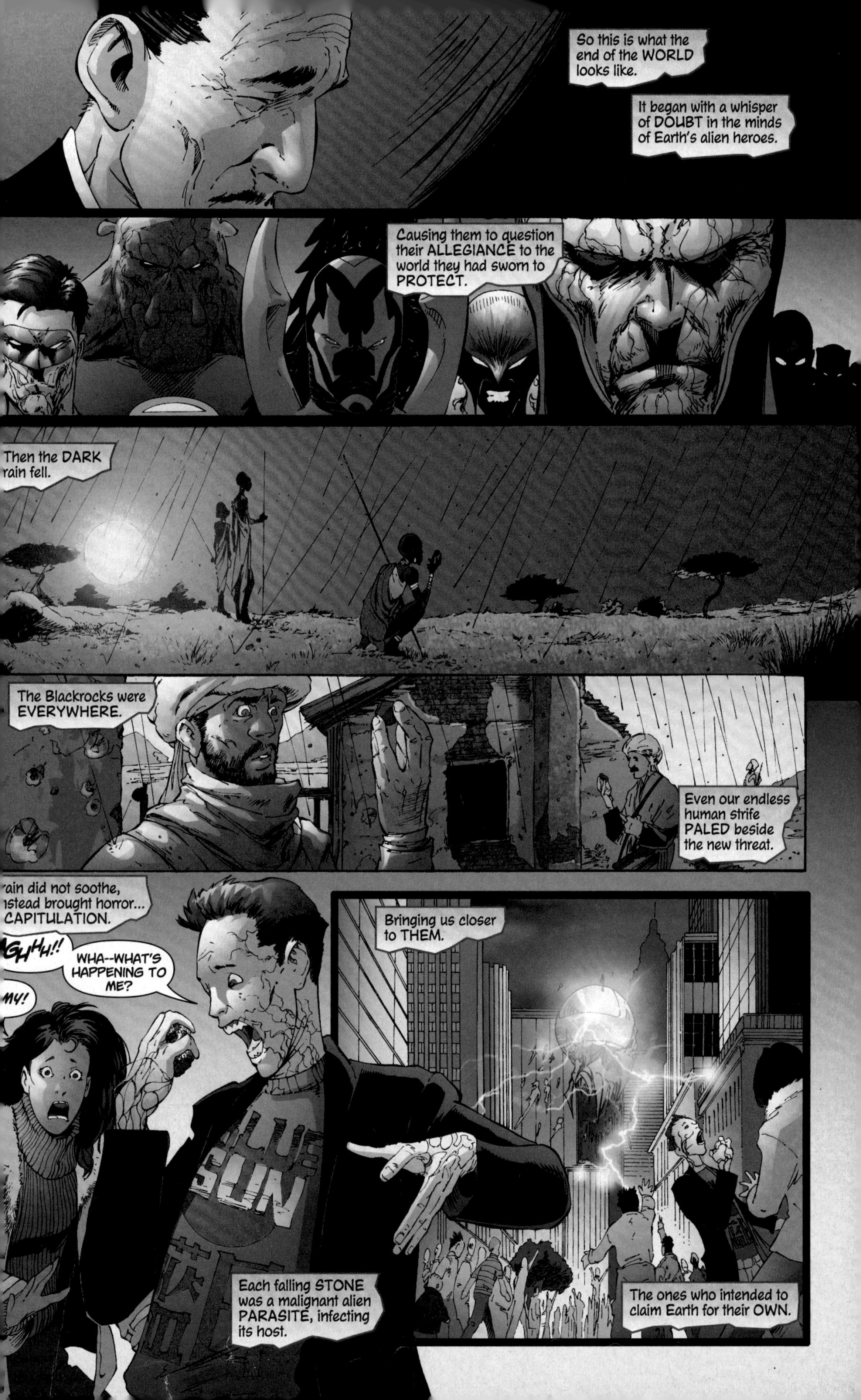

So this is what the end of the WORLD looks like.
It began with a whisper of DOUBT in the minds of Earth's alien heroes.
Causing them to question their ALLEGIANCE to the world they had sworn to PROTECT.
Then the DARK rain fell.
The Blackrocks were EVERYWHERE.
Even our endless human strife PALED beside the new threat.
rain did not soothe, nstead brought horror... CAPITULATION.
WHA--WHAT'S HAPPENING TO ME?
Bringing us closer to THEM.
Each falling STONE was a malignant alien PARASITE, infecting its host.
The ones who intended to claim Earth for their OWN.

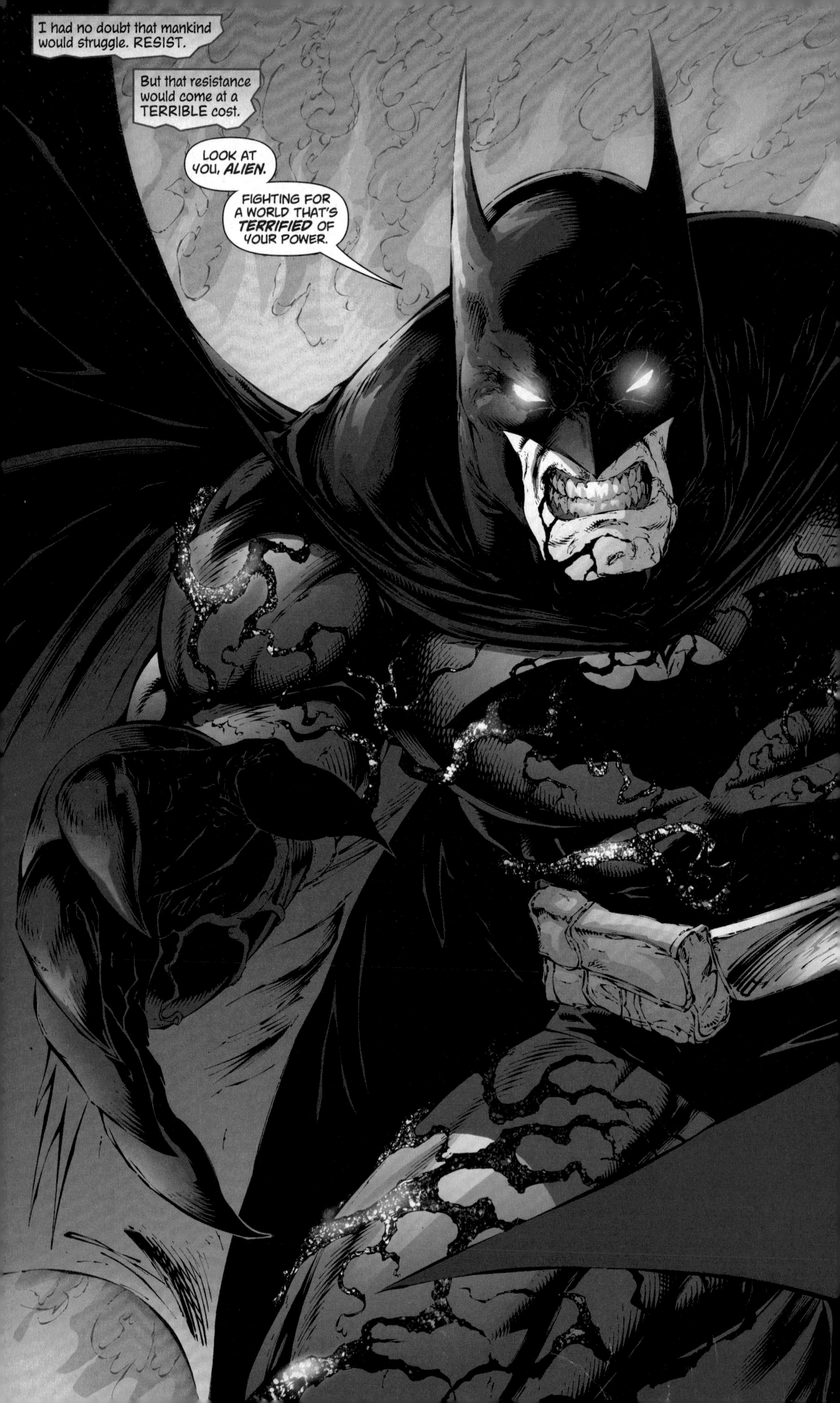

I had no doubt that mankind would struggle. RESIST.
But that resistance would come at a TERRIBLE cost.
LOOK AT YOU, ALIEN.
FIGHTING FOR A WORLD THAT'S TERRIFIED OF YOUR POWER.

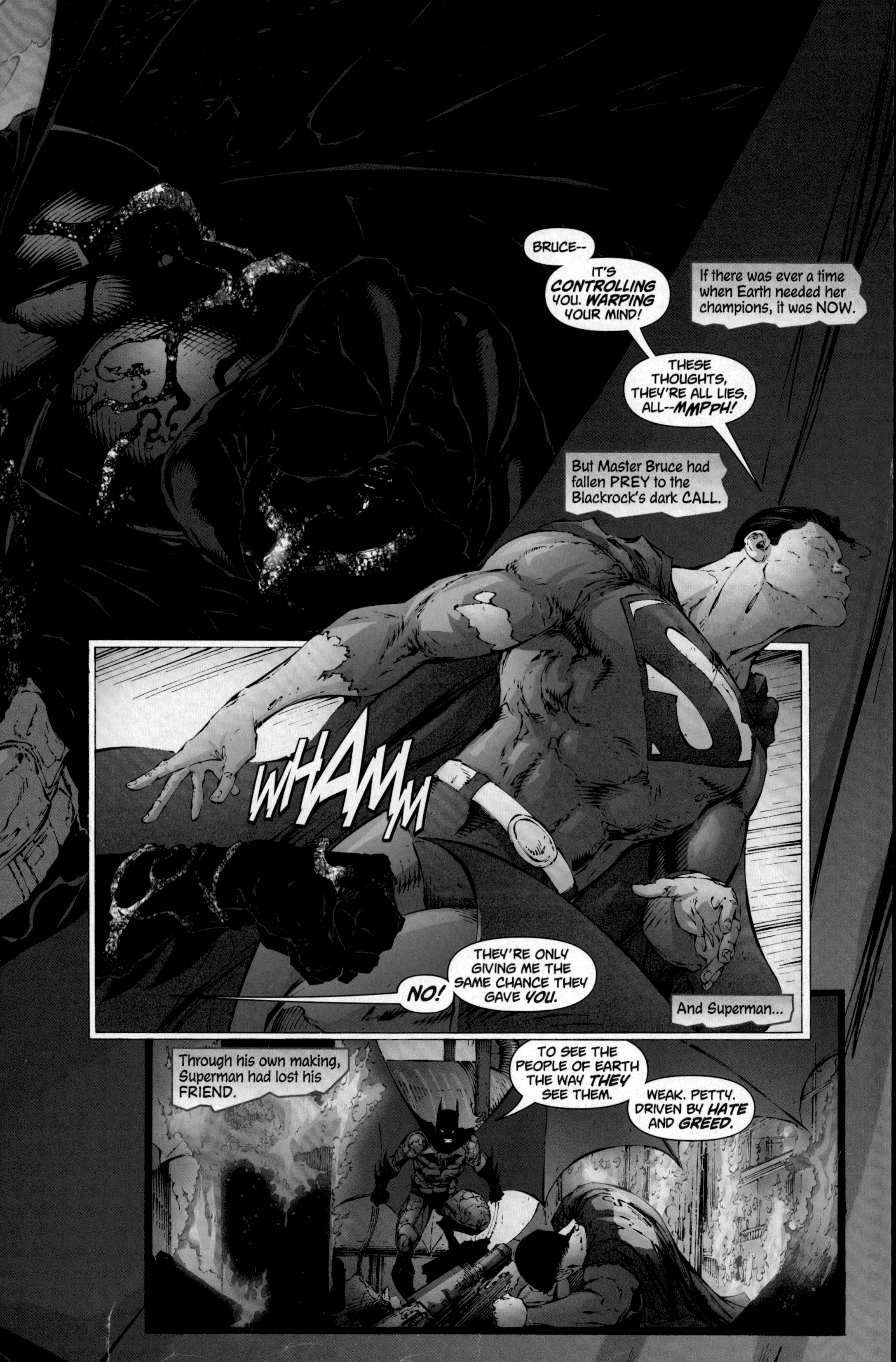

BRUCE--
IT'S CONTROLLING YOU. WARPING YOUR MIND!
If there was ever a time when Earth needed her champions, it was NOW.
THESE THOUGHTS, THEY'RE ALL LIES, ALL--MMPH!
But Master Bruce had fallen PREY to the Blackrock's dark CALL.
WHAMM
NO!
THEY'RE ONLY GIVING ME THE SAME CHANCE THEY GAVE YOU.
And Superman...
Through his own making, Superman had lost his FRIEND.
TO SEE THE PEOPLE OF EARTH THE WAY THEY SEE THEM.
WEAK. PETTY. DRIVEN BY HATE AND GREED.

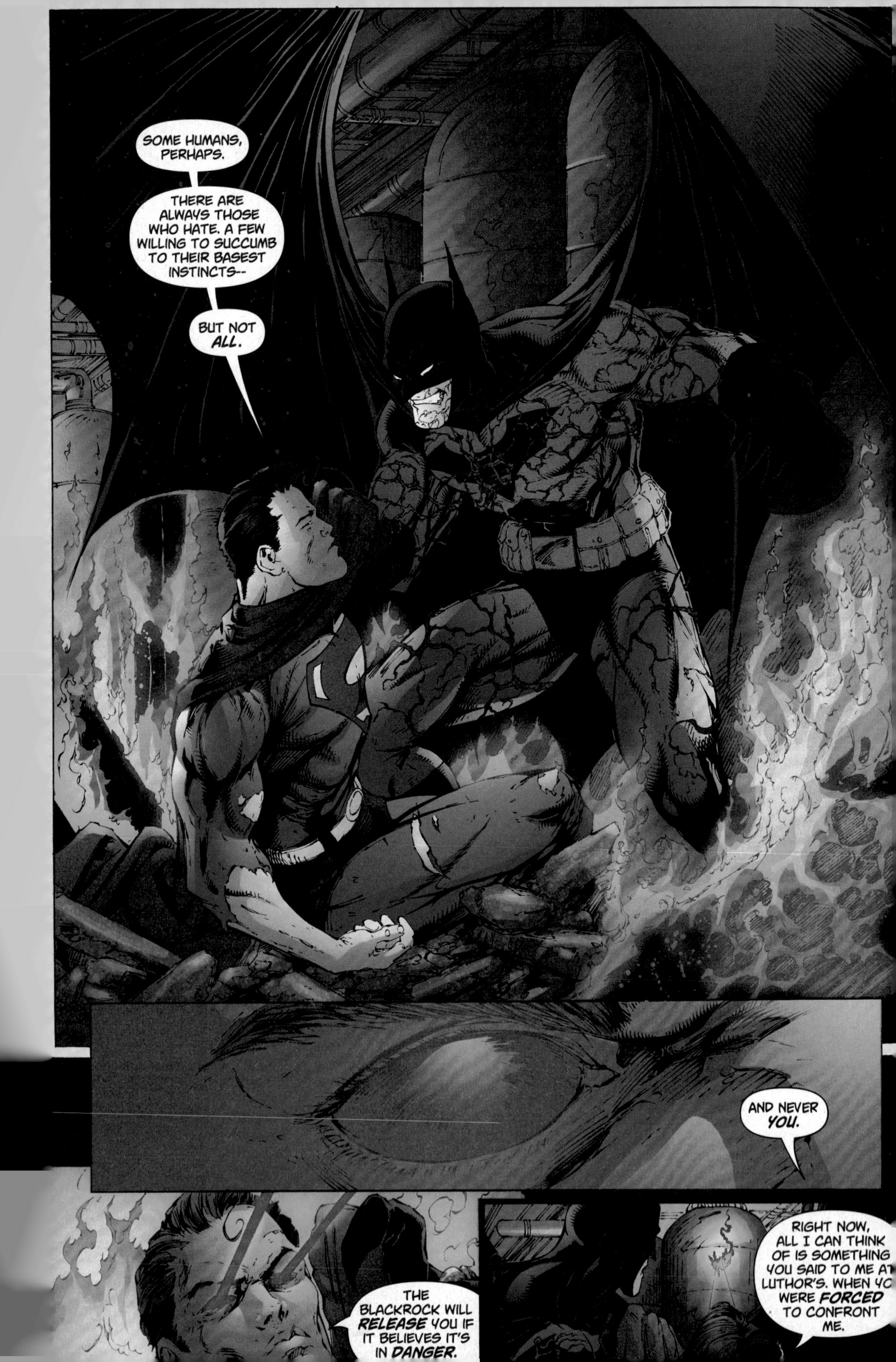
SOME HUMANS, PERHAPS.
THERE ARE ALWAYS THOSE WHO HATE. A FEW WILLING TO SUCCUMB TO THEIR BASEST INSTINCTS--
BUT NOT *ALL*.
AND NEVER *YOU*.
THE BLACKROCK WILL *RELEASE* YOU IF IT BELIEVES IT'S IN *DANGER*.
RIGHT NOW, ALL I CAN THINK OF IS SOMETHING YOU SAID TO ME AT LUTHOR'S. WHEN YO WERE *FORCED* TO CONFRONT ME.

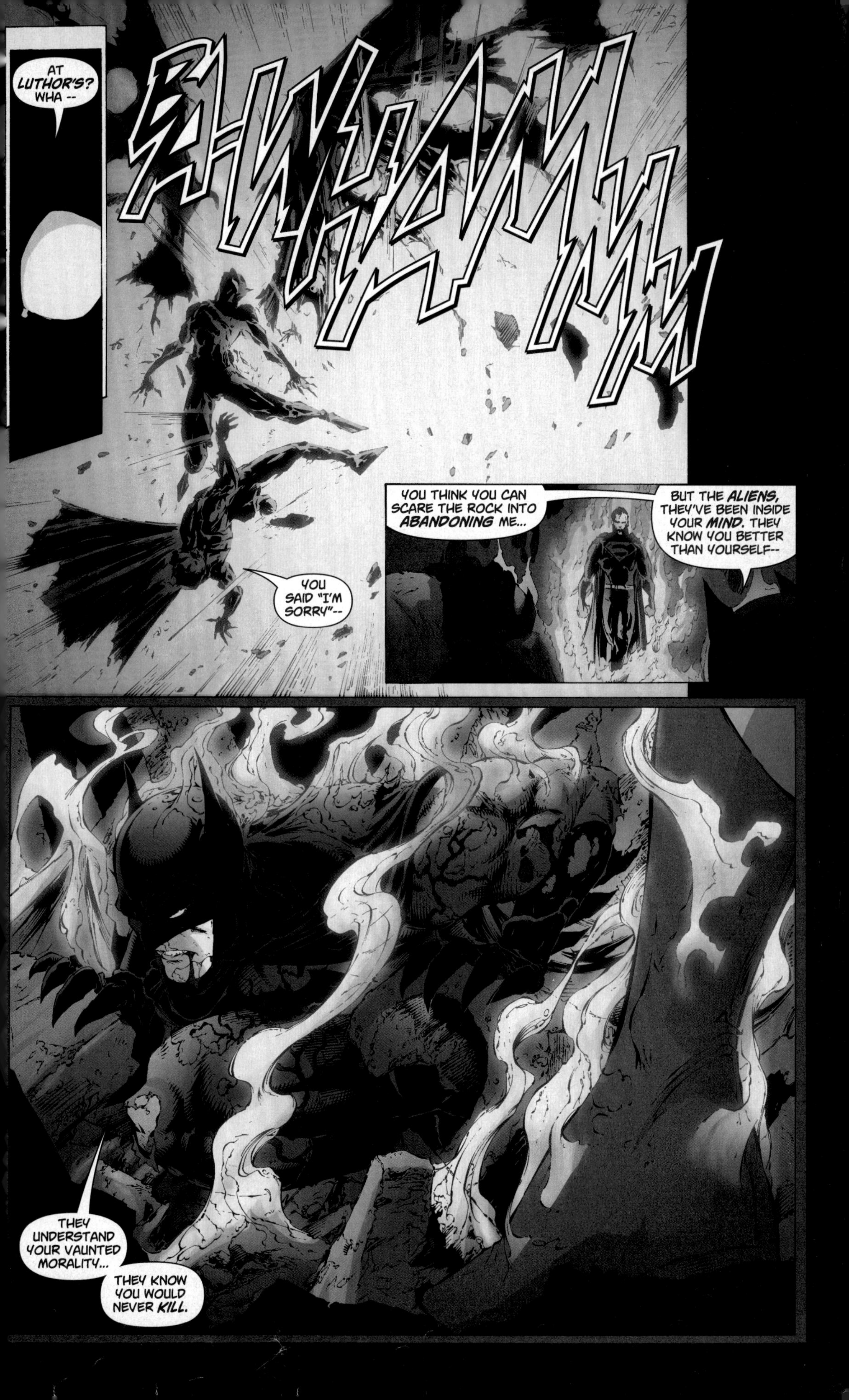
AT LUTHOR'S? WHA --
BWHAMM
YOU SAID "I'M SORRY"--
YOU THINK YOU CAN SCARE THE ROCK INTO ABANDONING ME...
BUT THE ALIENS, THEY'VE BEEN INSIDE YOUR MIND. THEY KNOW YOU BETTER THAN YOURSELF--
THEY UNDERSTAND YOUR VAUNTED MORALITY...
THEY KNOW YOU WOULD NEVER KILL.

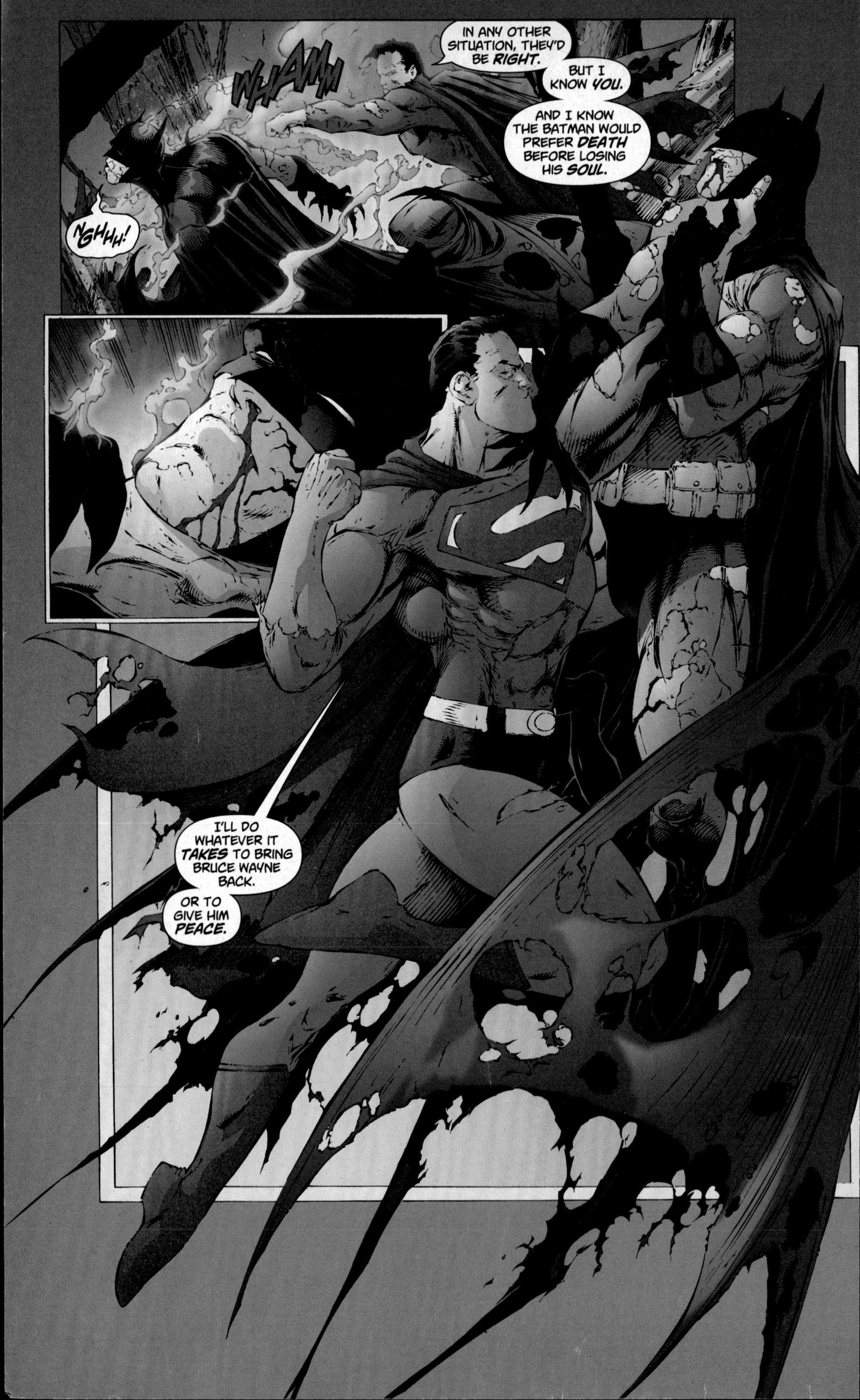
WHAMM
NGHHH!
IN ANY OTHER SITUATION, THEY'D BE RIGHT.
BUT I KNOW YOU.
AND I KNOW THE BATMAN WOULD PREFER DEATH BEFORE LOSING HIS SOUL.
I'LL DO WHATEVER IT TAKES TO BRING BRUCE WAYNE BACK.
OR TO GIVE HIM PEACE.

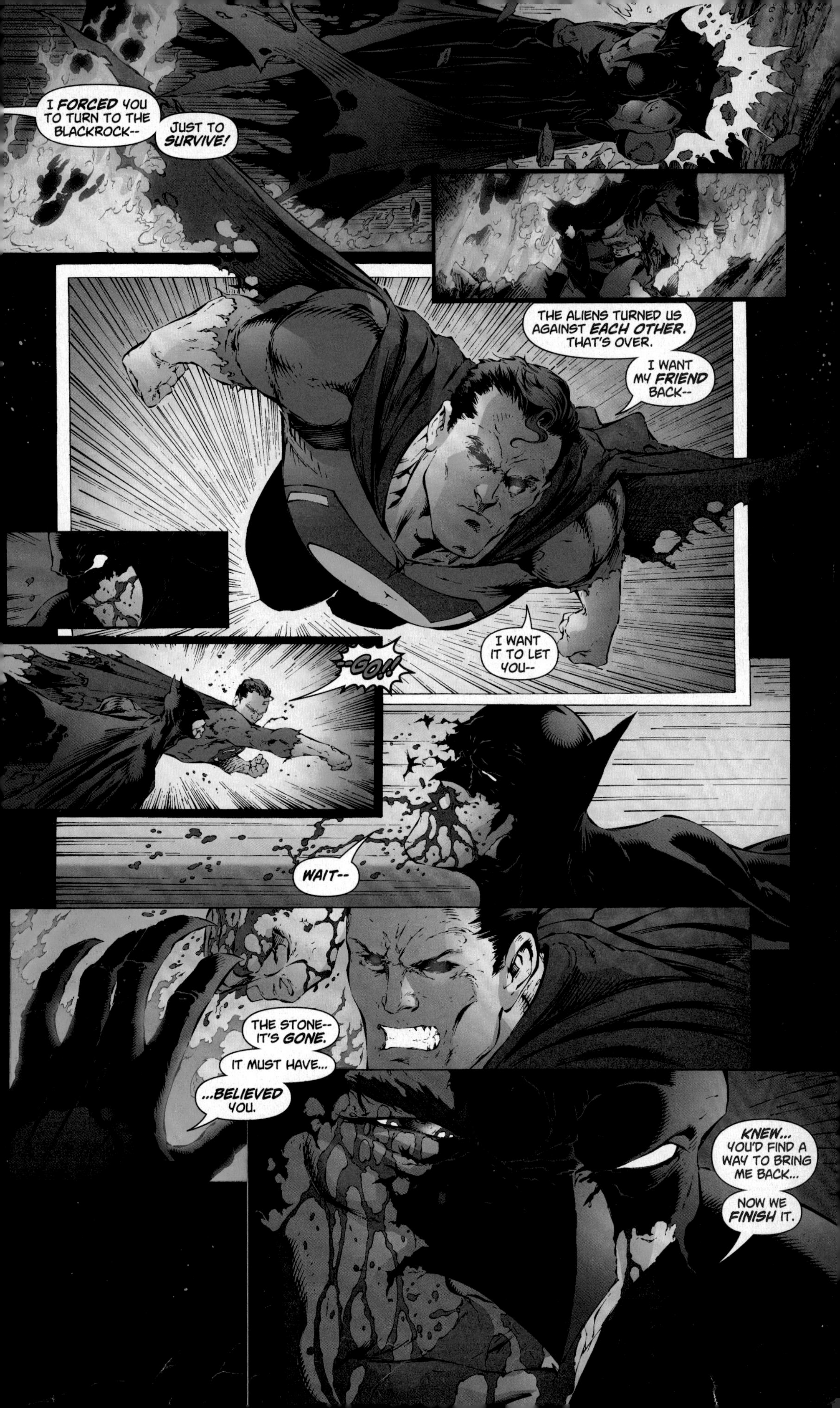

I FORCED YOU TO TURN TO THE BLACKROCK--
JUST TO SURVIVE!
THE ALIENS TURNED US AGAINST EACH OTHER. THAT'S OVER.
I WANT MY FRIEND BACK--
I WANT IT TO LET YOU--
--GO!!
WAIT--
THE STONE-- IT'S GONE.
IT MUST HAVE...
...BELIEVED YOU.
KNEW... YOU'D FIND A WAY TO BRING ME BACK...
NOW WE FINISH IT.

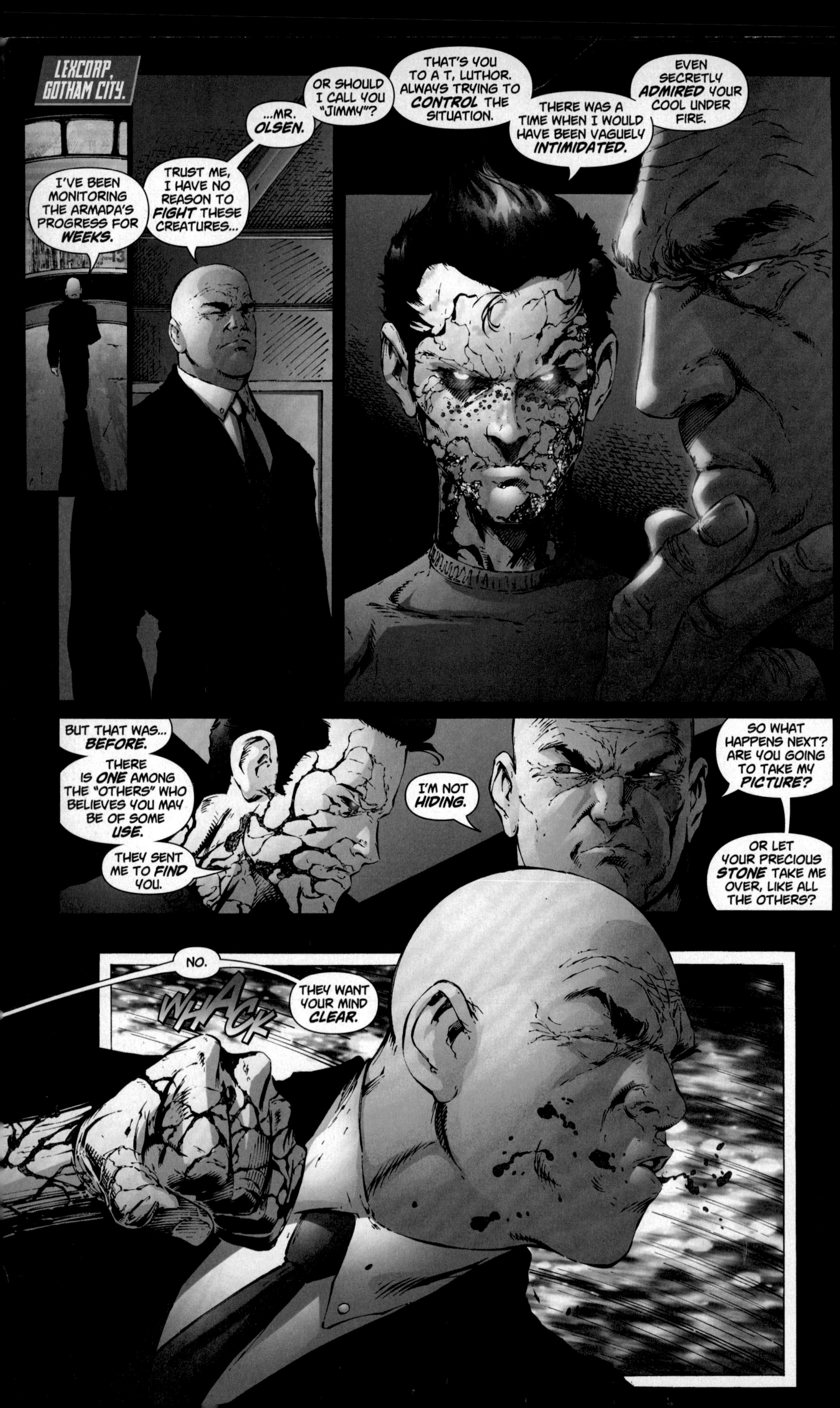
LEXCORP, GOTHAM CITY.
I'VE BEEN MONITORING THE ARMADA'S PROGRESS FOR WEEKS.
TRUST ME, I HAVE NO REASON TO FIGHT THESE CREATURES...
...MR. OLSEN.
OR SHOULD I CALL YOU "JIMMY"?
THAT'S YOU TO A T, LUTHOR. ALWAYS TRYING TO CONTROL THE SITUATION.
THERE WAS A TIME WHEN I WOULD HAVE BEEN VAGUELY INTIMIDATED.
EVEN SECRETLY ADMIRED YOUR COOL UNDER FIRE.
BUT THAT WAS... BEFORE.
THERE IS ONE AMONG THE "OTHERS" WHO BELIEVES YOU MAY BE OF SOME USE.
THEY SENT ME TO FIND YOU.
I'M NOT HIDING.
SO WHAT HAPPENS NEXT? ARE YOU GOING TO TAKE MY PICTURE?
OR LET YOUR PRECIOUS STONE TAKE ME OVER, LIKE ALL THE OTHERS?
NO.
WHACK
THEY WANT YOUR MIND CLEAR.

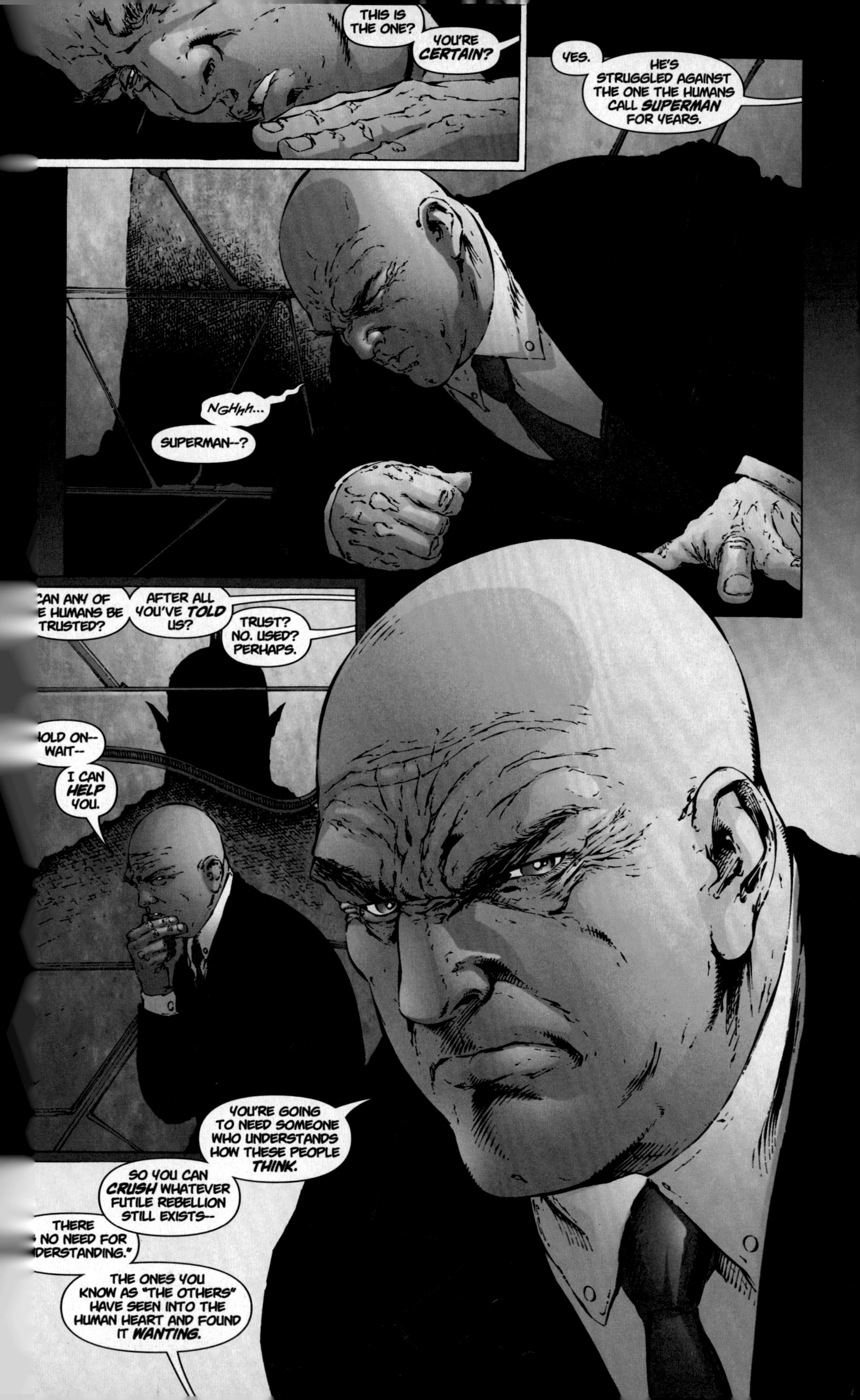
THIS IS THE ONE?
YOU'RE CERTAIN?
YES.
HE'S STRUGGLED AGAINST THE ONE THE HUMANS CALL SUPERMAN FOR YEARS.
NGHhh...
SUPERMAN--?
CAN ANY OF E HUMANS BE TRUSTED?
AFTER ALL YOU'VE TOLD US?
TRUST? NO. USED? PERHAPS.
HOLD ON-- WAIT--
I CAN HELP YOU.
YOU'RE GOING TO NEED SOMEONE WHO UNDERSTANDS HOW THESE PEOPLE THINK.
SO YOU CAN CRUSH WHATEVER FUTILE REBELLION STILL EXISTS--
THERE S NO NEED FOR NDERSTANDING."
THE ONES YOU KNOW AS "THE OTHERS" HAVE SEEN INTO THE HUMAN HEART AND FOUND IT WANTING.

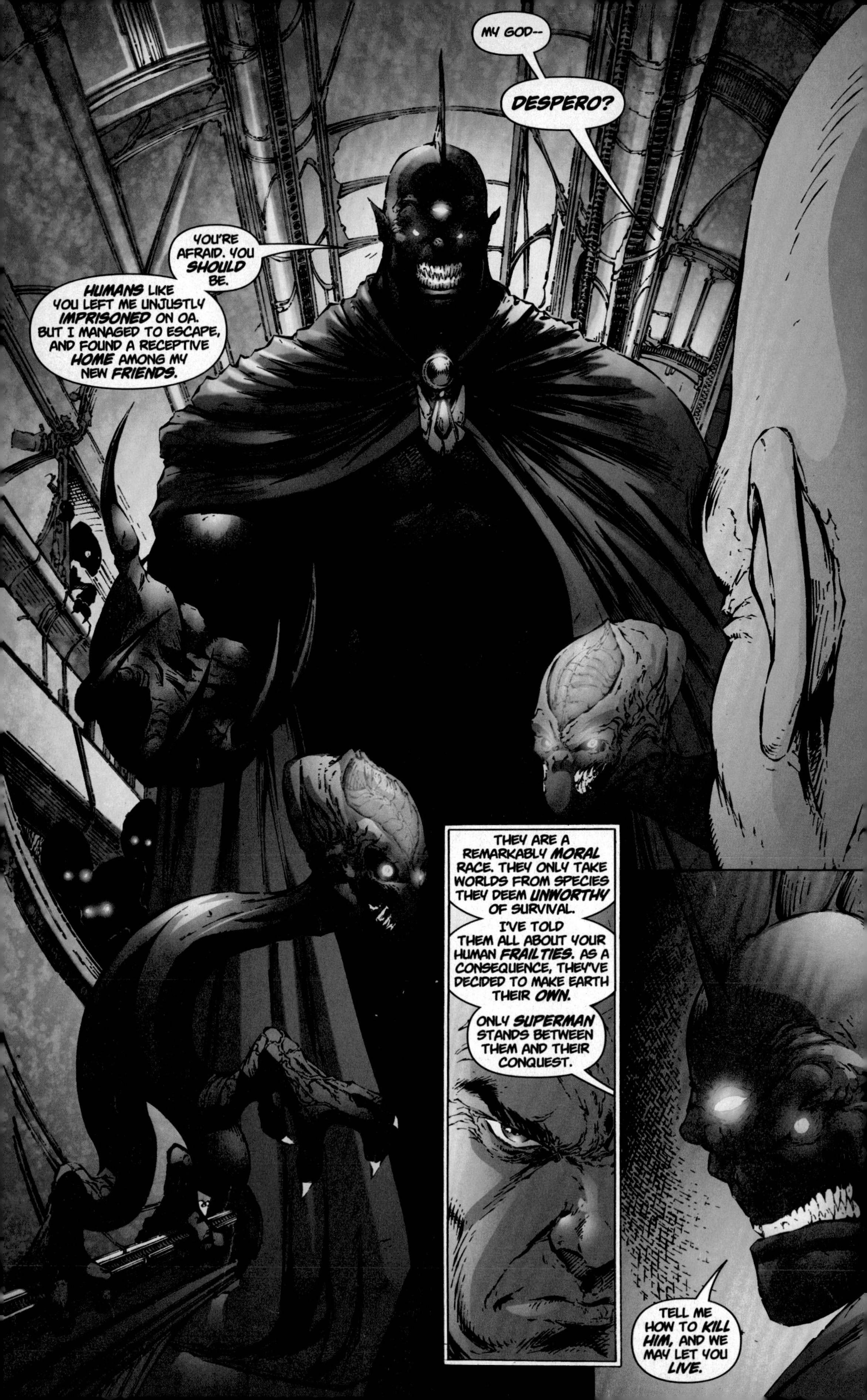
MY GOD--
DESPERO?
YOU'RE AFRAID. YOU SHOULD BE.
HUMANS LIKE YOU LEFT ME UNJUSTLY IMPRISONED ON OA. BUT I MANAGED TO ESCAPE, AND FOUND A RECEPTIVE HOME AMONG MY NEW FRIENDS.
THEY ARE A REMARKABLY MORAL RACE. THEY ONLY TAKE WORLDS FROM SPECIES THEY DEEM UNWORTHY OF SURVIVAL.
I'VE TOLD THEM ALL ABOUT YOUR HUMAN FRAILTIES. AS A CONSEQUENCE, THEY'VE DECIDED TO MAKE EARTH THEIR OWN.
ONLY SUPERMAN STANDS BETWEEN THEM AND THEIR CONQUEST.
TELL ME HOW TO KILL HIM, AND WE MAY LET YOU LIVE.

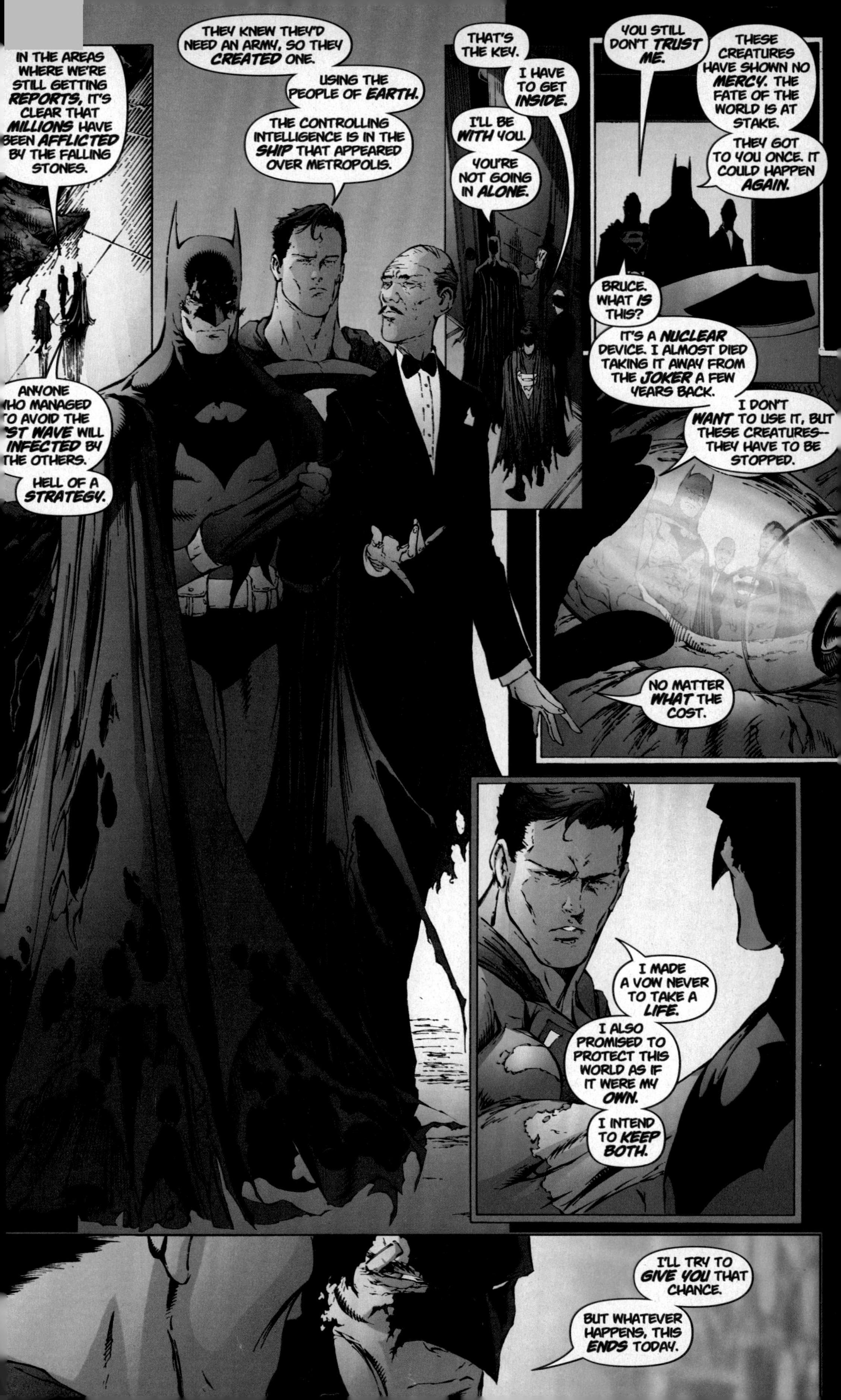
IN THE AREAS WHERE WE'RE STILL GETTING REPORTS, IT'S CLEAR THAT MILLIONS HAVE BEEN AFFLICTED BY THE FALLING STONES.
THEY KNEW THEY'D NEED AN ARMY, SO THEY CREATED ONE.
USING THE PEOPLE OF EARTH.
THE CONTROLLING INTELLIGENCE IS IN THE SHIP THAT APPEARED OVER METROPOLIS.
ANYONE WHO MANAGED TO AVOID THE ST WAVE WILL INFECTED BY THE OTHERS.
HELL OF A STRATEGY.
THAT'S THE KEY.
I HAVE TO GET INSIDE.
I'LL BE WITH YOU.
YOU'RE NOT GOING IN ALONE.
YOU STILL DON'T TRUST ME.
THESE CREATURES HAVE SHOWN NO MERCY. THE FATE OF THE WORLD IS AT STAKE.
THEY GOT TO YOU ONCE. IT COULD HAPPEN AGAIN.
BRUCE. WHAT IS THIS?
IT'S A NUCLEAR DEVICE. I ALMOST DIED TAKING IT AWAY FROM THE JOKER A FEW YEARS BACK.
I DON'T WANT TO USE IT, BUT THESE CREATURES-- THEY HAVE TO BE STOPPED.
NO MATTER WHAT THE COST.
I MADE A VOW NEVER TO TAKE A LIFE.
I ALSO PROMISED TO PROTECT THIS WORLD AS IF IT WERE MY OWN.
I INTEND TO KEEP BOTH.
I'LL TRY TO GIVE YOU THAT CHANCE.
BUT WHATEVER HAPPENS, THIS ENDS TODAY.

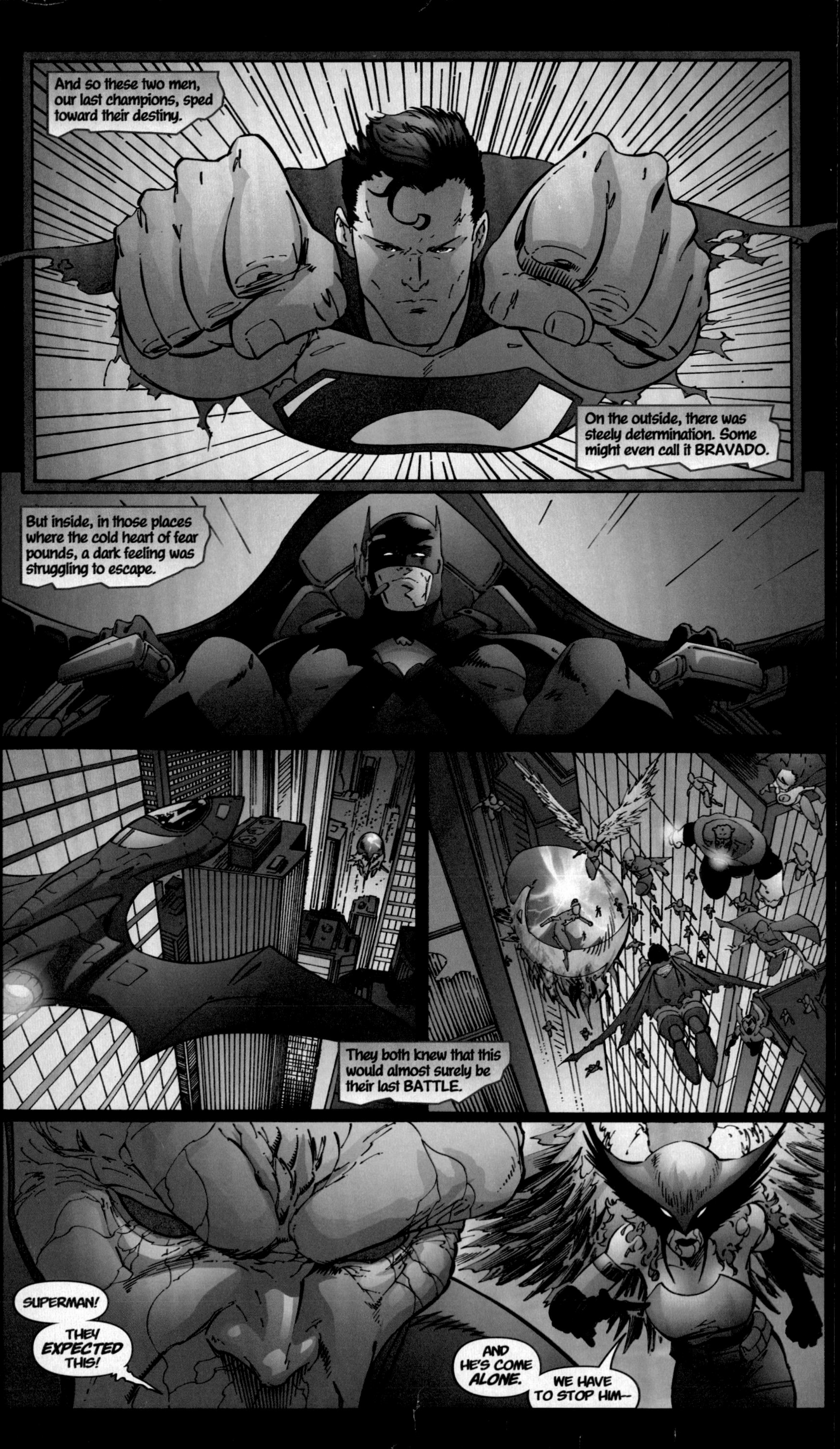
And so these two men, our last champions, sped toward their destiny.
On the outside, there was steely determination. Some might even call it BRAVADO.
But inside, in those places where the cold heart of fear pounds, a dark feeling was struggling to escape.
They both knew that this would almost surely be their last BATTLE.
SUPERMAN!
THEY EXPECTED THIS!
AND HE'S COME ALONE.
WE HAVE TO STOP HIM--

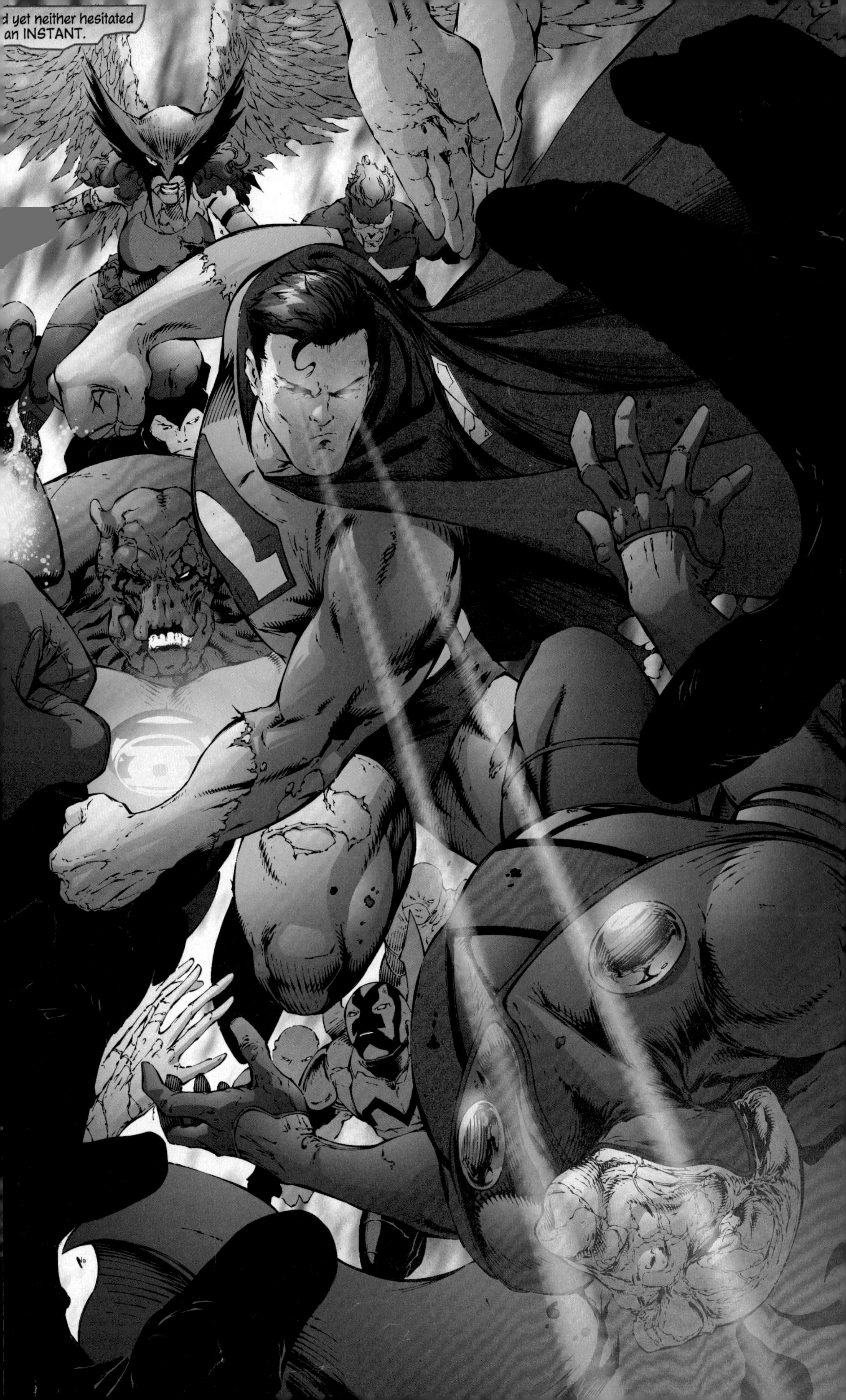
d yet neither hesitated
an INSTANT.

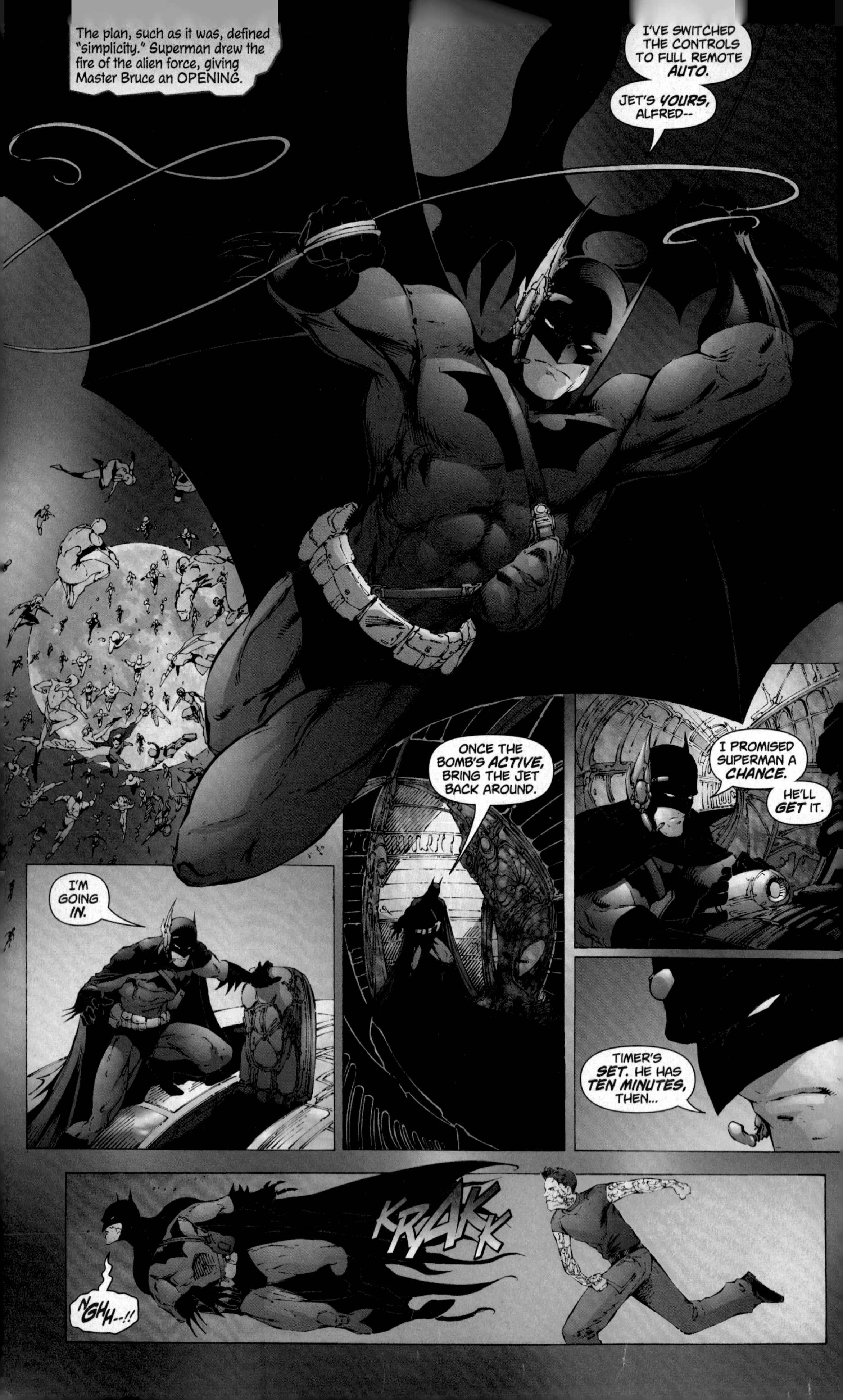

The plan, such as it was, defined "simplicity." Superman drew the fire of the alien force, giving Master Bruce an OPENING.
I'VE SWITCHED THE CONTROLS TO FULL REMOTE AUTO.
JET'S YOURS, ALFRED--
ONCE THE BOMB'S ACTIVE, BRING THE JET BACK AROUND.
I PROMISED SUPERMAN A CHANCE.
HE'LL GET IT.
I'M GOING IN.
TIMER'S SET. HE HAS TEN MINUTES, THEN...
KRAKK
NGHH--!!

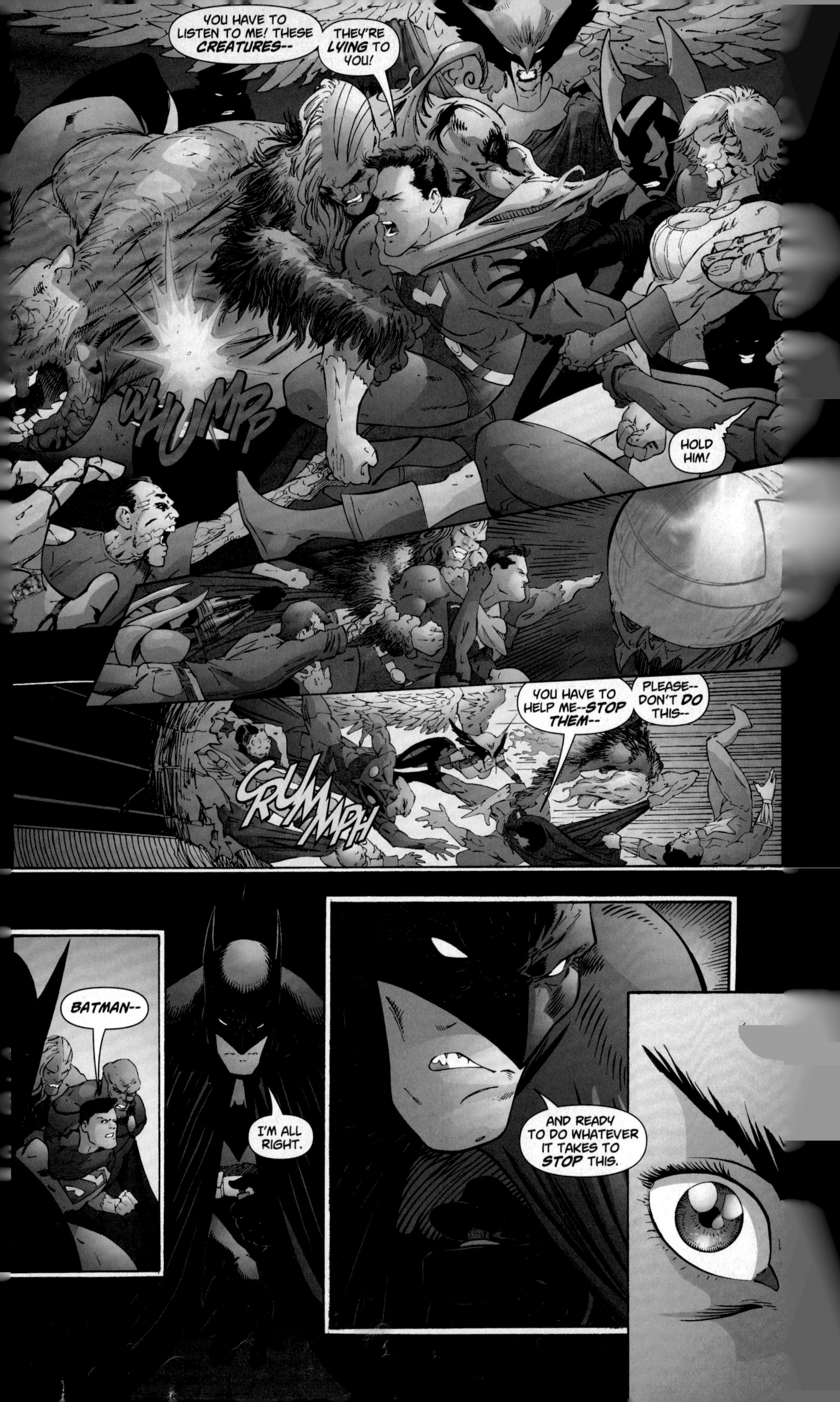

YOU HAVE TO LISTEN TO ME! THESE CREATURES--
THEY'RE LYING TO YOU!
WHUMP
HOLD HIM!
YOU HAVE TO HELP ME--STOP THEM--
PLEASE-- DON'T DO THIS--
CRUMMPH
BATMAN--
I'M ALL RIGHT.
AND READY TO DO WHATEVER IT TAKES TO STOP THIS.

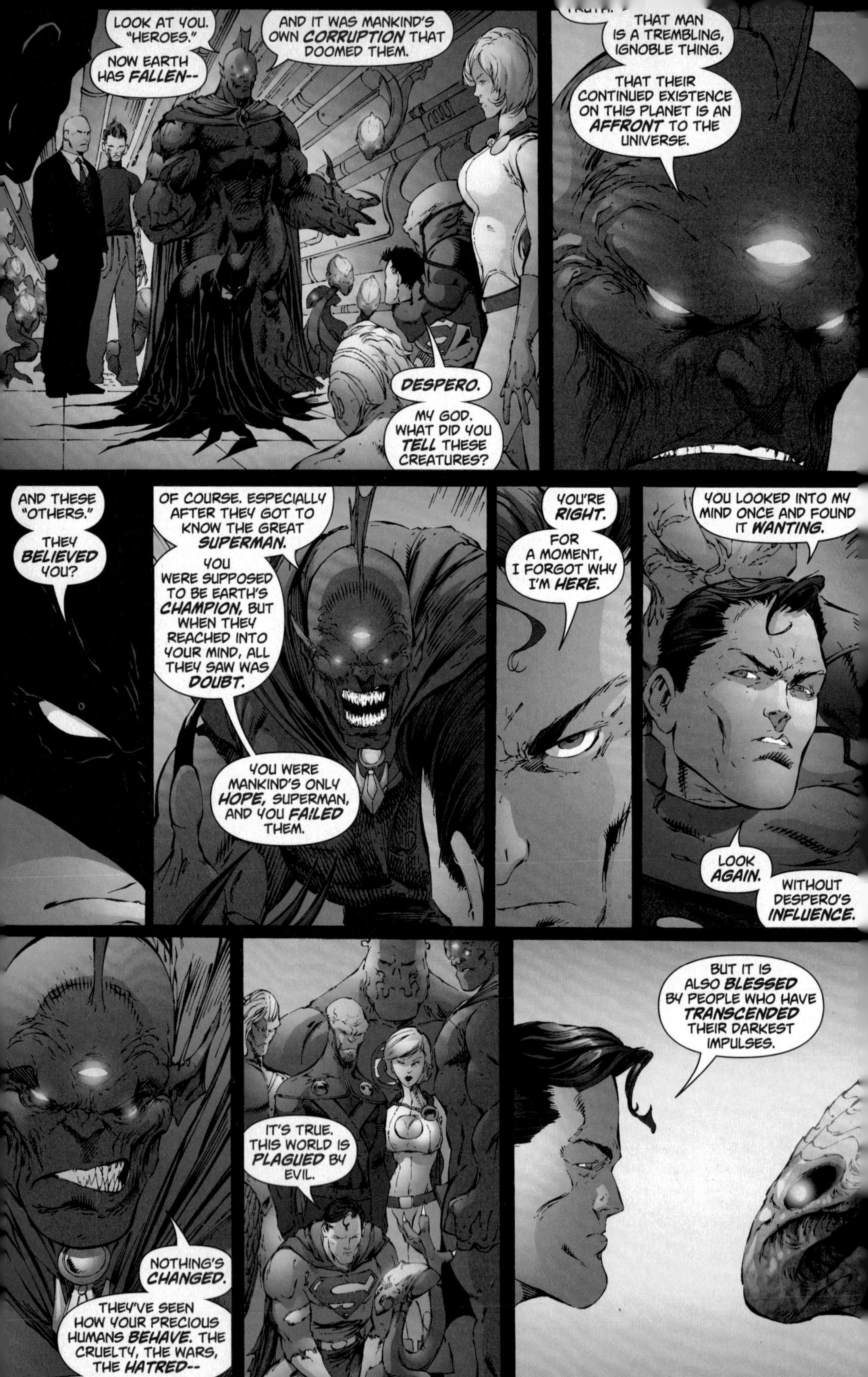

LOOK AT YOU. "HEROES."
NOW EARTH HAS FALLEN--
AND IT WAS MANKIND'S OWN CORRUPTION THAT DOOMED THEM.
DESPERO.
MY GOD. WHAT DID YOU TELL THESE CREATURES?
THAT MAN IS A TREMBLING, IGNOBLE THING.
THAT THEIR CONTINUED EXISTENCE ON THIS PLANET IS AN AFFRONT TO THE UNIVERSE.
AND THESE "OTHERS."
THEY BELIEVED YOU?
OF COURSE. ESPECIALLY AFTER THEY GOT TO KNOW THE GREAT SUPERMAN.
YOU WERE SUPPOSED TO BE EARTH'S CHAMPION, BUT WHEN THEY REACHED INTO YOUR MIND, ALL THEY SAW WAS DOUBT.
YOU WERE MANKIND'S ONLY HOPE, SUPERMAN, AND YOU FAILED THEM.
YOU'RE RIGHT.
FOR A MOMENT, I FORGOT WHY I'M HERE.
YOU LOOKED INTO MY MIND ONCE AND FOUND IT WANTING.
LOOK AGAIN.
WITHOUT DESPERO'S INFLUENCE.
NOTHING'S CHANGED.
THEY'VE SEEN HOW YOUR PRECIOUS HUMANS BEHAVE. THE CRUELTY, THE WARS, THE HATRED--
IT'S WHY I BROUGHT THEM LUTHOR. LIVING PROOF OF THIS WORLD'S INHUMANITY.
IT'S TRUE. THIS WORLD IS PLAGUED BY EVIL.
BUT IT IS ALSO BLESSED BY PEOPLE WHO HAVE TRANSCENDED THEIR DARKEST IMPULSES.

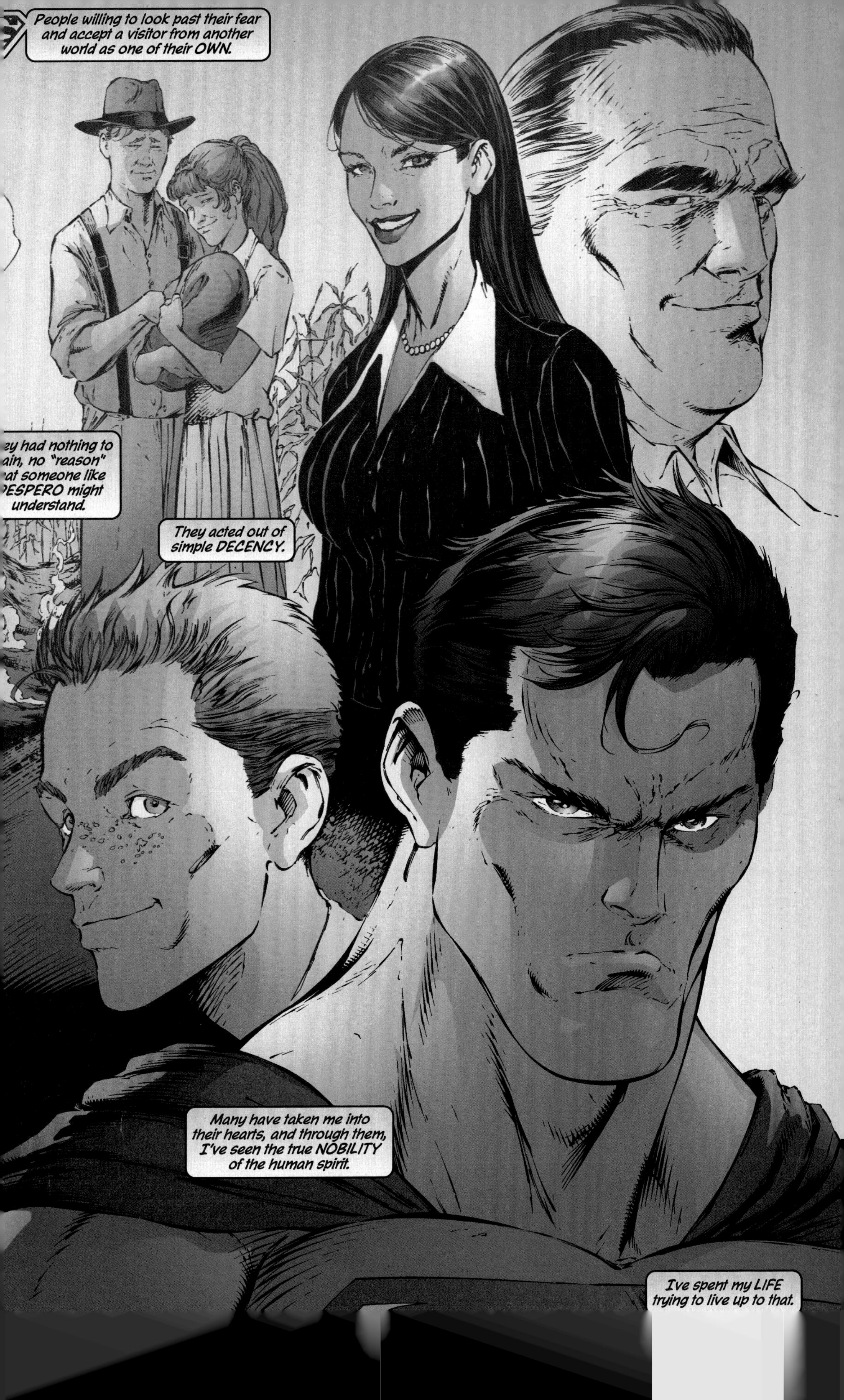
People willing to look past their fear and accept a visitor from another world as one of their OWN.
ey had nothing to ain, no "reason" at someone like ESPERO might understand.
They acted out of simple DECENCY.
Many have taken me into their hearts, and through them, I've seen the true NOBILITY of the human spirit.
I've spent my LIFE trying to live up to that.

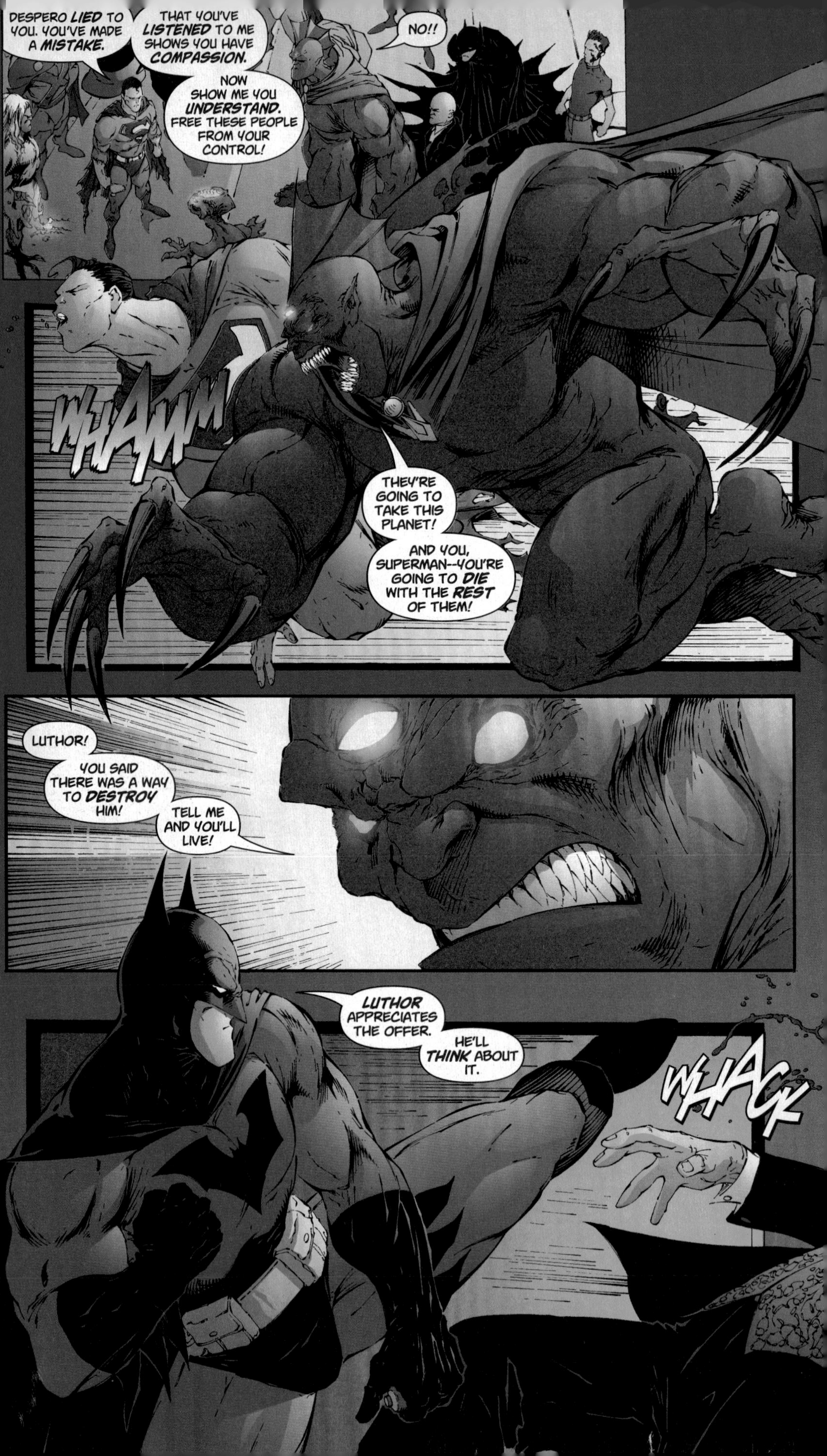
DESPERO LIED TO YOU. YOU'VE MADE A MISTAKE.
THAT YOU'VE LISTENED TO ME SHOWS YOU HAVE COMPASSION.
NOW SHOW ME YOU UNDERSTAND. FREE THESE PEOPLE FROM YOUR CONTROL!
NO!!
WHAMM
THEY'RE GOING TO TAKE THIS PLANET!
AND YOU, SUPERMAN--YOU'RE GOING TO DIE WITH THE REST OF THEM!
LUTHOR!
YOU SAID THERE WAS A WAY TO DESTROY HIM!
TELL ME AND YOU'LL LIVE!
LUTHOR APPRECIATES THE OFFER.
HE'LL THINK ABOUT IT.
WHACK

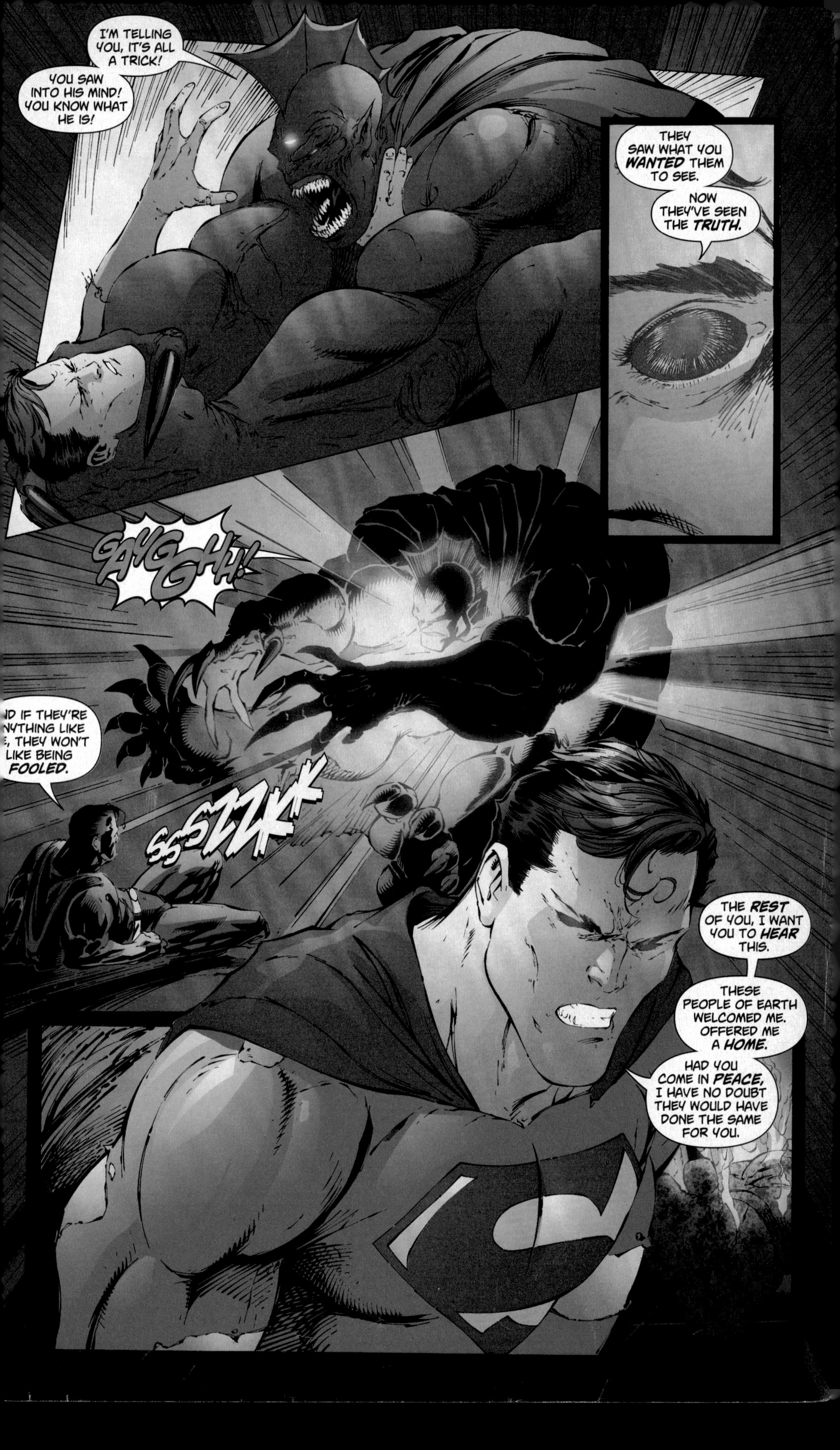

I'M TELLING YOU, IT'S ALL A TRICK!
YOU SAW INTO HIS MIND! YOU KNOW WHAT HE IS!
THEY SAW WHAT YOU WANTED THEM TO SEE.
NOW THEY'VE SEEN THE TRUTH.
GAYGGHH!
ND IF THEY'RE NYTHING LIKE E, THEY WON'T LIKE BEING FOOLED.
SSSSZZKK
THE REST OF YOU, I WANT YOU TO HEAR THIS.
THESE PEOPLE OF EARTH WELCOMED ME. OFFERED ME A HOME.
HAD YOU COME IN PEACE, I HAVE NO DOUBT THEY WOULD HAVE DONE THE SAME FOR YOU.

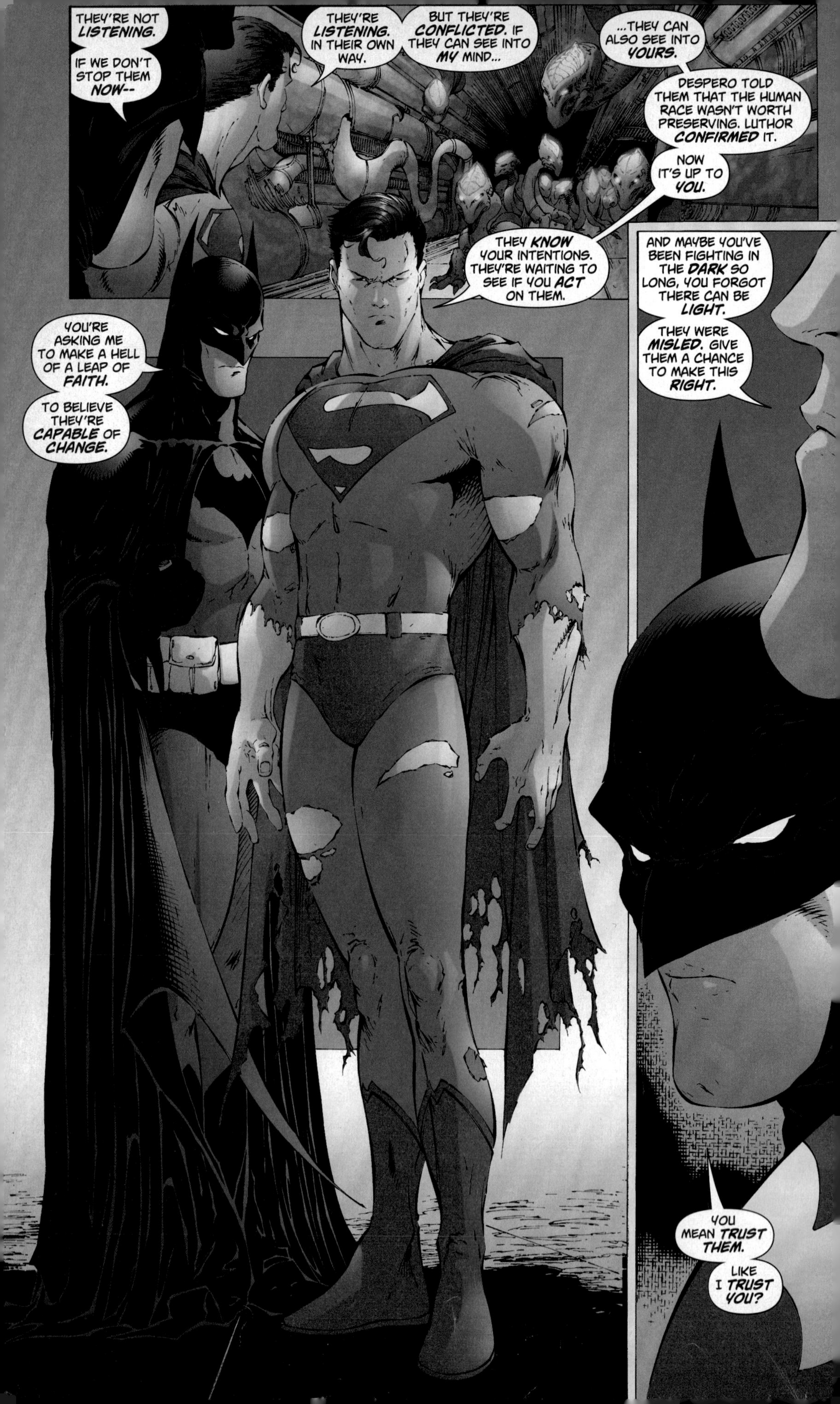
THEY'RE NOT LISTENING.
IF WE DON'T STOP THEM NOW--
THEY'RE LISTENING. IN THEIR OWN WAY.
BUT THEY'RE CONFLICTED. IF THEY CAN SEE INTO MY MIND...
...THEY CAN ALSO SEE INTO YOURS.
DESPERO TOLD THEM THAT THE HUMAN RACE WASN'T WORTH PRESERVING. LUTHOR CONFIRMED IT.
NOW IT'S UP TO YOU.
THEY KNOW YOUR INTENTIONS. THEY'RE WAITING TO SEE IF YOU ACT ON THEM.
YOU'RE ASKING ME TO MAKE A HELL OF A LEAP OF FAITH.
TO BELIEVE THEY'RE CAPABLE OF CHANGE.
AND MAYBE YOU'VE BEEN FIGHTING IN THE DARK SO LONG, YOU FORGOT THERE CAN BE LIGHT.
THEY WERE MISLED. GIVE THEM A CHANCE TO MAKE THIS RIGHT.
YOU MEAN TRUST THEM.
LIKE I TRUST YOU?

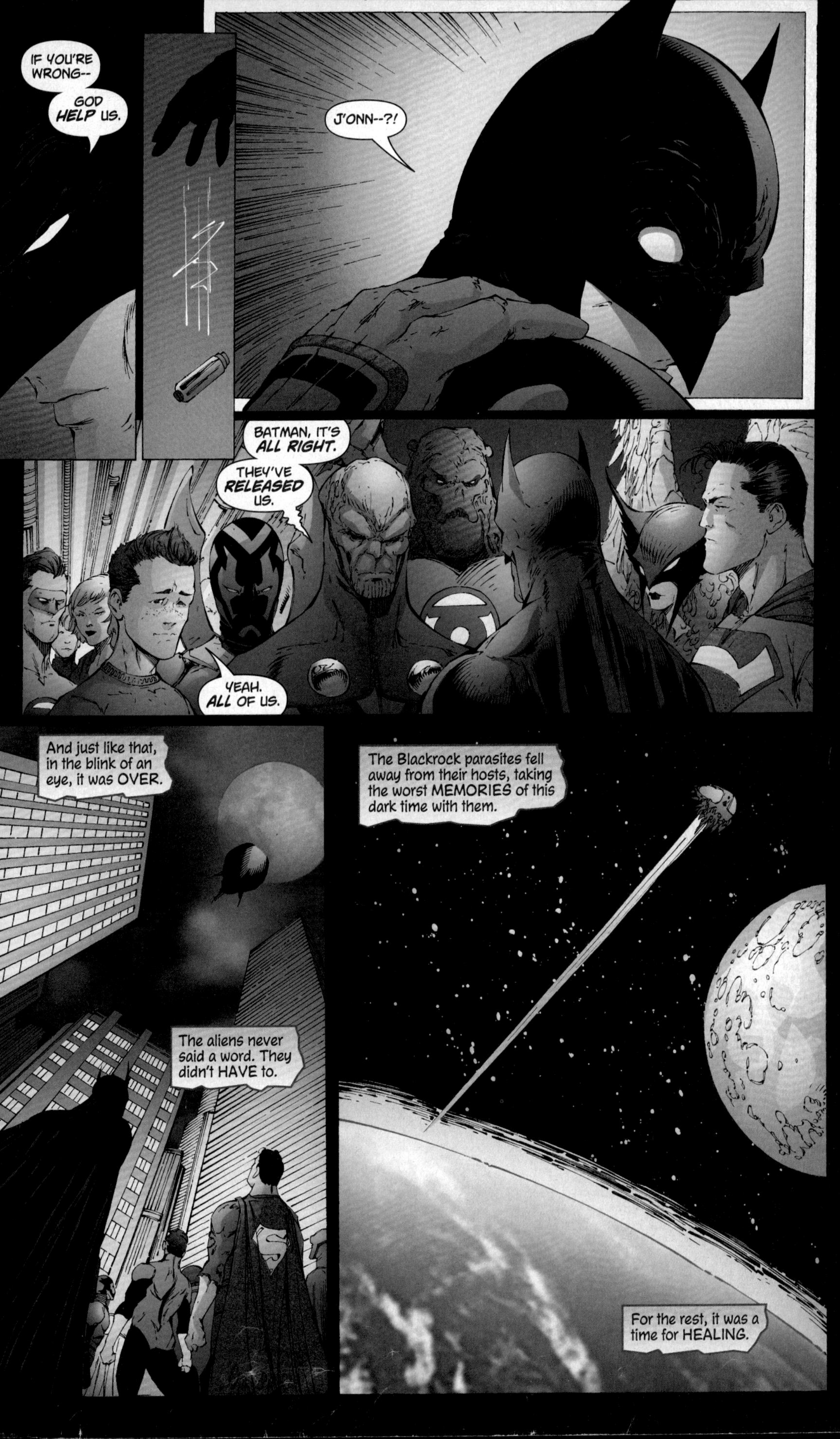

IF YOU'RE WRONG--
GOD HELP US.
J'ONN--?!
BATMAN, IT'S ALL RIGHT.
THEY'VE RELEASED US.
YEAH. ALL OF US.
And just like that, in the blink of an eye, it was OVER.
The aliens never said a word. They didn't HAVE to.
The Blackrock parasites fell away from their hosts, taking the worst MEMORIES of this dark time with them.
For the rest, it was a time for HEALING.

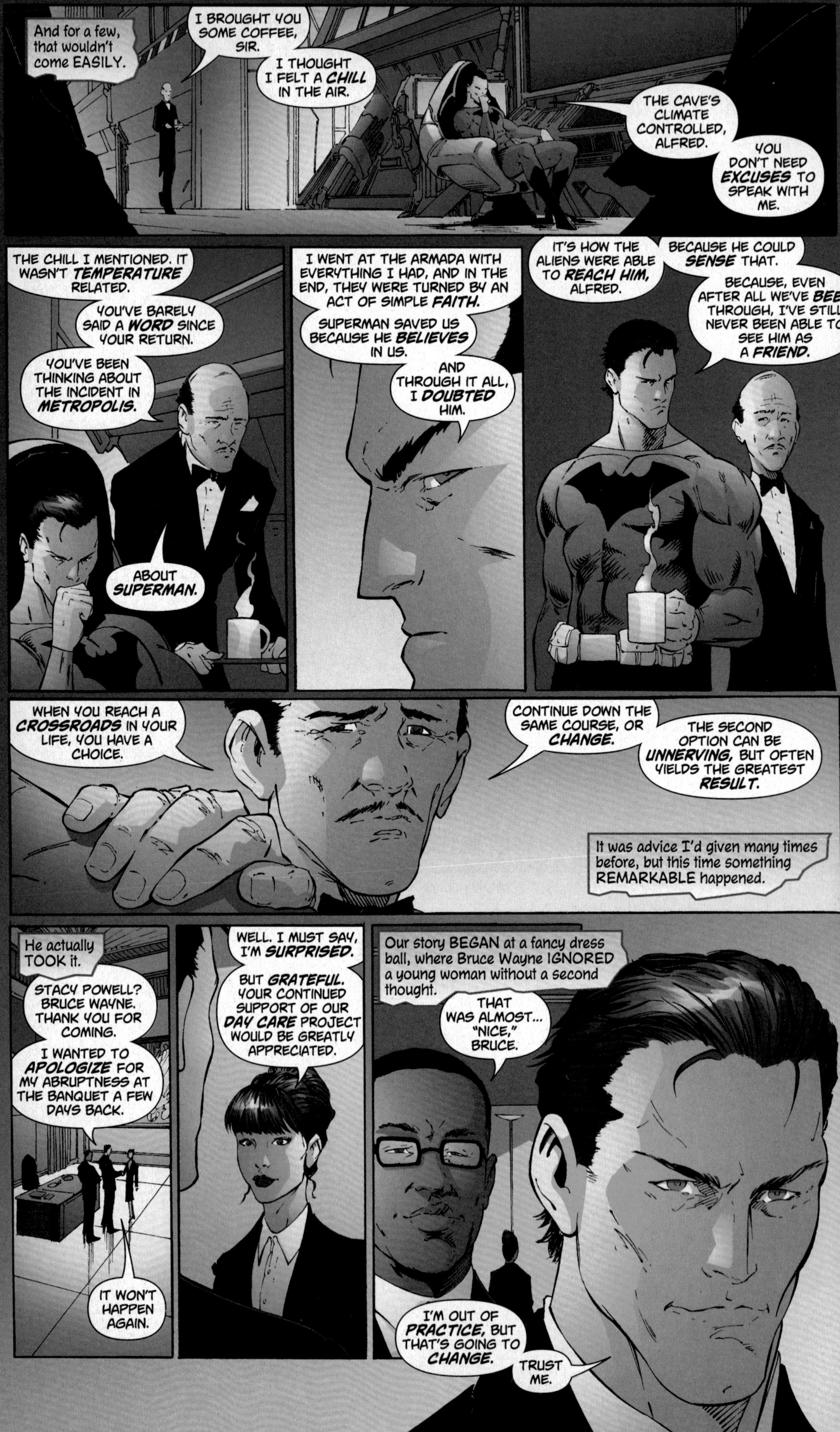
And for a few, that wouldn't come EASILY.
I BROUGHT YOU SOME COFFEE, SIR.
I THOUGHT I FELT A CHILL IN THE AIR.
THE CAVE'S CLIMATE CONTROLLED, ALFRED.
YOU DON'T NEED EXCUSES TO SPEAK WITH ME.
THE CHILL I MENTIONED. IT WASN'T TEMPERATURE RELATED.
YOU'VE BARELY SAID A WORD SINCE YOUR RETURN.
YOU'VE BEEN THINKING ABOUT THE INCIDENT IN METROPOLIS.
ABOUT SUPERMAN.
I WENT AT THE ARMADA WITH EVERYTHING I HAD, AND IN THE END, THEY WERE TURNED BY AN ACT OF SIMPLE FAITH.
SUPERMAN SAVED US BECAUSE HE BELIEVES IN US.
AND THROUGH IT ALL, I DOUBTED HIM.
IT'S HOW THE ALIENS WERE ABLE TO REACH HIM, ALFRED.
BECAUSE HE COULD SENSE THAT.
BECAUSE, EVEN AFTER ALL WE'VE BEEN THROUGH, I'VE STILL NEVER BEEN ABLE TO SEE HIM AS A FRIEND.
WHEN YOU REACH A CROSSROADS IN YOUR LIFE, YOU HAVE A CHOICE.
CONTINUE DOWN THE SAME COURSE, OR CHANGE.
THE SECOND OPTION CAN BE UNNERVING, BUT OFTEN YIELDS THE GREATEST RESULT.
It was advice I'd given many times before, but this time something REMARKABLE happened.
He actually TOOK it.
STACY POWELL? BRUCE WAYNE. THANK YOU FOR COMING.
I WANTED TO APOLOGIZE FOR MY ABRUPTNESS AT THE BANQUET A FEW DAYS BACK.
IT WON'T HAPPEN AGAIN.
WELL. I MUST SAY, I'M SURPRISED.
BUT GRATEFUL. YOUR CONTINUED SUPPORT OF OUR DAY CARE PROJECT WOULD BE GREATLY APPRECIATED.
Our story BEGAN at a fancy dress ball, where Bruce Wayne IGNORED a young woman without a second thought.
THAT WAS ALMOST... "NICE," BRUCE.
I'M OUT OF PRACTICE, BUT THAT'S GOING TO CHANGE.
TRUST ME.

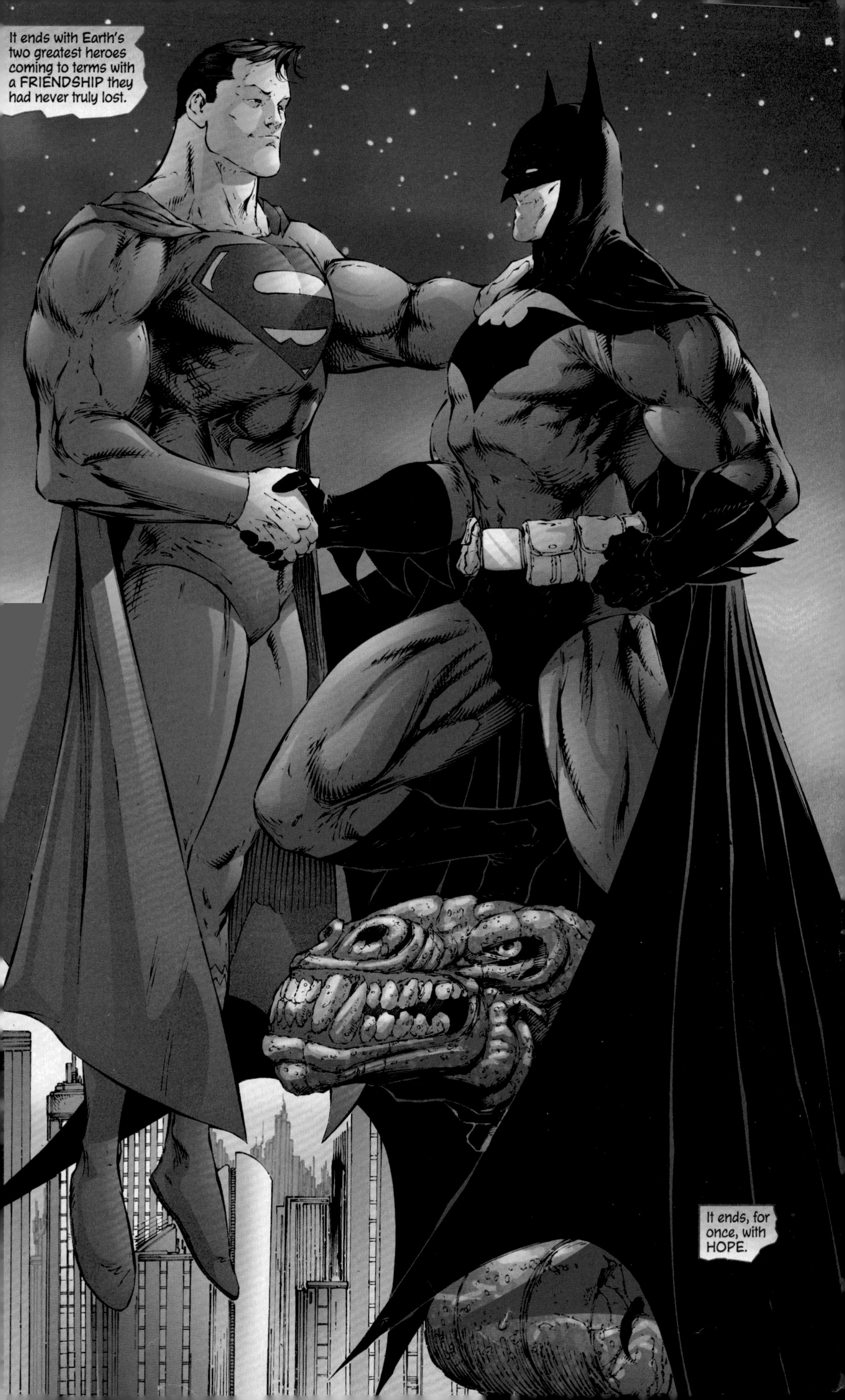
It ends with Earth's two greatest heroes coming to terms with a FRIENDSHIP they had never truly lost.
It ends, for once, with HOPE.

AFTERWORD BY MARK VERHEIDEN
"EEK! ONE OF THE VENOMEE HAS CHANGED MANHUNTER INTO A FISH!" ZOOK, HOUSE OF MYSTERY #145

Let me put something on the table, right at the top. I love Silver Age DC Comics. It's more than empty nostalgia for days gone by, and it's not a "guilty pleasure," a term I frankly find obnoxious. If you need some pretentious analysis to make it more palatable, okay, try this: there is a magic realism to the DC Silver Age that's simultaneously surreal and often emotionally affecting. That's a combo you don't find very often, especially in today's post-ironic, uber-cynical world, and it's something comics can do standing on their proverbial head.

Me? I'm constantly astounded by the "anything goes" spirit that infused so much Silver Age work. It was a time when Lana Lang could grow an insect head. Our old friend Batman could be zebra-striped, rainbow-hued, or transformed into a diapered baby, and that would only be the beginning of the story. I mean, Superman and Batman could challenge one another to an "amnesia contest" not because they'd been fooled into it by one of their foes, but just because they **felt** like it. There were rules to this universe, but they were remarkably elastic and utterly dispensable if they interfered with telling a cool story. So, how can you tell when you're reading a really great Silver Age adventure? Pause for a second and try to apply any sort of real-world construct to the drama. Trust me, your head will explode. And then you'll probably turn into a baby.

Aside from super-guys, the Silver Age DC universe was populated with an astonishing array of alien life forms. There were, of course, the alien heroes themselves, like Martian Manhunter, Hawkman, the Guardians of Oa and, of course, the big daddy of them all, Superman. But there were also a slew of bizarre creatures that erupted from the pages of STRANGE ADVENTURES, HOUSE OF MYSTERY, HOUSE OF SECRETS, and MY GREATEST ADVENTURE, as well as many of the superhero titles. What was great about DC's aliens was that even the most minimal concepts of physics and natural law were tossed into the trash pile when it came to their abilities. These things could fly, cross dimensions, shape-shift, time-travel… heck, you name it, and there was probably an alien doing it.

Mind you, I'm not talking about the drippy creatures torn out of H.R. Giger's psyche or the visceral horrors of "The War of the Worlds" (George Pal or Steven Spielberg version), or even the wonderful but somehow more prosaic Fin Fan Fooms and Gorgamms that populated the Marvel/Atlas line of the time. No sir. When DC said "alien," they meant frakkin' ALIENS.

These dudes came in all colors, often multi/hued in garish pinks, yellows, reds and purples. They could have beaks. Multiple arms. Tentacles. Claws. Fur. Feathers. Gaping eyes with triangles for pupils. They were usually really big (though not always) and if they were at all sentient, they were usually nursing a secret that only our heroes could divine. Most important, with the exception of the outright villains, most of the DC aliens weren't inherently "evil" but misunderstood, in that "there's a gigantic monster threatening our city and he just crushed the Municipal Bank Building, but I don't think he really **meant** it" sort of way.

Anyway, when I first started thinking about the "Enemies Within" arc for Superman/Batman, I had three main objectives. One, I wanted to somehow recapture the "anything goes" spirit that infused the Silver Age DC books, and that meant bringing back the most impossible of characters. Perhaps my favorite "get" was resurrecting "The Creature Who Could Not Die," a critter I discovered while plowing through the SHOWCASE issues of "GREEN LANTERN." What intrigued me about this fellow was not just the fact that he was one of the Lantern's earliest and deadliest opponents, but that "The Creature Who Could Not Die" in fact died in his very first outing. Remember what I said about the remarkably elastic rules of the early DCU? Reviving this palooka seemed to fit right in with the plan.

Two, I wanted to use some of DC's greatest villains, and one of them had to be a gorilla. Dr. Phosphorus and Doomsday fit squarely in the villain category, but Titano the super ape was my glorious two-fer. I know what you're asking yourself: "How in the ever-loving world can the skeletal structure of a primate support the weight

and mass of a 75-foot-tall-gorilla?" Thing is, you're not asking the right question. What you really want to know is: "How in the world can the skeletal structure of a primate support the weight and mass of a 75-foot-tall gorilla - and look so **darn cool** while doing it?"

And three, I wanted to bring Zook back into the current DCU. Not only bring him back, mind you, but make him the central player in our little drama. A tall order, but the challenge was half the thrill.

Ahh, Zook, "we hardly knew ye." Barely a blip in the short run of Martian Manhunter stories that ran in DETECTIVE COMICS, then HOUSE OF MYSTERY, in the mid-'60s, Zook was the Manhunter's alien sidekick and nominal comic relief. But there was more to the Zookster than your everyday alien pet sidekick. For one thing, Zook was instrumental in saving the Manhunter's bacon on several occasions. Take HOUSE OF MYSTERY #146 for example. The Emerald Investigator found himself paralyzed as he faced the hands (well, claws) of "Chulko," the red, shambling, virtually featureless offspring of "Aroo," which was itself a big yellow creature with a dog's head, rabbit-ear antennae and red underpants. In this nine-and-a-half-page tale, the Manhunter finally falls prey to the Chulko's deadly eye beam, leaving it to Zook to save the day. Needless to say, Zook came through like a champ, dispatching Chulko post haste by melting a large bar of ice over his head and causing the creature to "fade away." Which sounds better than "die," I guess, though it's pretty much the same thing...

Did I mention that the rules in this earlier DCU were remarkably elastic?

Anyhow, what struck me about Zook and his relationship to the Martian Manhunter was that somehow, even though Zook was just as smart and almost as powerful as the big green guy, he didn't get the accolades or attention because he just didn't look the part of a hero. Indeed, poor Zook was Nicole Ritchie to the Manhunter's Paris Hilton, as the glow from the more glamorous of the pair often blinded the world to the other's abilities. Even though Zook spoke in a semi-literate patois ("Yipes! Green ring now drawing you in, Manhunter - because you **green!**"), he was clearly as intelligent as any of the other heroes. Yet because he was small, orange and had a physique reminiscent of the freakish child in those "dancing baby" videos, he would never get his shot at the pantheon.

So the "Enemies Among Us" arc was created in part to explore Zook's attitude toward Earth's heroes, and to give him one more shot at immortality. Of course, that meant making him the villain, albeit an unwitting one, but sooner or later he'll come around. Meanwhile, for those who picked up the series in monthly form, let me just ask - did **any** of you guess Zook was the one behind the mayhem?

In the end, I just hope that this isn't the end of folks strategically plumbing DC's vast alien reservoir. The anarchic imaginations that invented these diverse and bizarre characters deserve to be venerated and carried on, because as long as there are comics, we're going to need Purple Demons, the Beings in the Color Rings, Doom Shadows, King Zoldi and dying Creatures That Cannot Die.

MARK VERHEIDEN is currently the co-executive producer of **Battlestar Galactica** and writer of the live-action **Teen Titans** movie for Warner Bros. He lives in Los Angeles, California.

READ MORE OF THE
MAN OF STEEL'S
ADVENTURES IN
THESE COLLECTIONS
FROM DC COMICS:

SUPERMAN

SUPERMAN: FOR TOMORROW VOLUME 1

Brian Azzarello, Jim Lee and **Scott Williams** tell the epic tale of a cataclysmic event that strikes the Earth, affecting millions – including those closest to the Man of Steel.

"A BIG HERO NEEDS A BIG STORY, AND THIS TEAM DOESN'T DISAPPOINT."
– THE WASHINGTON POST

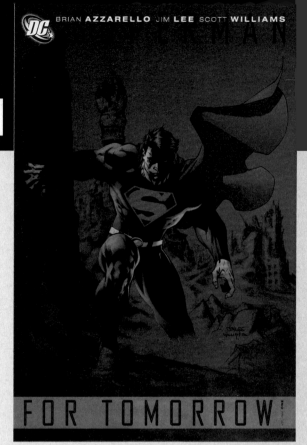

BRIAN **AZZARELLO** JIM **LEE** SCOTT **WILLIAMS**

FOR TOMORROW

SUPERMAN: THE MAN OF STEEL VOLUME 1

**JOHN BYRNE
DICK GIORDANO**

SUPERMAN FOR ALL SEASONS

**JEPH LOEB
TIM SALE**

THE DEATH OF SUPERMAN

**DAN JURGENS
JERRY ORDWAY
JACKSON GUICE**

SEARCH THE GRAPHIC NOVELS SECTION OF
WWW.DCCOMICS.COM

READ MORE OF THE DARK KNIGHT
DETECTIVE'S ADVENTURES
IN THESE COLLECTIONS
FROM DC COMICS:

BATMAN

BATMAN: HUSH VOLUME 1

Jeph Loeb, Jim Lee and
Scott Williams tell an epic
tale of friendship, trust
and betrayal, in the first
volume of a tale that
spans a lifetime of
the Dark Knight.

*"THE ACTION IS EXCITING AND THE DETAIL
IS METICULOUS."*
— **CRITIQUES ON INFINITE EARTHS**

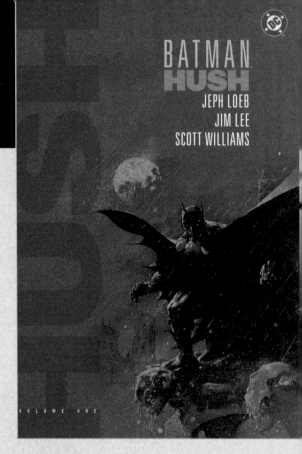

BATMAN
HUSH
JEPH LOEB
JIM LEE
SCOTT WILLIAMS

VOLUME ONE

BATMAN:
THE DARK KNIGHT RETURNS

BATMAN:
THE LONG HALLOWEEN

BATMAN:
YEAR ONE

**FRANK MILLER
KLAUS JANSON
LYNN VARLEY**

**JEPH LOEB
TIM SALE**

**FRANK MILLER
DAVID MAZZUCCHELLI**

SEARCH THE GRAPHIC NOVELS SECTION OF
www.DCCOMICS.com
FOR ART AND INFORMATION ON ALL OF OUR BOOKS!